Good Medicine
and Good Music

Good Medicine and Good Music

*A Biography of Mrs. Joe Person,
Patent Remedy Entrepreneur and
Musician, Including the Complete
Text of Her 1903 Autobiography*

DAVID HURSH *and*
CHRIS GOERTZEN

McFarland & Company, Inc., Publishers
Jefferson, North Carolina, and London

LIBRARY OF CONGRESS CATALOGUING-IN-PUBLICATION DATA

Hursh, David, 1962–
    Good medicine and good music : a biography of Mrs. Joe Person, patent remedy entrepreneur and musician, including the complete text of her 1903 autobiography / David Hursh and Chris Goertzen.
    p.   cm.
    Includes bibliographical references and index.

    ISBN 978-0-7864-3459-6
    softcover : 50# alkaline paper ∞

    1. Person, Alice Morgan, 1840–1913. 2. Businesswomen— North Carolina—Biography. 3. Folk musicians—North Carolina—Biography. 4. Women folk musicians—North Carolina—Biography. 5. Patent medicines—North Carolina— History. 6. Folk music—North Carolina—History and criticism. 7. North Carolina—Social life and customs—19th century. 8. North Carolina—Biography. I. Goertzen, Chris. II. Person, Alice Morgan, 1840–1913. III. Title.
CT275.P496H87   2009
975.6'03092—dc22
[B]   2009021371

British Library cataloguing data are available

©2009 David Hursh and Chris Goertzen. All rights reserved

No part of this book may be reproduced or transmitted in any form or by any means, electronic or mechanical, including photocopying or recording, or by any information storage and retrieval system, without permission in writing from the publisher.

On the cover: Cabinet card portrait of middle-aged Alice appearing on the first edition cover of *Popular Airs* collection, 1889 *(courtesy North Carolina Office of Archives and History, Raleigh, NC)*; Empty remedy bottle from Alice's Tarboro days *(courtesy of Donna and Gary Cunard)*

Manufactured in the United States of America

McFarland & Company, Inc., Publishers
  Box 611, Jefferson, North Carolina 28640
    www.mcfarlandpub.com

To Louise Scott Stephenson

Table of Contents

Acknowledgments ix
Introduction 1

BOOK I: "The Chivalry of Man as Exemplified in the Life of Mrs. Joe Person": Alice Morgan Person's Story in Her Own Words, 1858–1892

Preface 7
Foreword 9

PART I

1. The Origin of Mrs. Joe Person's Remedy 11
2. Castles in the Air 14
3. The Development of the Remedy 20
4. More Castles in the Air 22
5. The Chivalry of Man 25
6. More Chivalry 29
7. Clouds—Sunshine: "After the Alps Comes Italy" 35
8. I Go to Church 38
9. More Chivalry 40
10. Partner No. 2 47
11. Tarboro and Tarboro Ways 50
12. Partners, Adieu! 52

PART II: NOTES BY THE WAYSIDE

Flowers Plucked from the Hedges and Thorns from the Briar-Bushes 55

Poor John!	59
"Sonny"	59
Not My Daughter, Oh No!	60
What Is Happiness?	62
Big, Rich and a Strong Pillar	64
An Honest Man Is the Noblest Work of God	65
A Woman's Opinion	66
Finale	66

Book II: A Life Out of the Ordinary: Alice's Story in the Words of Others

Part I: The Woman

1. Daughter and Sister	71
2. Wife and Mother	85
3. Medicine Maker and Musician	103
4. Public and Private	129

Part II: Reflections on the Medicine and the Music

5. Snake Oil or Native American Medical Marvel?	137
6. The Remedy and the Turn-of-the-Century Patent Medicine Trade	151
7. Alice and Music in Fashion	167
8. *Popular Airs, Blue Alsatian Mountains,* and Nostalgia	179
Appendix: Timeline of Alice Morgan Person and Her Company	189
Chapter Notes	193
Bibliography	201
Index	205

Acknowledgments

An endeavor such as this would not be successful without the help of numerous organizations and individuals, and I am grateful to them all. I first thank those organizations that considered Alice worthy of research travel funding: the Music Library Association for the Dena Epstein Award for Archival and Library Research in American Music, and Dena Epstein herself for endowing the award; The North Caroliniana Society for the Archie K. Davis Fellowship; and the Southern Regional Education Board for a Faculty Grant Award.

The research assistance of the dedicated librarians, archivists, and government employees at the following institutions and organizations was invaluable to my research: Duke University; UNC–Chapel Hill; East Carolina University (ECU); the Virginia Historical Society; the North Carolina and Virginia state libraries and archives; the county courthouses in Louisburg, Henderson, Tarboro, and Charlotte, North Carolina, and Petersburg, Virginia; and the United States Patent and Trademark Office.

Many thanks to my ECU colleagues who made it possible for me to conduct my research and write: Dr. Larry Boyer, dean of Academic Library Services, for allowing me to take time from my daily duties to realize this project; my wonderful ECU Music Library colleagues Judy Barber, Kevin-Andrew Cronin, Sarah Davis, Harry Frank, Nara Newcomer, and Jeffrey Tuthill for covering for me in my absence, and for reading and critiquing the manuscript; and graduate assistant Emily Smith for her assistance with transcribing hundreds of letters, documents, and journal pages.

Special thanks are due to Mary Moulton Barden, Harmon Person, Louise Scott Stephenson, and Alice Ritter. Mary Barden, a granddaughter of Mary Morgan Moulton (widow of Alice's brother Rufus), shared her collection of letters between Alice, Rufus, and Mary, and introduced me to retired North Carolina state archivist Steve Massengill, to whom thanks are also due for sharing his research on Rufus. Alice's great-grandson Harmon Person owns Alice's family Bible, and kindly shared digital scans of the marriage, birth, and death records recorded there by Alice. Posthumous thanks are due to Louise Scott Stephenson for her encouragement, and also for creating the typescript of "The Chivalry of Man as Exemplified in the Life of Mrs. Joe Person." Alice Ritter, Louise Scott Stephenson's niece and estate executrix, happily granted copyright permission for the use of her aunt's typescript.

The final group of people I wish to thank forms a serendipitous—some might say supernatural—chain. This chain begins with Franklin County, North Carolina, native Franceine Perry Rees. A chance mention of my Alice Person project within hearing range of Franceine at a meeting of the Friends of Joyner Library resulted in her presenting me with contact information for three Franklin County historians familiar with Alice: Joseph Pearce, Jr., Joseph Elmore, and Thilbert Pearce. All three men provided me with helpful information, but Thilbert Pearce's directions to the house in which Alice lived when her love affair with the remedy began led to the next link in the chain— present-day residents Libby and Wyatt McGhee III. The McGhees not only shared their knowledge of Alice and their unopened bottle of her remedy, they also shared their home when I made an overnight trip to central North Carolina to conduct my research.

If any link in this chain could be considered supernatural, it is the next one. As I was bringing my research to an end in the spring of 2007, I received a call from Wyatt McGhee III. He and his wife had just been visited by Alice's great-great-grandson, Michael Boyce. Boyce had recently heard Alice may have lived in the McGhee's home. With the hope that the current residents were either Person descendents or knew something about Alice, he paid the McGhees a visit. In so doing, Boyce learned that Chris Goertzen and I were writing a book about the woman of which his elders spoke in reverent tones. Boyce knew at once he had finally found the reason he had been storing two large boxes of Alice's journals, papers, and business ledgers in one of his barns. He was not only anxious to share them, he was also anxious to give them to me for addition to Joyner Library's collection so they would no longer be subjected to the damaging effects of the southern climate. On a warm evening in June of 2007, Boyce and his wife opened their home to me and we sorted through hundreds of items that Alice's son Rufus left to his son Rufus, Jr., who left them to his daughter, Sallie Person Kelly, who left them to Boyce. But the chain does not end there; Boyce provided me with the final link— T.T. Beckham. Beckham is a Kittrell, North Carolina, native whose grandfather, W.M. Beckham, owned a business a few doors from Alice's Kittrell laboratory. Beckham kindly spent an evening with me walking the Kittrell street on which Alice's laboratory once stood and sharing his collection of

Kittrell memorabilia, which includes a Mrs. Joe Person's Remedy shipping crate containing eight remedy bottles.

Ultimate thanks are due to Harry Stubbs, without whom there would have been no need for the assistance of those already listed. Not only did Harry see the value in his great-great-grandmother's decaying sheet music when he discovered it in his deceased father's attic, he also had the foresight to bring it to my attention and arrange for me to meet Louise Scott Stephenson. Without Harry, the complete story of Alice's inspiring life would have reposed indefinitely in a fractured state — scattered among private and institutional owners oblivious to each other, and perhaps lost forever.

David Hursh

Introduction

Life in the post–Civil War South was difficult. The atrocities of war, the loss of loved ones and personal property, and the arduous task of rebuilding the economy intensified physical infirmities untouched by mid–nineteenth-century medical practice. These circumstances drove Southerners to seek ways to heal both body and soul. The passionate search of one Southerner, Mrs. Joe (Alice) Person, resulted in a unique combination of medicine and music, a synthesis that became the hallmark of a remarkable life that would not soon be forgotten. Indeed, nearly one hundred years after Alice's death her descendents enthusiastically claim her as an example of what women can accomplish in the face of adversity. This familial enthusiasm was the impetus for the publication of this book.

In my capacity as head music librarian at East Carolina University (ECU) in Greenville, North Carolina, I receive numerous gifts from generous donors. Harry Stubbs, ECU alumnus and a great-great-grandson of Alice Person, is one such donor. Stubbs approached me in the fall of 2000 about donating two of Alice's published arrangements of southern folk tunes. As I examined the well-used, century-old sheets, Stubbs related snippets of the composer's colorful life. My curiosity was piqued, and further research led me to conclude I must do what I could to preserve Alice's crumbling musical legacy. My interest in Alice spurred Stubbs to arrange dinner with his cousin and Alice's great-granddaughter, Louise Scott Stephenson. At our dinner I learned that Stephenson, or "Scottie" as she preferred to be called, donated a collection of Alice's papers to the Southern Historical Collection at the University of North Carolina at Chapel Hill (UNC-Chapel Hill) in the mid–1970s. Before doing so, however, she produced a typescript of the handwritten manuscript of Alice's unpublished autobiography, a copy of which she presented to me for addition to the music library's collection. Pleased to learn of my desire to preserve her cousin's donation, Scottie was certain there were more pieces of sheet music that should be preserved and she set about to locate them. Unfortunately, she passed away before she could complete this task.

Though I had already committed myself to preserving Alice's music, the passing of this great lady and champion of Alice's memory moved me to go one step further. I had to publish Alice's story—a project both Alice and Scottie had hoped to accomplish, but never did. My initial commitment has been fulfilled in two ways. First, the frayed music is safely encased in acid-free boxes and stored in a climate-controlled environment in ECU's J.Y. Joyner Library. Second, an award-winning online exhibit featuring the digitized graphic and audio versions of Alice's known sheet music publications, as well as letters, newspaper clippings, and photographs not contained in this book, is available at *http://digital.lib.ecu.edu/music/person/*. With the publication of this book, I fulfill my second commitment and finally accomplish the century-old aspiration of two special North Carolina women.

This book is divided into two parts. The first part, "The Chivalry of Man as Exemplified in the Life of Mrs. Joe Person: Alice Morgan Person's Story in Her Own Words, 1858–92," is Louise Stephenson's typescript of Alice's manuscript. The arrangement and titles of this part are exactly as they appear in the manuscript. Unfortunately, Alice's account covers only the years 1858–92, leaving readers in the dark with regard to the early and late periods of her life. The research I conducted while creating the digital exhibit indicated that noteworthy events occurred during the years omitted by Alice in her work, and further research proved that observation to be true. The second part of the book, "A Life Out of the Ordinary: Alice's Story in the Words of Others," completes Alice's story, provides additional information about the years she covered in her work, and discusses her role in the history of American patent medicine and popular music. As an aid to reader comprehension, the book closes with a timeline of important events that comprised or surrounded Alice's life.

In order to complete Alice's story, I traveled to places as diverse as local, state and federal government offices, university manuscript and special collections, and central North Carolina farms. The government offices I visited include the county courthouses in Louisburg, Henderson, Tarboro, and Charlotte, North Carolina, and Petersburg, Virginia; the North Carolina and Virginia state libraries and archives; and the United States Patent and Trademark Office. I also searched the manuscript and special collections of Duke University, UNC-Chapel Hill, ECU, and the Virginia Historical Society in Richmond. Last, but certainly not least, I visited the Wake Forest, North Carolina, home of Sheila and Michael Boyce, as well as the Franklin County, North Carolina, home of Libby and Wyatt McGhee III. Michael Boyce, one of Alice's great-great-grandsons, provided me with a priceless collection of primary source materials in the form of Alice's journals and business records. These papers, stored in one of Boyce's barns for many years, are now part of the Joyner Library Special Collections at ECU. The McGhees own and occupy the house in which Alice lived when she first began producing her remedy, and my visits with them allowed me to step back in time and imagine what life must have been like for Alice and her family.

My research also led me to my coauthor, Dr. Chris Goertzen, whose 1991 article on Alice's arrangements of southern folk tunes was one of only two publications dealing with Alice that I located early in my research.[1] As an ethnomusicologist and folk arts specialist, Chris is uniquely qualified to write about both the music and the medicine, which he does in the final four chapters of this book.

The title, *Good Medicine and Good Music*, was inspired by an announcement in a Greenville, North Carolina, newspaper. The announcement, which heralds Alice's arrival in Greenville for the purpose of selling her medicinal and musical products, refers to her as "perhaps the best known woman in the State" and tells readers that "good medicine and good music have made her name a household word."[2]

While Alice's fame originated with her medicine and music, it was sustained by her exceptional character. The following quote from the preface to Alice's autobiography is an indication of the respect she had for all people, a respect that in turn earned her theirs: "For fifteen years I have led a drummer's life, have come into contact with all manner of mankind, high and low, sick and poor, patricians and plebeians, knights and cowards, and it must be an opaque nature that could not, in turn, learn a lesson from each as they came along."[3] John Baseler of Richmond, Virginia, was one of the knights to which Alice refers in this quote. She bestowed this title on Baseler for the kindness he showed her by transcribing the musical notes that were in her head on to paper, free of charge, while she repeatedly played them on the piano for more than two days.[4] Just as Baseler recorded Alice's music, so have Chris and I unearthed and recorded her story for the benefit of future generations, an effort I trust would have earned us knighthood in Alice's eyes.

David Hursh

Book I

"The Chivalry of Man as Exemplified in the Life of Mrs. Joe Person"

Alice Morgan Person's Story in Her Own Words, 1858–1892

Preface

The interest of many people has been awakened in regard to my work. How did I ever happen to think of it? How did I start to take hold of it? Why did I choose such a life? And similar questions have been asked me hundreds of times. This little book is intended as an answer to all.

For fifteen years I have led a drummer's life, have come into contact with all manner of mankind, high and low, rich and poor, patricians and plebeians, knights and cowards, and it must be an opaque nature that could not, in turn, learn a lesson from each, as they came along.

Every conversation, every incident narrated is an actual FACT, given exactly as it occurred. In no sense of the word is it an advertisement, but an account of my work, concentrated into its title — The Chivalry of Man, as exemplified in the life of Mrs. Joe Person.

Dedicated to my beloved children, for whom I have lived and learned.

Foreword

My life has been out of the ordinary run of woman's life. Circumstances have forced me to the front, where I have met both Knights and Cowards. Circumstances have compelled me to stand my ground and fight the great Fight single-handed and alone. Sometimes a suspicion has been born in my mind that undue credit for a courage I did not really possess, had often been accorded me by a Public, generally kind and oft times just.

A soldier goes into battle, there is an unseen Power behind with the point of a bayonet pressed to his very back; to waver would be death and destruction, and so he fights onward, cheered by the multitude, while his ears are deaf to the applause: HE only knows he dare not halt; HE only feels he must not stop — there is work to do, and there is the Power behind. Is he a brave man because he fights and presses on?

PART I

Chapter 1

The Origin of Mrs. Joe Person's Remedy

I was born and reared in Petersburg, Virginia, where I lived until December 1857, when I was united in marriage to Joseph Arrington Person, a prosperous farmer of Franklin County, North Carolina. We came direct to his lovely country home, where I was surrounded by all of the comforts and many of the luxuries attending such a life in the old days of the South. My husband was possessed of independent means and I found that my lines had indeed been cast in pleasant places. Not a care, not a responsibility, not a thought or fear for the future did I have. We both came from old families, who had never known aught save of the elegancies and refinements of life, and no one could have felt more secure than I. That I should lose it all, that I should have to work for my bread, that I should be poor, had never occurred to me. What a blessing it is that the future should be revealed a page at a time! We could never have strength for the conflict did we know what was before us, and we should flinch and we should quail before the ordeal, regardless of, and notwithstanding that mighty Power; so, as it is, is best.

The first heart trouble I ever knew was when my husband organized a company of volunteers in '63 and told me he felt he must leave me at his country's call. In command of the company he left and life seemed over for me. The world was dark, nothing was left, my husband was away and in danger. It was at that time that my heart first really turned to God. My life became a long continued prayer — a prayer that God would send my husband back to me, and I am afraid now that I did not care very much how he came back, I only wanted him to come, and am afraid that my affection was stronger than my patriotism. I sought comfort in my Bible, and I found that God wanted me to fast as well as pray; as a condition for an answer to prayer I entered into the cause and thought, "Well, my Father, I will do anything you ask of me or require, if it will cause you to send my husband back to me," and so I divided my days between God and between Nature. One day I would eat, the next I would fast; not a morsel or crumb of anything would I touch, not a drop of water for twenty four hours. Then my usual meals, never more, and so I alternated the days, rigidly fasting every other day for three weeks.

How I promised my God if he would only grant my prayer, that I would serve him the balance of my days.

One day, sitting in my room, with the burden almost greater than I could bear, one of the Negroes came in almost shouting, "Oh mistress, the Master's coming," and I went to the door to meet my husband, honorably discharged, as totally unfit for military service. He had, years before, been thrown from his horse in a fox hunt, and his leg been badly broken in two places, and he could do nothing as a soldier, so once again life began for me in earnest.

At the first visit of Bishop Atkinson in '63, I was confirmed a member of the Episcopal Church.

Three bright and beautiful children came to bless our union and we were very happy. My husband was one of the handsomest men I ever saw, and he retired in perfect health one memorable night, but awoke me before morning and told me he was paralyzed and directed me to summon the physician from Franklinton. It was a terrible stroke, affecting his whole left side, and for weeks he hovered between life and death. For weeks he could not even move a muscle, but nature and a strong constitution helped the cause and conquered, in a measure.

Then came the Surrender, which was only another chapter of calamity and so the shadows of life had indeed begun to fall across my path.

At one fell stroke our means of income were swept away and we were left, as were so many Southerners, with only a tract of land, which my husband was powerless to look after, and a family of little children depending upon us. Our income became less and less and I knew we were becoming poorer and poorer each year, and I also knew we were powerless to stem the tide. My husband's condition improved so that he could walk-around some, look after his stock, hitch his horse to the buggy and visit his neighbors, could saddle his horse and ride to town, but, as a man of business, his career was ended.

In the course of time I saw that the health of one of our little ones was failing and we called in the services of a physician, who pronounced the trouble Scrofula.* This sounded like a death knell to me. Regardless of every care

---

*In existence for thousands of years, scrofula, or tuberculous cervical adenitis, is a form of tuberculosis spread via infected cow's milk. While pulmonary tuberculosis affects the lungs, scrofula inflames the glands of the neck causing painful sores. Grzybowski and Allen, "History and Importance of Scrofula."

and attention that could be given, the child became dangerously ill, and we felt that the end was near. Before leaving one afternoon, the doctor said, "Mrs. Person, as long as there is life there is hope, but I do not think your child can possibly stand it another night. I think she will pass away before morning."

While my child was in this condition and virtually at death's door, a woman living near came to see me and said she heard I had a child afflicted with Scrofula, and she had come to cure her! I could but smile at her earnestness, and told her she came too late, that I looked upon our child as dying and past all hope, and I did not expect her to live until morning. She said if the child was bound to die, it could do no harm to try her medicine. I protested. I did not wish to torture the child with any more medicine, as I felt it would be useless. She again appealed to me, saying, "I came to save your child, and you will not even let me try; you do not know what you are doing." She said an old Indian gave the recipe to her father, and she had never known it to fail.

Impressed by her earnestness, we concluded to try it, so together we went to the woods and gathered the ingredients—the identical ingredients of which my Remedy is made today. She showed me how to prepare the medicine and we gave some to the child. Before leaving me she told me to continue to give it regularly through the night, and I would see the ground she had for her great faith in it. I followed her directions, with not a shadow of faith or hope.

The next morning the child was better, and in three weeks, she was well! <u>This was the origin of my Remedy.</u>

Chapter 2

Castles in the Air

Upon what apparently small events the tide of one's whole life may turn!

The coming of that Good Samaritan to my home that evening changed life for me, as well as for hundreds of others.

I knew that something very valuable had been placed within my grasp, and I treasured it as I would a precious jewel. I told my husband I was as good as elected and expected to be worth a million of dollars yet. And live in a brown stone front. He laughed and said, "Surely you are not going to turn Scrofula-doctor, are you?" I told him I did not know how I should work it, but I expected to be worth a million of dollars yet.

My family continued to grow, and it was all out-go and no income. I had to decide between two things: to make household drudges of my girls and myself, put my boys to the plow handle and thus save the land and home, or else continue the advantages we had always enjoyed, educate our children, entertain our friends, keep servants to wait on us, and let the land go to pay for it, and I chose the latter.

Many a one living now can tell of the good times at the old home — the dances, the picnics, the company, the music, the fun, the good cheer! How like a dream it seems now, and how I revel in the recollection, and am thankful for it. "'Tis better to have loved and lost than never to have loved at all!" All these things brightened life for my afflicted husband and for us all, and made it better worth the living. Still, I knew it was too bright to last and the change was bound to come, but I always had an abiding faith in God's goodness and felt that, "It may not be in my way, it may not be in thy way, but in His own way, God would provide."

Meanwhile, I kept my eye on that wonderful remedy of mine, and every time I heard of a case of blood trouble I made some of the Remedy and sent to the parties, and I never failed to cure a single case. Then people commenced to write to me for it, and it soon became the source of considerable income to us.

As cure followed upon cure and was reported to me, I became an enthusiast on the subject. I could do what no one else had ever been able to do, and the thought was inspiring. I had found the antidote for blood impurity and I could prove it. I feared no test, for I knew my cause would come out triumphant. The more I thought and studied over the matter the more I became impressed with its importance, not only to me, but to the wide field of suffering humanity. The issue was irresistible and led me on.

Night and day did I dream of the visions unfolded in my imagination. I felt the weight of the tremendous issue. I felt it was a power too great to be in the hands of any one person, the power to cure, the power to heal, <u>every time</u>, what no physician had ever been able to do, and it was MINE, but a power I had NO RIGHT to use solely for the purpose of making money from the sufferings of the afflicted. My work had become to me something very sacred, almost a religion. I thought if the physicians could only know what I could do to relieve suffering, if I would only prove it to them, what an avenue of relief would be opened to the afflicted, and at the same time a gate of triumph would be opened for me to pass through, to receive the crown of recognition that I felt my work so richly deserved.

So one morning I awoke and found myself A Woman with a Mission. I told my husband I was going to Raleigh and lay my cause before the Medical profession of the Capital of our grand old State, that I was going to tell them I could cure any case of scrofula or blood impurity that might be submitted to me. That I should ask them to give me any number of test cases that would be necessary to convince them of the truth of my claim, and I would furnish the medicine free of charge and cure them. I would ask them to examine the cases for me and watch the result, and if I cured every one, which I knew I would do, I felt as if my discovery was entitled to the honorable recognition I would respectfully ask them to accord me. My husband, laughing, said, "What a poor little fool you are! Do you not know they are not going to have anything to do with anything of the kind, and were you to go there and cure a hundred cases, they wouldn't have anything to do with it or you. Do you suppose they would be so blind to their own interest to acknowledge you could do a thing they could not do, or even want you to do it? Take my advice and let doctors alone." But I was now a full-fledged woman with a mission, and would not "down." So to Raleigh I went, a bundle of inspirations, aspirations, hopes, visions, ideas, dreams, castles and unlimited possibilities generally. A farmer's wife with a farmer's life, for a quarter of a century, and then to go to the city, on a mission! May the Saints defend all such!

How I tremblingly rang the medical door bell and was first ushered into the august presence of Dr. Royster. I can feel the lump in my throat now, as I told him what I came for.

He gave me attention most respectful and then with his habitual courtesy, he told me he did not care to have anything to do with it, and that a sense of professional duty and etiquette would compel him to decline to witness any of those wonderful cures I claimed I could make. So, just a little crestfallen and just a little shaky about the knees, I went to the "next door neighbor" and called on Dr. Hines, and to him presented my claims and views. That I wanted to prove to the medical profession of Raleigh that I could take any given number of cases of scrofula or blood impurity, and cure every one. I would not fail in a case. I urged that it was a question of sufficient importance to the afflicted and to the cause of science, to merit investigation, and I asked him would he be willing to examine any test cases that might be submitted for my treatment. He replied that it was a part of his professional duty to examine anyone physically who needed his services, and he was willing to do so. To be assured fully of my position I also called on Dr. E.B. Haywood and Dr. James McKee, who took a similar stand in regard to the examination.

So, on the strength of these views I inserted the following card periodically for one month in the *Raleigh News-Observer*, and the *Raleigh Evening Visitor*, and submit the result to show the public just how I was treated.

- A CARD -

In order to prove to the medical fraternity and the public generally, that my Remedy is an infallible cure for all diseases of a scrofulous taint, or impurities of the blood, I propose to submit it to a public test in the city of Raleigh, N.C., and most respectfully ask those afflicted with scrofula, or kindred diseases to meet me at the Yarboro House on March 16, 1882, from 9 o'clock A.M. to 12 P.M., and from 2 to 4 P.M. bringing with them their physician's certificate that their disease is scrofula, when they will be cured free of charge. The physicians are invited to bring forward their incurable cases. Correspondence may be opened with me at address given below.

I am — Very truly —

Mrs. Joe Person
Franklinton, N.C.

Dr. McKee met me on broader and more liberal grounds than anyone else. I came to Raleigh on the 13th March, called on Dr. McKee on the morning of the 14th and told him if I obtained the test cases, I wished him to examine them for me, which he willingly agreed to do, and I then and there agreed to pay him five dollars for each case he might examine. At 12 noon, on the 16th I had selected five test cases, and repairing to Dr. McKee's office, left a note for him to be at the Yarboro at 4 P.M., according to promise, as I had obtained the cases. Four o'clock came, but no Dr. McKee. I explained to the cases, now increased to eight, that I had been disappointed in procuring the services of a physician, and required them severally to promise to meet me again at 4 o'clock the next evening. That afternoon Dr. McKee explained to me on the street that he did not get my note in time to attend. I told him all right, it made but little difference, as they would come again the next evening at 4 o'clock, and he <u>again promised to be on hand to examine them</u>. To make assurance doubly sure, I went to his office on the morning of the 17th and he, having been up all night, had not arisen, so I sent a note of the following import to his room: "Dr. McKee, Your appointment this afternoon must be unquestioned and undoubted. One of the cases comes eight miles and another twelve, and there must be no doubt in the matter. Can you attend, without a fear of failure, this afternoon at 3:30 o'clock, at the Yarboro?" He sent me word, all right, <u>he would be on hand at the appointed time</u>. Four o'clock came, and so did the cases, but <u>again no Dr. McKee</u>, but instead, he sent me the following letter which I received while the cases were a second time awaiting him:

> March 17, 1882
> Mrs. Joe Person: Madam,
> After careful deliberation on the propriety of examining the subjects sent you for treatment, I am convinced that it would be wrong, and must therefore decline. In the first place, a public test of a <u>secret patent medicine</u> is not feasible. Second you are pursuing a course just adversely to the admonition extended to you by two other physicians. If I examine anybody for you now, I, of course, connive at the effort to enrich the owner of a patent secret remedy. To show you that I am friendly disposed to you, ask me to do something else, that I may manifest it.
> Very truly yours,
> James McKee, M.D.

In reply to the above I wrote, I <u>do</u> ask you then to pay me a professional visit at your very convenience and oblige, etc. I waited some time and as he did not come, I wrote him the following: "Dr. McKee: I regret you did not 'manifest' the 'kindly disposed' by paying me the visit I requested. Allow me to add, that by failing to keep your promised appointment, you have succeeded well in rendering all my efforts null and void, and had you done so in time for me to have procured the services of another physician, which I could have done, your object would not have been so apparent." I wrote this letter to him which fully explained my views at the time, but, upon reflection, concluded I would not send it until I could see him and give him a chance to explain. I saw him later that afternoon, and he told me he was actuated as much by consideration of my good as by a sense of professional duty, and that I would see the day when I would thank him for his course.

Honestly believing that I had in Dr. McKee a friend, I called on him on Tuesday, May 2, and told him that after mature deliberation I had concluded to follow the "admonition extended to me by the physicians" and <u>give</u> my discovery to the world through the medical profession; that I wished to do this in person at the medical convention to be held in Concord, May 11, and claim through that body the credit of the discovery. That I desired introduction there by the medical fraternity of Raleigh, and to this end I requested to be <u>allowed to prove to them</u> that I had made the discovery which supplies one of the greatest wants of medical science, that I had brought <u>proofs</u> that I had found the vegetable antidote for scrofula and its kindred complaints.

Dr. McKee replied: "Madam, if you have discovered this remedy, you are a made woman; it is a remedy that has been unsuccessfully sought for hundreds of years, and if you can prove this, you are entitled to honorable recognition. Your name will have an honored place, not only in the medical journals of the United States, but of Europe, and because this discovery was made by you, and by one outside of our profession, is no reason why it should not be recognized by us. I am sure you are not the lady to let a few thousand dollars stand between you and fame, and I approve your resolution and applaud your efforts."

He said he would not attend the medical convention or he would gladly introduce me, but as <u>he believed from the proofs</u> I had shown him, that I <u>was</u> in possession of a remedy which would be of incalculable benefit in relieving suffering humanity, he would speak to Dr. Hines on the subject.

I asked him would he express to Dr. Hines his unqualified belief that I <u>could</u> prove what I claimed. His reply was, "Most assuredly, I will."

I called on Dr. Hines, Dr. E.B. Haywood, Dr. Ellis, and Dr. McGee, and explained to them my position: That ten years ago I discovered the vegetable specific for scrofulous taint; that I had spent the last several years in perfecting it, and I now wished to take it out of the rank and file of patent medicines, and elevate it to its legitimate place among the great discoveries of medical science. I proposed to <u>give</u> it to the medical profession, to make known my formula, only asking from them the acknowledged credit of the discovery, and the benefit of their adopting it in their practice. To place myself on a footing where the Raleigh physicians could accord me this recognition, and would be justified in introducing me to the medical convention, I asked permission to attend a meeting of their medical board held Wednesday night, in Raleigh, where I might be allowed to present proofs to substantiate my claim. All I wanted and asked was a hearing. Dr. Hines, Dr. Ellis, and Dr. McGee said they thought I was entitled to it; the last named, on the score of courtesy to a lady. Dr. E. Burke Haywood was characteristically non-committal.

At their meeting Wednesday night a hearing was denied me, merely on the score of its being an "irregular proceeding," and <u>not one voice</u> was raised to demand in public what they assured me privately was my right.

I leave the public to pronounce a verdict.

So endeth the second chapter.

Blessed is the man who never said "I told you so."

Note. I received letters from all sections of the State, asking the result of my treatment of the test cases, and to explain it to all interested, I incorporated the foregoing statement in the next pamphlet I issued, under the heading:

A SOLID CHAPTER OF SOLID FACTS.
MRS. JOE PERSON AND THE RALEIGH DOCTORS.

Chapter 3

The Development of the Remedy

The sales of my Remedy were fast becoming a tangible reality, but still I was restless. It was not what it should be. The field was too limited. I wanted to fly but had no wings. The want grew until it controlled me, and I astonished the household one day by telling them I was going to Charlotte in the interest of my Remedy.

Had I said I was going to the moon on business, they would not have been more surprised. Since my Raleigh contretemps, I had subsided so completely and had so entirely stopped talking about "hopes" and "aims" that I do not think it ever entered into their heads to suppose I would ever have another one.

But in the fall of '82 I boarded the train at Franklinton, with a ticket to Charlotte and $17.50 in my pocket, all the available funds I had in the world but all the same, I drove up as big as life to the Central, and registered as if I had had many thousands.

I asked Mr. Eccles his terms, which he gave me. I told him I only took two meals a day, breakfast and supper, and he, little dreaming of my expedient to stretch my money, gave me corresponding reduction of rates.

The next morning I started out "in the interest of my Remedy," and Mr. William M. Wilson of Charlotte is the first man I ever approached to sell a bill of goods to. With my most winning smile I told him I had come in to sell him a dozen bottles of my Remedy. He said "What remedy, Madam?" I told him "Mrs. Joe Person's Remedy, of course." "Why Madam," he said, "I never heard of it!" I told him that was the reason I wanted to sell him a dozen, so that he would hear of it, and see what it would do.

I think Mr. Wilson appreciated my position and its pathos, for then and there, after finding this was my first effort, he so kindly explained to me the law of supply and demand, that it robbed the bitterness of my disappointment of its sting.

He said, "I believe you have a good thing, and I hope you will succeed with it, but if you had a medicine that would raise the dead, and people knew nothing of it, and did not call for it, I couldn't afford to put my money in it, because I couldn't sell it. You create the demand and I'll buy! Put out your circulars in the houses here and if people call for it, I will certainly send you an order. That is all I can do." I knew he was right and I wouldn't have had him to do more, but the disappointment was bitter and hard to bear.

I called on Dr. T.C. Smith and Dr. McAden, with the same result, of course. Not a bottle did I sell as the result of my first day's work in Charlotte. I returned to the Hotel, disheartened, and lay awake that night chewing the cud of sweet and bitter phantasies.

It was at that time that I met with the dearest friend of my after-life, Mrs. Eccles. She came around to my room, and to her sympathetic and willing ear, I told "my tale of woe," and I felt better, a stranger in a strange land, for knowing her. May God bless her always! When the days were dark with me, then and afterward, she it was who strengthened me and ever reminded me of the sunshine which always follows the clouds.

I had but few circulars, as I was only able to have five hundred at a time, so the next morning I went to the *Observer* office and had some gummed slips printed, reading "Please read this circular and preserve it. I will call for it tomorrow." I pasted one on each circular and carried them myself to each house on one of the principal residence streets. The next day, I went the rounds again to gather them in, and many of the ladies invited me in, and showed me kind attention and gave me encouraging words. I can never forget. They wanted me to tell them of this wonderful Remedy of mine, which I was only too glad of the chance to do.

I worked two days with my circulars in Charlotte, but did not sell a bottle. I then returned to my home, sad and thoughtful, I must confess. In less than two weeks I received an order from Mr. W.M. Wilson for two dozen Remedy, and in a few days this was followed by an order from Dr. T.C. Smith, for two dozen, and in that way my trade was established which has sold me thousands of bottles in Charlotte. I continued this plan in the various towns and cities of the State, thus introducing my Remedy with most gratifying results.

Chapter 4

More Castles in the Air

I passed one of the mileposts of my life in Salisbury.

Early in '83, I was in the Hotel parlor one evening with quite a number of the guests and boarders, when the conversation turned upon my work, its nature, and so on. I remarked that it had so permeated my whole life that whenever I passed people on the street, I could not help from looking at them and wondering if they did not need my Remedy.

I was soon after introduced to a Mr. George Davidson, who seemed particularly interested in my work, and asked me a great many questions concerning it. He was one of a company of men engaged in mining in Western Carolina, and I was told he was a man of great wealth.

In May '83, I received a letter from Mr. Davidson saying that he, in company with other capitalists, was thinking of putting big money into the Remedy, and if I was willing to sell out, wholly or in part, it might pay me to come to Salisbury and talk the matter over.

The next day I went to Salisbury, saw Mr. Davidson that night, and he appointed ten o'clock the next morning for an interview.

Punctual to the appointment, I met him.

He asked me the first-thing if I would be willing to sell a half interest in my Remedy? I told him "I would."

"Would you sell a two-third interest?"

"I would not. That would relegate me to a minority voice and I would not so sell."

"Would you sell your entire interest?"

"I would."

"For how much?"

I told him I was not prepared to answer that question, but would give him an answer at ten o'clock the next day.

"<u>Will you take twenty thousand dollars for it?</u> I am authorized to offer you that, payable on or before the 1st day of September."

("Oh, my heart be still," I said) but to him I replied, "I would not sell for that amount unless I reserved a royalty."

"Of how much?"

"Just what I have always paid to the government in the form of internal revenue, four cents on each bottle."

He said he was not authorized to pay me any royalty, but asked me to remain with his wife that night and he would go to High Point and consult the other gentlemen interested, as they were there — his father and a Mr. Geo. Wilson, all of Pittsburg, Pa., being the ones alluded to.

He said if we came to terms, they had decided to put two hundred and fifty thousand dollars into it at once, and advertise it from Maine to Florida, and from the Atlantic to the Pacific.

The next morning, the tenth day of May, 1883, Mr. Davidson returned from High Point with the contract written.

On or before the first day of September, he was to pay me twenty thousand dollars in Cash. The first year I was to receive no royalty. The second year I was to receive one cent on each bottle sold, the third year two cents, the fourth year, three cents, the fifth and each succeeding year, I was to receive four cents royalty on each bottle sold.

Upon the payment of the money, I was to transfer to him my trademark and all rights pertaining to the same.

I was almost overwhelmed at the magnitude of the transaction, but made a noble effort for self-control.

Mr. Davidson took $100 out of his pocket and handed it to me. I asked him,

"What is that for?"

"That seals the contract and makes it binding; five dollars would make it just as binding, but I pay you this as evidence of good faith on my part." He had two copies of the contract, one for him and one for me. He passed them over to me to sign.

I laid down the paper and pen, and, without touching his money said, "Mr. Davidson, before signing this contract, let me say a few words. This matter between us represents to us two entirely different things. To you, it is but a mere matter of business, a bargain and sale, a question of dollars and cents, such as come into your life at any time. To me, it is something far different. To me it means SUCCESS. It means the fulfillment of the dearest hopes I have on earth, the realization of my brightest dreams. To me, it is EVERYTHING, and let me beg you now, before we go any further, if there is any doubt in your mind, not only of your ability, but of your intention to comply with this contract, by everything you hold sacred, withdraw now, and go no further. I would only go home a little disappointed —<u>but</u>, were you to go into this thing and then disappoint me, it would be a death blow to me; I could never live through it."

He replied, "Mrs. Person, we are men of business and see in your remedy a big field for investment. If I had not meant to go into it, do you think I should have written for you to come here, would have written that contract, would have paid you that one hundred dollars? You need have no fear, the contract will be carried out."

Then he added: "Suppose on or before the 1st day of September we were to pay you ten thousand dollars and secure you in the balance, would you comply with the contract?"

"I would not. I shall want all or none."

"You shall be paid it all, every dollar."

"One word more, Mr. Davidson, and I am done. When you pay me, do not bring me a check or draft, for I do not want it. I want you to pay me in greenbacks."

"A check or draft would be much more convenient and easy to carry and would be just as good."

"That may be so, but I do not want it. I want, once in my life, to look at a great big pile of greenbacks and know that they are mine and I made them."

"You shall be paid in greenbacks, on or before the 1st day of September."

I signed the contract and received the $100.

It was agreed between us that when the time of payment came, he was to write to me to join him somewhere, and I selected Messrs. Fuller & Snow's Office in Raleigh, as the place.

It was a big deal for me to make, and I felt it so, but resolved not to let the transaction be known, even to my husband or family, until I got the money into my possession. I would give them no hint of it.

With such a resolution formed, I was not equal to going among them yet awhile and keeping my big secret, so I went to Charlotte and confided to my dear friend, Mrs. Eccles, what I had done, and bound her to secrecy. She said my enthusiasm made her tremble. She begged me not to be so confident. Somehow, she mistrusted the contract, and quoted "There's many a slip, 'twixt the cup and the lip," but I laughed at her fears and was not afraid.

I stopped in Raleigh on my way home, deposited the contract with Messrs. Fuller and Snow, who examined it and said it was all right.

While there, I met with my husband's nephew and my friend, Dr. Hal Harris, of Wake Forest. He had been kind to me in an hour of need, and extended to me a helping hand when I sorely needed it. I knew I had his sympathy in my work and to him I also confided the glorious finale which now awaited me.

I then returned to my home and kept my own counsel.

Chapter 5

The Chivalry of Man

How I lived through those days God alone knows!

The passage of each day meant so much for me, twenty four hours nearer the goal!

How long the days were. How endless the weeks!

How often did I lie awake at night, and go through the whole transaction. The letter of appointment that was bound to come! How often I read it over in imagination!

How I would go to Raleigh and how I would receive the money! Twenty thousand dollars in greenbacks! Only to think of it!

And all that was coming right to me!

Each time I awoke in the morning, it was twenty four hours nearer me! It was bound to come; no earthly power could stay it!

I would go to Raleigh. I would bring the money back. I would stop at Franklinton, pay off the heavy mortgage hanging over our home, and pay every dollar my husband owed.

I would get the mortgage papers and all the receipts and hand them to him, and then I would take out my great big pile of greenbacks and show to him and the children, and tell them that was what I had been working for so long, and what they had laughed at me so often for!

Now, wasn't that glory enough to last one woman a lifetime?

And after I had straightened out our money matters, I was going to build a huge platform, and invite all of my friends to come and rejoice with me, and I would have celebration and jollification that would make the "welkining," and that old Franklinton had never known before!

Oh, the halcyon days of that bright Fool's Paradise I lived in then!

A great Joy is as hard to bear as a great Sorrow.

In June I received a letter from Mr. Davidson asking many questions about the manufacture of my Remedy, the machinery necessary, etc. I could not answer with cold pen and ink, but went at once to Salisbury and saw him.

It was a kind of escape valve for a surcharged engine.

Mr. Davidson said he would establish his Laboratory at Pittsburg, Pa., and he would soon go on to begin operations. He said, "It will not be long now, Mrs. Person, before you get your money," and I again returned home.

Late in July I heard from him again. He was in Pittsburg, and wrote me he was rapidly pushing everything to completion.

The first day of August dawned, and I knew that my days of waiting were drawing to a close.

I wrote to my dearly loved sister, and told her she must come and be with me the last of the month, and the same to a friend in another part of the State.

I wanted them with me in this, my hour of triumph, tho' I gave them no hint.

On the twenty third day of August, they were both there.

The tension was almost unendurable.

Towards evening I told my son, Robert Lee, that I was looking for a letter either from Pittsburg or Salisbury; that I wanted him to go for it, and if he brought it for me I would reward him.

We lived four miles in the country; he had to walk and it was late when he started. The household retired early that night, and all, save me, were asleep when he returned.

He came in with a beaming face, said he had my letter from Salisbury, and claimed his reward.

There it was! At last!

My waiting was ended! It had come at last! My call to Raleigh had come!

Oh, My God, can I stand it!

It was some minutes before I could nerve myself to open the letter and read it, and when I did, <u>this</u> was what I saw:

> Salisbury, N.C. Aug. 22 '83
>
> Mrs. Joe Person: Madam,
>
> Upon reflection we have concluded to invest our money other than in the Remedy, and hereby withdraw from our contract. I am,
>
> Very truly,
> Geo. Davidson

Only that, and nothing more!

I read it and read it and read it over and over again. Then I went and woke up my husband and household. I told them what I had done, and how I had lived since May and "This is the end of it all!"

5. The Chivalry of Man

There was no more sleep for anyone in that house that night.

I told them I should have to go somewhere, I hardly knew or cared where, but inactivity would kill me. I could not stay still; I must go. The first train going South passed Franklinton about sunrise, and I was there ready to take it. I went to Raleigh.

About ten o'clock I went to Messrs. Fuller and Snow's office, with Davidson's letter of withdrawal.

How Col. Fuller's great big honest-looking eyes sparkled with indignation!

"My dear Madam, a contract like this cannot be so easily broken in North Carolina, and when a man does not wish to stand up to a contract of his own making, there is a way to make him do it, or else to make him pay. The Law will protect you and I shall stand by you. It is infamous, and we will show him that a Yankee cannot come down here and treat a woman of our State in this way. Madam, you have a good case against him, a No. 1 case, and I shall, at once, institute suit against him for thirty thousand dollars, and I shall win it for you, too."

He cited a case wherein heavy damages were recovered for failure of contract to furnish some windows, sashes, doors, etc., which he said was a case similar to mine.

Col. Fuller told me he wished I could contrive an interview for him with Davidson. This gave me something to do, and was better for me.

That afternoon, I kept on to Salisbury, saw Mr. Davidson, who had but little to say and nothing to explain. They had changed their minds. That was all in it. He said as he had business in Raleigh, he would go on as I did, but I need not ask him to see Messrs. Fuller and Snow, as he did not intend to do so.

Before leaving Salisbury, I wired Fuller and Snow, "Meet me at Yarboro when bus comes from train." Mr. Snow was there to meet me. As Davidson alighted from the bus, I introduced him to Mr. Snow, but without noticing or acknowledging the introduction, Davidson hurriedly left and walked up Fayetteville Street, thus eluding us.

When he came to the Hotel to dinner, I sent him word I wished to see him in the parlor for a few minutes, and he sent me word, "All right."

I hastily dispatched a message for Col. Fuller to come at once, and while I was talking to Davidson, Col. Fuller came in, and I had them face to face. Col. Fuller asked him if he had made a contract with Mrs. Person, and so and so on. He replied that he had. Col. Fuller then formally tendered compliance on my part, and he, on his part, refused compliance. Then and there Col. Fuller notified him of the suit he intended to bring against him.

Col. Fuller then requested me to go to Louisburg, see Capt. C.M. Cooke and Capt. Jos. Davis, tell them all the circumstances of the case, and ask them if they would not join him in prosecuting the suit.

I went at once to Louisburg and saw Capts. Cooke and Davis, and they heartily and cheerfully agreed to cooperate with Col. Fuller.

They said it was a duty they felt called upon to perform, and would gladly champion my cause, which was a good one and just. I had the Law on my side and the Right, and Davidson should see he could not treat one of our women in any such way, with impunity.

So with these three Towers of Strength and noble Champions on my side, I returned home, feeling a little better than when I left. Then I had nothing to look forward to; now I really enjoyed the change of pace, and already anticipated The Great Fight of the Three Giants, and almost persuaded myself that I had as soon get Davidson's money that way as the other — as long as I couldn't get the other. At the next term of Court, the case was duly docketed.

A suit for damages for thirty thousand dollars against George Davidson!

Wasn't it a big thing!

Let us send up three cheers for the Chivalry of Man!

What would become of the weaker sex without this Chivalry to defend us!

Shall we not return thanks that the Knights are not all dead yet?

At the next term of Court the case was "continued."

At the next term of Court the case was "continued."

At the next term of Court the case was "continued" ... AND

That was the end of my big Davidson case!!!

True, years afterwards, to clear the case from the docket and get rid of it, the Court adjudged me actual damages of $1,250, but my big case never came up for trial.

<u>My lawyer never once appeared in its behalf.</u>

Davidson had too much money for me and got ahead of me at last.

Moral: Never go into a Lawsuit with big money on the other side.

Chapter 6

More Chivalry

My work in and around Charlotte was beginning to bring me tangible results, and early in '84 I received a letter from a citizen of Charlotte, offering to put money into the Remedy if I would form a co-partnership with him and establish my headquarters at Charlotte.

It had now been many years since my husband was paralyzed and our principal was slowly but surely going. I saw at a glance the advantages which would accrue from such a move, and I wrote a favorable reply. A few days after, he came to my home.

He offered to put in one thousand dollars in Cash, furnish all the capital, advertising, etc., to build up the business. In return I was to transfer to him a one-half interest in my Trademark, right to manufacture, etc.

We were to equally divide the profits, and the Company, composed of him and myself, was to pay me $75 a month and my expenses for my services to manufacture and sell the Remedy.

I signed the contract, and on the 31st day of January, 1884, I went to Charlotte to begin work.

It was a move of love and duty for my household idols, not of choice and preference. Somebody had to work and the place was mine.

I contracted with my married daughter to take my place by her father's side and look after my little children, so that I knew they were well cared for.

I went to work in earnest and put up 3000 bottles of Remedy, my partner furnishing all the material. I had 2000 bottles of my own in stock at my home in Franklin County, which the Company bought for actual cost. This gave us a stock of 5000 in February.

I went on the road advertising, selling, drumming, talking, doing everything in my power to force sales, sending in the orders to Charlotte where my Partner attended to the shipping, kept the books, collected and so on.

I went home in March on a visit, and left all well and happy, except that I was not there. In April, while I was at Monroe, I was recalled home by a dispatch. My husband had died suddenly of heart disease. Suddenly had the summons come, while he was sitting in the porch waiting for the mail, for the letter I sent him daily.

I hastened home and we will touch lightly upon this part of my life. I stayed there three days, at the old home, without him; three desolate, wretched, miserable days, and then I felt that any other place was preferable to me now. I could not stay and then there was no need. The living needed me.

Two of my daughters were married now, and they took charge of my youngest children. Leaving one of my sons in charge of the farm, I returned to my work the following Monday.

I went direct to Wilmington and from there to Fayetteville.

I went into Mr. E.J. Hale's office one morning to see him in regard to an advertisement and he asked me why was it that Dr. Yates had made the attack upon me that he had?

"An attack upon <u>me</u>? What have I done? I know nothing of it."

"Yes," he said, "a most unprovoked and unwarranted attack, but one that cannot harm you," and he showed me the <u>Raleigh Evening Visitor</u>, and for the first time I read:

> Raleigh Doctors.
> Correspondence of the Evening Visitor.
> Wilmington, N.C. April 17, 1884
>
> Dear Visitor,
>   This seems to be a day of pretentious humbug, and, unfortunately the <u>hum</u> of the bug seems to be in the direction of the established order of the things that have been approved by the test of ages. There are certain great bulwarks of religion, civilization and liberty, finding their expression in the physician, minister of the gospel, lawyer and school teacher, against which the isms and humbugs of the day dash their waves. Society is especially interested in having these bulwarks properly supported. We may concede honesty to a man, and, at the same time condemn his reasoning, who, because he has run upon a small island, persists in his claim to have discovered a continent.
>   Yesterday, an advertising pamphlet was thrown into my yard. It contained a handbill stating that Mrs. Joe Person's medicine was extraordinarily good. I concluded to buy some; but looking at the pamphlet, I discovered a tirade of abuse of the Raleigh physicians. The effort seems to have been made to force the Raleigh physicians to notice the patent medicine mentioned above. They properly refused to do so, and hence their names are spread abroad in this pamphlet as deceivers, and if what this villainous pamphlet says be true, scoundrels!

6. More Chivalry

Who believes that Haywood, Hines, McKee, Royster, McGee and others are such men as this pamphlet makes them? And, if not, what shall be said of such attacks as these upon men, without whom society would be poor indeed!

I determined not to buy the medicine, of course; for I saw there must be something rotten in Denmark. For why try to rise by pulling others down? Why force a great principle as maintained by physicians for the good of society to yield to the claims of a secret remedy, even if it was discovered by a woman. If it is good in itself, push it properly. Good is a unit. It is not divided against itself. There is no necessity for abusing physicians.

Besides, it shows the cloven foot at once, for that cannot be good that tries to force itself over the levees of civilization, and that would inundate society with free doctors, lynch law, free love, sans religion, sans virtue, sans everything.

Yours as ever,
E.A. Yates

Speechless indignation expressed my feelings, but on my return home I replied:

Franklinton, N.C. April 29, 1884
Dr. E.A. Yates,
Minister of the Methodist Church,
Wilmington, N.C.

Dear Sir,

I have just seen the Raleigh Evening Visitor of April 17, in which appears your personal attack upon me.

1. Your attack was uncalled for — a copy of the "villainous pamphlet" was, weeks ago, mailed to each of the Doctors you go so far out of your way to defend. Months ago, they read the article to which you take such violent exception and they have always treated me with the respect and courtesy due a lady from a gentleman. I submitted the statement to the principal ones concerned — Dr. James McKee and Dr. McGee — for their correction and approval before it was sent to press, and I am at a loss to discover why you should have constituted yourself the champion and defender of the professional honor of the Raleigh Doctors, when they are all alive and so fully competent to take care of themselves. I DENY that I have ever uttered one word of abuse against the Raleigh Doctors, or any other member of the Medical Fraternity, and had I done so, the complaint should have come from them — not you.

2. Clothed in your ministerial garb, you have uttered a slander which, divested of it, you would never have dared to utter.

3. Your attack was upon one quietly pursuing the vocation which duty had assigned her — one who never did you a harm. You dealt a blow calculated to injure one you thought powerless to defend herself.

Had you turned to the back of that same pamphlet, for references for my personal reliability, you would have found as high names as Carolina could afford. If they are unknown to you, let me ask you to write to Col. Thos. C. Fuller, of Raleigh, write to Dr. G.W. Blacknall, Mr. John Nichols, Gov. Jarvis, Dr. Eugene Grissom, Raleigh; write to my minister, Rev. R.B. Sutton, D.D. Kittrell; write to your brother, Mr. W.J. Yates, of Charlotte; nay more, write to the Raleigh Doctors; ask any or all of them if you had ANY RIGHT to use my name in connection with the closing clause of your attack, and I am confident a sense of honor and right will cause you to offer me the amende honorable, and to acknowledge through the columns in which your attack was made, that it was unjustifiable and wrong. I am,

Very truly,
Mrs. Joe Person.

The "amende honorable" never came.
Letter from Mrs. Mary Bayard Clark and Dr. Yates' reply:

New Bern, N.C. June 3, 1884
Editors of Evening Visitor
Raleigh, N.C. Gentlemen:

Will you allow me space as a North Carolina woman to enter my protest against the attack made in your paper on Mrs. Joe Person, by Rev. E.A. Yates, of Wilmington, N.C.

Admitting, which I by no means do, that Mrs. Person had attempted to force a secret remedy on the profession, or even more (which again I do not do), that she did abuse the physicians of Raleigh, is that any reason why Dr. Yates, or anyone else, should accuse her of trying to "inundate society with free doctors, lynch law, free love, sans religion, sans virtue, sans everything"?

The charge is almost too ridiculous to be offensive!

So far from wishing to "force a secret remedy on the profession," Mrs. Person, in her "villainous pamphlet," offers "to give" the medical society her formula, only asking from them the acknowledged credit of the discovery.

Every woman, who, like Mrs. Person, is working for the support of her family, ought to rise, not in her defense, for she has, in her reply to Dr. Yates, shown herself quite equal to him and the occasion, but in self-defense. Dr. Yates has done her no harm in her business, on the contrary, his attack will doubtless benefit her pecuniarily; but he has needlessly wounded her feelings, for pursuing a legitimate business in an energetic manner. I have no personal acquaintance with Dr. Yates, but, from his reputation can but believe that he would never have written so harsh a letter about a lady had he been in good health. It shows "bad blood," and, as Mrs. Person's Remedy is a well known blood purifier, I think if he were tried by a Jury of women, he would be sentenced to one year's use of it, to the great improvement both of health and temper.

Wishing him nothing worse, I am

Yours respectfully,
Mary Bayard Clarke

Yates' reply:

Mr. Editor,

This excellent lady has wholly mistaken the animus of my article touching a certain publication connected with an advertisement of a patent medicine. The pamphlet was brought in and laid down in my piazza and I think it was therefore a lawful subject of criticism, whether written by a lady or gentleman. In point of fact, I did not think at the moment that it was the work of a lady; perhaps that fact might have caused me to be silent. Mrs. Clark will doubtless agree with me that there is a lamentable tendency to iconoclasm in much of the current thought of the day.

If the long established and fundamental principals that constitute the moorings of our splendid civilization are loosened, society must float out to unknown and stormy seas. A true philosophy concretes itself in the question: If the foundations be removed, what can the righteous do? My Scotch blood is ready to start up and antagonize every such attack. I do not say that the publication I criticized was necessarily such an attack, but to my eye, it had that complexion.

I am glad my fair reviewer thinks I have done no harm to Mrs. Person's business. I assure her that such was not my object. In fact, I had about reached the conclusion that I was among the last men who would willingly hurt a lady, and I still so feel. I would not only, Sir Walter Raleigh–like, lay down my cloak to keep her feet from the mud, but, if necessary, would put my hand beneath her foot.

A sharp argument is not suited to tender feelings and Paul was right, "It is good not to touch a woman." But, although, bee-like, they gather sweetness all the day, they can sometimes sting. And this is right; they ought to have the means of defense. Only in this case these excellent ladies are mistaken as to the object and animus of the attack.

I have not the pleasure of an acquaintance with either of these ladies. I have seen Mrs. Clark once or twice and that "divine brow and eye of infinite depth" misleads my judgment if, after mature thought, she does not agree with me as to the justness of my criticism. She kindly lays my supposed error to poor health. Thanks. But while I weigh 152 pounds and am able to be about a little, I am still much obliged for any means of escape. Indeed, I would "give my kingdom for a horse."

Woman's genius for war is incomprehensible. Mahomet II could not have taken Constantinople had it not been for the women, who beat back his flying soldiers, their husbands and brothers, and compelled them to stand to their posts.

And it may be doubted whether the genius of a Narses or a Bellisariess could make much headway against a Jeanne d'Arc.

Well, let it all go. These good ladies will please consider my hat off. "I take it all back," and in the next war, the Raleigh doctors may shift for themselves.

E.A. Yates.

The mountain labored and brought forth a mouse.

Chapter 7

Clouds — Sunshine: "After the Alps Comes Italy"

I worked on until May, when my partner recalled me to Charlotte to put up more Remedy, as the stock was nearly exhausted.

I put up another lot of 5000 bottles, and again went on the road to sell it. I was again recalled in September to put up more, as my partner wrote me it was nearly all sold.

Subdued by my old experiences, I tried not to build any more castles but I was bound to be very hopeful at the outlook.

In September, I returned to Charlotte to put up my third lot of Remedy. According to my partner's instructions, I went to the House of Messrs. Elliott and Remley, and ordered ten barrels of whiskey sent to the Laboratory. Two barrels were sent and then the supply seemed to stop. I went to the store to see what was the matter, and one of the proprietors said to me: "Mrs. Person, I have something to say which I regret to say to you, but business is business. When your Company pays me for the whiskey I have already furnished, I will be glad to send up all you need. You now owe me $540 for what I furnished in February and May, and until it is paid, I cannot furnish any more."

I was shocked at such a state of affairs. I knew we had done a big business, and I had no idea we owed a dollar.

Knowing that we had bought our bottles from Dr. McAden, I went direct to him and asked him how much we owed him for bottles. He told me we owed him for all we had used; between three and four hundred dollars, he believed, as we had never paid a dollar on them.

I couldn't exactly take it in, how such a thing could be.

Ten thousand bottles sold, and the whiskey and bottles not paid for! I couldn't understand it.

More dazed than ever, I went to my partner, and told him the situation.

I asked him what it meant, and how we were going to put up any more Remedy. He said he was sure he "didn't know" and he didn't suppose we could put up any more. "And the fact of the business is, we're busted, Mrs. Person, broke, dead broke, and we will just have to go to work and wind up the concern."

I asked him how much money was on hand; he said he would "see." He went and took out a little drawer and brought it forward and said: "Exactly one dollar and fifty cents."

One dollar and fifty cents in Cash, less than a gross of Remedy in stock, and $1700 in debt, was the outlook.

I called for the expense book. There was none.

My partner said he had had no time to keep a record of the expenses; he only knew the medicine was all sold and the money all spent — for expenses.

He added that all the available assets on hand now was the Trademark; he supposed that would bring something; in fact, he might buy it himself, and he should, at once, advertise it for sale at the Courthouse in Charlotte to the highest bidder, within 30 days.

Sell my Trademark! Why that meant robbing me of everything! Taking from me all means of earning my living!

It meant ruin in its "baldest meaning"!

All other sorrows I had seen seemed naught compared with this. To take from me the right to put up my own Remedy and sell it to someone else! It was monstrous. It was inhuman and yet it was before me.

The fiat had gone forth and the deed was to be done.

In the depth of my despair, I went to Dr. John. H. McAden and told him of the great wrong going to be done me and all it meant to me, and we can draw aside the curtain here and give you a glimpse of a scene that must have made the angels in Heaven rejoice: the sight of a rich man who was good, and noble, and true, and loyal to his manhood — a man who, for humanity's sake, put his hand into his pocket to relieve the distress of one whose narrative meant an appeal.

He told me my Trademark should not be sold, that he would save it for me. He asked me how much money would be required to save it. I told him if I could put up five thousand bottles of Remedy and have control of the sales, I could not only repay the expense of their cost, but could also pay every dollar we owed and my Trademark would be saved.

Dr. McAden asked me how much would that cost.

I told him, "Every cent of a thousand dollars."

He said he would advance it for me, and not only said so, <u>but</u> he did it. He at once ordered whiskey, bottles, everything necessary to put up five thousand bottles of Remedy. I put them up and we were solvent and — I was saved.

I then forced a dissolution of co-partnership, as I told my partner I would never work with him another day, as a partner. He transferred back to me his interest in my Trademark, while I relinquished all interest in the stock and he assumed the debts. This was satisfactory to Dr. McAden, who, in his turn, gave me a release in full.

I then agreed to work for my partner at the same salary for six months, to help him dispose of the stock, which he could not have done alone.

This act of Dr. McAden's was one of those grand acts sometimes done that redeem mankind and hold us on to our faith in man, but I shall always believe it never could have happened anywhere except in Charlotte and never would have been done except by a Charlotte man. Dear, dear Charlotte! There is no place like it, and she may well be called the garden spot of the Old North State.

Writers ascribe her prosperity to the progressiveness of her citizens, to their liberality and public-spiritedness, but the cause reaches higher and further and beyond that.

It is because they are animated by that broad spirit of Humanity, which makes one man extend a helping hand always to his brother in need; they had rather help than hinder, build up than to tear down. They had rather see a man rise than fall, and if he does not rise it will not be their fault. They have the kind word and broad sympathy which brings a man nearer his brother man, and keeps one's faith in human nature firm and unquestioned.

Chapter 8

I Go to Church

It must not be supposed that my life was altogether prosaic and practical, for many enjoyable episodes were interspersed as I traveled onward.

My business again called me to Wilmington in May, and one morning a gentleman's card was handed me. I went into the parlor and met a stranger. After introducing himself, he said: "Mrs. Person, I am one of the stewards in Dr. Yates' church, and, at the suggestion of several members of his congregation, I have called on you. We have read his attack upon you, and we wish to express our disapproval of it. He should never have done what he did, and we want you to know that his congregation denounces the act. I have heard but one sentiment and that was in your behalf." Before leaving, he said: "If I can serve you in any way, Mrs. Person, command me." Quick as the lightning's flash came the uttered thought. "I accept your offer — you can serve me. Tomorrow will be Sunday and I shall go to hear the Reverend Dr. Yates preach. Will you render me the kindness to let him know it? To let him know that it is I, sitting right in front of him, looking right at him, listening right to him, standing in God's pulpit, expounding God's gospel?

"I have a curiosity to see the Reverend gentleman posing in his professional character, but it would not do me any good unless he could know it."

My visitor laughed and said: "Well, I cannot blame you; I think I should feel so myself."

I told him I should go up the middle aisle to about four seats from the pulpit, and he promised to let him know.

And the next day I did go, and I did walk up the middle aisle, and I got a choice seat, where I could have a good view of him, and he knew who was looking at him, and listening to him preach "good will on earth." I wouldn't have had to preach that sermon for a good deal more than he got for it. And his prayer! I can never forget it. In his stentorian voice he prayed: "God grant that every one who has entered the holy sanctuary of God this day may have been prompted hither by pure and holy motives!"

"AMEN," said I, in tones equally stentorian.

Revenge is sweet, and it was mine.

Chapter 9

More Chivalry

I am here compelled to enter more into the particulars of one of my cases than I desire, and yet it is necessary because it was the pivot around which revolved many important incidents. It is but a chapter in the history, without which there would be a missing link.

In July '84 I first went to Tarboro to introduce my Remedy, and after remaining a few days, I had everything in readiness to leave the next morning, but in the afternoon a lady, Miss Pattie McDowell, drove up to the Hotel and said she came for me to go and see Miss Mary Staton, who was almost crazy from the effects of poison oak. I told Miss Pattie I would not like to go to a case of that kind, as it was something I did not recommend my Remedy for. She said Miss Mary Staton wished me to go and see if I could not give her some relief, and had requested her, as her friend, to bring me. She added, "We do not think she can live the night through, unless something can be done to relieve her."

Again I protested, I did not wish to go, for should she die while I was there, it might do me great harm. Mr. and Mrs. Bryan, and several gentlemen present, heard the conversation and advised me to go. They said the case had been given up by the doctors, who could do nothing for it, and were she to die, it could do me no harm, as everyone was expecting it. So, under protest, I went.

It was a case of great suffering, but I went to work and administered my Remedy and Wash and anxiously awaited the result. I remained with her that night. By morning she was better, and by four o'clock the next evening, the disease was under perfect control. Three days after, I went to see her again and found her up and dressed and in the regular prosecution of her household duties.

These facts are verified by a written statement given me for publication, and which I still use in my pamphlet, signed by Miss Mary Staton, Nicholas

Staton, Cornelius Staton, Felix Staton, and Miss Pattie McDowell, who were all eye-witnesses of my work and its results.

On my second visit to Miss Mary Staton, I told her and the family that it was impossible for an extreme case like that to be <u>cured</u> so soon, and as I thought it was liable to break out again at any time, I would not leave Tarboro yet awhile, but would remain a few days, so as to be near when she needed me, and every member of the family expressed themselves as gratified at my decision.

I have never seen anything equal to the enthusiasm that prevailed in Tarboro when the result of my treatment of Miss Mary Staton's case became known. People flocked to see me as if I had been a show, and as for the Remedy, we could not get it there as fast as we needed it.

I had several dozen lots scattered along at the towns on the Wilmington and Weldon Railroad, which I ordered to Tarboro by telegram, and every bottle was sold before I could get it there.

I ordered a gross from Charlotte, but it was nothing to what the demand called for, and I ordered another.

People would come and pay me the money for it before the Remedy came, to make sure they would get it and not be put off.

Those who were sick wanted it so they might get well.

Those who were well wanted it in case they should get sick.

It seemed that in one day I had become famous. Enthusiasm ran high.

Among the physicians who had attended Miss Mary Staton, there was one little fellow named Baker, who was reported to be considerably annoyed by the result of my work. I was told that "the boys" had been "guying" him unmercifully and that he had a long face in consequence. I was also told that he was a bosom friend of the Staton boys, but I did not attach much importance to that fact at the time, or realize all that it meant to me.

<u>But</u>, while I was waiting on Miss Mary Staton as I said I would do, she had, as I had predicted, a recurrence of her trouble and, instead of sending for me, they had actually sent for this little Baker, because he had told them that it was not Mrs. Joe Person's Remedy that had done Miss Mary the good, but "the medicine <u>I</u> had given her had just taken effect," and, as incredible as it may seem, it actually turned the tide against me for a while.

People who had spoken for the Remedy came and told me they did not want it. "When I spoke to you for it I thought it was your medicine that 'hoped' Miss Mary Staton, but Dr. Baker says it was his!" Some would add, "And we know him and don't know you."

Several who had paid me wanted their money back, giving the same reason. In every instance, I paid it back, until I had refunded $17! and I abided my time.

I am a great believer in Right is Might.

In company with Miss Pattie McDowell — dear Miss Pattie, faithful and good, staunch and true — I went again to see Miss Mary Staton, to see why they should have treated me as they did, after giving me their written testimony as to what my Remedy had done for her.

The Staton boys said the same thing I had heard that Dr. Baker said — it was his medicine that had just taken effect, and not mine that had done the good.

Miss Mary said, "I could not help myself, Mrs. Person. You are here today and gone tomorrow. Dr. Baker is here all the time and the boys wanted to send for him, but I know it was your Remedy that did me the good. Then it was that Dr. Baker went on the streets and said the people of Tarboro would let any humbug come along and fool them with his quackery."

I was thoroughly indignant and aroused.

I did not seek Miss Mary Staton's case. I did not even wish to go to it. I went because I couldn't well help myself and as an accommodation to the family. I saw no sense or justice in any doctor hounding me down because I had relieved a suffering woman.

If he could have done it, they would never have sent for me. Could he have relieved her, they would never have thought of sending for me; there would have been no necessity. I was a last resort, after he failed.

Two and two always made four, so, in my righteous indignation I wrote him the following:

> Tarboro, N.C. July 18, '84
>
> Dr. J.M. Baker,
>   I have been informed that you have stigmatized me as a humbug, and my work as quackery. Please let me know whether this is true or not, as I have no desire to do you an injustice, even in my thoughts, unheard.
>
> Respectfully,
> Mrs. Joe Person

The following is his reply:

> Tarboro, N.C. July 19 '84
>
> Mrs. Joe Person,
>
> Dear Madam,
>   Your note of July 18 was handed me a few minutes ago. In reply I would say I have no desire to injure you in any particular. If there is virtue in your medicine you deserve and will receive the approbation of humanity. A quack is a boastful pretender to medical science or art, of which they know nothing, an irregular, tricking practitioner of

physic. A humbug is an imposition, a hoax, a deception. Until you show the medical profession that yourself and your Remedy, neither, can be placed in such a category, we are compelled to look upon you as such and treat you accordingly. I am not one of those persons who think everything out of the legitimate bound of the professional code should be hooted at, but will acknowledge merit wherever found. I assure you, Madam, that whatever I have said or will say in regard to your Remedy or your quackery is meant as no reflection on you personally. I do not now recollect applying the epithets to you, you refer to, but may have done so without any semblance of hypocrisy.

Very truly yours,
Julian M. Baker

Tarboro, N.C. July 19 '84

Dr. J.M. Baker,

Dear Sir,

In reply to your favor of this morning, I write for information. Will you be kind enough to tell me <u>in what way</u> I would be allowed to prove to the medical profession that myself and my Remedy, neither, can be placed in such a category as "quacks" and "humbugs"?

I send you one of my pamphlets. Read that "Solid Chapter of Solid Facts," and you will see that I <u>did</u> go to the medical profession of Raleigh, and offer to cure free any and all cases of blood impurity they might submit to me as a public test that my Remedy would do all I claimed for it. The privilege was denied me on the ground that "it would be conniving, at the effort to enrich the owner of a patent secret remedy." This presupposed success, as there would be no enrichment to me, had I failed, even in a single case.

Again, I came into your community, had the most extreme case I ever met taken from your hands and placed in mine. I treated the case twenty hours, with such marvelous success that the whole community was stirred, the news spread like wildfire, the feeling amounted to enthusiasm, when, <u>seeing your danger</u>, you came to the front and denounced me as a humbug and my work as quackery. Lacking moral courage to come forward, and, for humanity's sake, congratulate me upon having a remedy which could relieve what you proved you could not reach, you did come forward, but it was to make the effort to take from me what you knew belonged to me, and appropriate it to yourself.

If you will not look, how can you see?

You say you are not one who thinks everything out of the legitimate bounds of the professional code should be hooted at, but will acknowledge merit wherever found.

How can you find it if when brought right before you, you close your eyes? If, when the great problem is being worked and the answer is being developed on the tablet of events, you not only ignore the worker, but shielded under a great cloak, <u>get before her</u> and seriously announce to an admiring and applauding public, "I DID THAT"!!

Hoping you can throw some light on a subject which is to me, so far, a mystery, I am

Respectfully,
Mrs. Joe Person

Tarboro, N.C. July 20 '84

Mrs. Joe Person,

Dear Madam,

Your note of yesterday would have been answered sooner, but I have been too busy to attend to it until now.

I do not propose to be the instrument by which you can bring yourself and your remedy into notoriety, and answer your note to remove the delusion from your mind.

You entirely misrepresented the case of Miss Staton and in so doing take occasion to insult me, and, no doubt, as you had a right to do, hold up the petticoat as protection. Be that as it may, I will be candid and just enough, to give you a correct account when you will see the folly of your position and appreciate the ridicule to which you are subjected.

Miss Mary was seen by my father, Dr. J.H. Baker, only one time previous to the attack in which you saw her, the result of his visit (she being in one of her paroxysms) was to give her <u>immediate</u> relief.

The next week the trouble returned, he was sent for again, visited her, and made a prescription, telling her that relief would be felt as soon as the medicine had time to take effect, making another prescription, which had to be gotten in town. When you saw her, she was under the influence of the medicine he had given in the morning.

You say you relieved her and can have it so if you like, as it signifies nothing, as hundreds of times before had Dr. Speed and others relieved her, and never considered it a matter of any importance whatever. When the trouble returned after you took her in charge, a faithful application of the medicine only aggravated the itching, giving no relief whatever, so that my father was sent for in the night. The result was he gave her <u>instant</u> relief, after your medicine had failed, the same medicine he used then she is using now and every time it is applied.

The lady has been in town since and says the attack which came on after using your medicine was the most violent she ever had in her life. Miss Staton was not seen by my father or myself, until sent for after your remedy failed. Your name was never mentioned by me to Miss Staton or any member of the family, nor have they ever mentioned your name to me but once, and then it was in the spirit of ridicule, in which, Madam, I took no part. If there is any virtue in your medicine, it is certainly not suited to such cases as Miss Staton's.

If it affects others as it did her, I advise you to trade it off for a dog, give him half a dozen bottles, stoppers and all and if that don't kill him, shoot him. I have devoted as much time to you and your remedy as I intend to; my time is too valuable for such recreation, so do not write me any more love letters.

Respectfully,
Julian M. Baker

Instinctively I acted:
I got ½ dozen bottles of the now famous Remedy, put them on a waiter, and spread a napkin over it.
Instinctively I wrote:

Dr. Baker,
In compliance with your prescription, I send you a half dozen bottles of my Remedy. Please take it, stoppers and all, and if it don't kill you, let me know and I will come over and shoot you.

Very truly,
Mrs. Joe Person.

N.B. This is not intended as a love letter.

After impulse came reflection, and I saw that I could not afford to reply to such a missive, and did not reply.

Why give a letter I never sent? Because I am dealing with FACTS and giving them as they actually occurred.

I knew he was unjust and un–Christian, but I did not know he was <u>dirty</u>, and I truly regretted that I had dignified him by notice, or put myself in touch with a man of his caliber, but I was a stranger then to Tarboro and Tarboro ways.

Circumstances again forced me to the front and to explain so, I published a Card in the <u>Southerner</u>, explanatory of the situation and left it to the Public to decide how unjust it was for them to take Miss Mary Staton's case from me and give it to Dr. Baker, when their published statement, signed by every, member of the family and by Miss Mary, would show what my Remedy had done for her, and the absurdity of his claim, and again the Public was with me and knew I was right, and again the demand for my Remedy was started and continued on a solid basis.

This is evidenced by the following letter, which showed the stand my Remedy had taken in Tarboro <u>seven months</u> after the Staton case, <u>regardless</u>.

Tarboro, N.C. Feb. 4, 1885

Mrs. Joe. Person, Madam,

    Ship at once five gross of your Remedy and two gross of your Wash. We are doing well with it in Tarboro, and sales are rapidly increasing. It has given satisfaction, so far as we have learned, in every case.

Respectfully,
E.B. Hodges & Co.

And this order for five gross was duplicated in less than sixty days.

Chapter 10

Partner No. 2

When I was in Tarboro in January, '85, Mr. E.B. Hodges made me a proposition of Partnership, on the same basis of my Charlotte contract, which I, unhesitatingly, declined. The sales had grown and the demand increased so steadily and rapidly, that he became almost demoralized on the subject of the Remedy. He saw as many castles as I had ever seen and dreamed as many dreams. His enthusiasm knew no bounds. He asked me upon what terms I would take him in as a co-equal partner, and I told him, which he declined. After remarking to a citizen of the plan, that I was the biggest fool he had ever met to suppose for a moment that he would accept any such proposition, when I was in Charlotte, in March, he wrote me he would accept my terms.

The time had nearly expired that I had promised to work for my Charlotte partner, and as this Tarboro outlook was the best that presented itself then, I accepted the situation, and formed a co-partnership with him under the name of The Mrs. Joe Person Remedy Co. Mr. Hodges was to put in two thousand dollars in cash, and be the business manager of the concern. The Company was to pay me one hundred dollars a month and expenses, for my services, and we were to divide equally the profits. In consideration of this I was to transfer to him a half interest in my Trademark. He came to Charlotte on the 31st day of March, as he wanted it clinched beyond all hope of recall.

As my Chivalrous defender, Col. T.C. Fuller had my Davidson case in hand, I would not agree for anyone else to write the contract. So together we went to Raleigh.

We explained to Col. Fuller our business and I told him I had a great deal of trouble with my last partnership, and unless I could make a solid and good contract I did not want any. I told him that Mr. Hodges was a minor. I told him how near I came to losing my Trademark in Charlotte, and that I wanted it protected this time so that I could not lose it. Col. Fuller talked with Mr. Hodges, and found that in all things Mr. Hodges acted for the Company in his firm, the Company being his father. He told Col. Fuller that his father had given him absolute power of attorney, to manage his money and business.

Col. Fuller said that recognized him <u>a man</u> in law, and any contract made by him would be valid.

I was satisfied and signed the contract.

I then returned to Charlotte to wind up my business, which I soon did.

Oh, the sadness of that last leave-taking of Charlotte! I could not control my feelings and would give vent to them at every sad "Goodbye" given me. It is a terrible thing to leave friends, tried and true, to go among strangers to find — who knows what?

To leave CHARLOTTE to go to Tarboro! What a transition!

How little did I dream then all that it meant!

In April, 1885, I moved to Tarboro, and the first I did was to have my contract with Mr. Hodges recorded in the Clerk's Office.

A few days after that I was reading the contract over and my consternation was great when I found that not one word had been inserted in the contract to protect my Trademark. My partner had the same <u>power</u> to involve it that my first partner had, and, by one of those inadvertencies we cannot account for or explain, I had read it over and signed it, without noticing the omission. I went to my room, copied the contract exactly as it had been written by Col. Fuller, but inserted this additional clause:

> AND IT IS HEREBY AGREED BETWEEN. E.B. HODGES AND MRS. JOE PERSON THAT HER TRADEMARK SHALL NOT BE HELD LIABLE FOR ANY DEBTS THAT MAY BE CONTRACTED BY E.B. HODGES IN THE MANAGEMENT OF THE MRS. JOE PERSON REMEDY COMPANY.

I carried this second contract to Mr. Hodges, told him of my oversight and asked him to sign it. He positively refused to do so.

I told him, as it stood, I was completely, in his power. He said he couldn't help that, he had gone to my own lawyer, I had read it over and signed it, the contract had been recorded and the transaction was final. Feeling the helplessness of my position, I determined to abide my time and "watch" as well as "pray."

The following Monday, Mr. Hodges and I went to Baltimore to buy supplies for the Laboratory.

Under a contract to put in two thousand dollars only, he bought at one stroke ten barrels of Alcohol, for which he paid over one thousand dollars, with all material necessary for putting up ten thousand bottles of Remedy!

I begged him to go slow. I told him it was so much better to begin small and work up big. No, the money was his, he knew what he was doing and he was the business manager of the Co.

What could I do? I saw that his first move brought the Company in debt to him, that my Trademark was again in danger and I trembled and was afraid.

SELF PRESERVATION IS THE FIRST LAW OF NATURE.

In the course of time the materials for putting up the ten thousand bottles of Remedy began to come in. The ten barrels of Alcohol had come, the vegetable ingredients were there, ten thousand bottles with our name blown in them were on the way, ten thousand cartons were in press!

Mr. Hodges came into the Hotel one morning, jubilant and exultant, and said, "Well, Mrs. Person, the Alcohol and ingredients are here, come on and, let's go down to the Laboratory and start things to work. We have got everything in readiness to start this morning."

I went to my room and got the contract I had written. I carried it to Mr. Hodges and asked him to sign it. He said, "Mrs. Person, I will not sign that contract. I have told you so before and I positively refuse."

"Then," said I, "I positively refuse to strike one lick of work in the Remedy. If you will not sign this contract, protecting my Trademark, I shall not go near the Laboratory. I will not put up a bottle or have anything whatever to do with it."

His face blanched to the pallor so well known by those who know him, and he said, "You do not mean that, surely."

I told him I meant every word of it, that unless he signed the contract that I wrote, I would have nothing to do with any of it.

He signed it. I had it recorded, so there are now two contracts recorded in Edgecombe County, one the contract written by Col. Fuller, and one written by me, identical with the first, except the addition of one little clause, protecting my Trademark, and making it impossible for my partner to engineer it from me.

Experience is a dear teacher, but it is certainly a good one. I then went to work with a will, but from this time, my partner never had the same interest in the work. He had put so much money into the stock that he had none left to push the business, and it was uphill work altogether. Mr. Hodges had employed Mr. Murphy Dodd of Fayetteville, and Mr. Ben Hardy, so well and favorably known in North Carolina, both loyal men, honest and true, to travel and sell the Remedy.

Sales were good, and I was, even now, hopeful of the success of my second partnership business, but I soon found that Tarboro lacked a great deal of being Charlotte.

Chapter 11

Tarboro and Tarboro Ways

The people of Tarboro looked askance at me, as if I had no business there. I had "sassed" their doctor and they didn't like it. Things went from bad to worse. The tide was against me and I was virtually tabooed.

To the average Tarborean, an outsider is synonymous with an interloper, that is, if he comes as a worker.

It is well known to the citizens of Tarboro now, how I was treated in those days — to their shame be it said.

I could not even work at my place of business in safety, and was finally forced to appeal to the Court for protection.

The ladies, even of my own Church had nothing to do with me, the minister of my own Church did not come near me, and for nearly a year I was excluded from all Church privileges, and did not feel free, and welcome to cross its portals.

I can never forget one day, when Mr. Dodd — who was my friend as well as coworker — and I were going from the Laboratory to the Hotel. Three scions of the "upper ten" passed by us, two scions of the "lower five" — and the supercilious smile they gave us, and the Tarborean

An empty remedy bottle from Alice's Tarboro days. This bottle (from the private collection of Donna and Gary Cunard) is rare in that the company's name and location are blown into the glass rather than being printed on a paper label, as was the case with most of Alice's bottles (courtesy of Donna and Gary Cunard).

aspect of their upturned noses, as they gave us an all-searching gaze, and the contemptuous swish of their skirts as they passed, lest they should come into contact with a working woman! And how Mr. Dodd returned their gaze with a polite bow and said, "All it costs is five cents a look, ladies!"

Had I gone to Tarboro with the emoluments of wealth, my recollections of the place might have been different, would perhaps have been as pleasant as those of a lady boarding at the same Hotel that I was at the same time, who was visited, drived [sic], flowered, and ice creamed.

She was a Yankee, I a Southerner, <u>but</u> she wore diamonds and I — a working apron.

Encased in their little shell of exclusiveness, to them the World is bounded on the North by the Railroad Depot, on the South by the Tar River, on the East by Hendrick's Creek and on the West by Lloyd's field. See?

There were some few families there who were as kind and courteous to me as anyone could be, but they were few. There are as good people in Tarboro as one can find anywhere, but they are far between.

Dr. J.W. Jones and family, the Shacklefords, the Bryans, the Penders never meted me anything but kindness and courtesy, which I have never forgotten.

Chapter 12

Partners, Adieu!

My partner was a wonderful man of business in many respects, for his years, and if he had had money back of him, and not been afraid of Tarboro people, he might have made a success of his venture, but the outlook made him shaky and nervous. Things were not as he had calculated, the castles had begun to fall, the dreams to fade, and he had no money to keep the enterprise going, so he wanted to get out of it and dissolve the partnership. He said if he couldn't get out of it any other way, he would play the "Baby Act," as he was not of age when he made the contract. It was then that I learned, for the first time, that the contract of partnership that Col. Fuller wrote for me was not worth the paper it was written on. I wired to him at Raleigh: "The contract you gave me has been decided worthless. If you are willing to protect its validity, come on first train; if not, I am ruined." As he was absent, the message was repeated to New Bern, and his answer came: "I expect to return to Raleigh tomorrow," and I saw at a glance where I was "at."

I found that the one clause I had inserted in the second contract was all that saved my Trademark, and stood between me and ruin. The Company was then indebted to my partner, as he had already spent more money than was stipulated in the contract, and it was, of course, charged against the Company. I put my case in the hands of Judge Howard and Mr. Jos. Martin, and well and faithfully did they protect my cause.

I told my partner that in my first dissolution I had been left high and dry without a dollar and I did not intend to be set adrift in the same manner a second time. I was willing to dissolve the Partnership, but he would not only have to give back to me his half-interest in my Trademark, but, for the inconvenience to which he had subjected me, he would have to make an assignment to me of the stock on hand, which would give me a start elsewhere, as I could not afford to leave stock of my Remedy, in other hands, behind me.

12. Partners, Adieu!

On these terms and none other would I agree to dissolve. In the light of everything that stood between us, my partner knew it was the best thing he could do, and on those terms we dissolved.

In April 1886, I shook Tarboro dust from my feet, and sufficiently amused with Partners and Partnerships, I moved to my adopted home in Kittrell, where I have since prosecuted my business in peace.

Men have long since ceased to fight me, because they know they cannot hurt me, and besides, my boys are grown and brave, and my Remedy is now established on a pedestal none can shake.

When I first went forward into the world, fifteen years ago, woman had not advanced to the front, as at the present day. It was then something new to see a woman, and a Southern woman at that, doing man's work. I suppose it did look strange to see a woman on the street posting bills and pasting up advertisements, but I hardly saw, and cared not for, the gaze of the curious. I only saw the little hands extended to me for aid. I only knew I stood a bulwark between them, and privation, and dependence.

In the fall of '84 my home and all I had was sold for the face of the mortgage. It took everything to liquidate the debts.

My three eldest children were independent and self-supporting, but I was left with six children totally dependent on me for food, clothing, education, everything — the youngest six years old, then little stairsteps, up.

My children are now grown and mostly self-supporting. My youngest boy and the last I have to educate is at College, and the lines are easier to me now. I have cared for them well, have clothed them well, and educated them well, so that they can take the stand in life they are entitled to. Seven of my children are now living, and they are prosperous and succeeding in life. I have five sons and not a dissipated or immoral one among them. Is not that a rich reward?

I have been spared to see my children grown and my happiness within them is complete. I have lived to enjoy the fruit of my labor, and the reward is worthy of the work. I have borne the cross, and I daily wear the crown. At a recent visit of the Bishop, four of my children were confirmed in the Church I love. My mantle must, ere many more years, fall upon my beloved boy, Rufus, who is well worthy to wear it. For years he has stood by my side and worked with me, and when I have crossed the River, he will take my place, and continue the good work.

I am often asked if I am not a woman's rights "man," and I emphatically answer <u>Yes</u>— a staunch believer in her "right" to earn her living, and be respected for it; in her "right" to defend herself from the assaults of men, when assailed.

I had to go. What else could I do? I could not beg and to steal I was ashamed. I could not keep house, for I had no house to keep. I could not stay at home, for I had none.

No, I have always felt I was doing the work my Father intended I should do. He gave it to me as a talent, and then made it a necessity that I should go and use it. He opened the avenue and showed me the way.

Believe me, no woman will voluntarily go out in the world among men, to do man's work. When you see one there pause, ere you condemn or smile.

There is a Power behind you cannot see, a mountain of Love you can know nothing of.

THE END.

PART II: NOTES BY THE WAYSIDE

Flowers Plucked from the Hedges and Thorns from the Briar-Bushes

I have made allusion in the first part of my little work to the music, company and bright days at the old home. In that way I kept up my music, playing principally bright lively pieces, and the old plantation melodies so dear to the Southern heart, and when my work called me forth into the world, I found that my music attracted attention, and gave pleasure and enjoyment that I little thought it capable of.

I visited the Raleigh Exposition one day near its close and some friends asked me to go into one of the musical Exhibitions, and "knock off" some of my old tunes, which I did.

I soon had a crowd around me that seemed to enjoy it vastly. My music was so different from the music of the present day, that it touched a responsive chord in the hearts of many a one present.

To my surprise, the owner of the Exhibition — a Richmond House — made me an offer to play for them at the Fairs to be held that fall.

I accepted this offer which brought me into closer touch with the people and gave me better chance to advance my work than anything that had yet presented itself.

I played for the same House for several consecutive years.

On one occasion I was in Charlotte, and my friend, Mrs. Eccles, with an eye always open to the possibilities of the future and the latent developments within me, asked me why I did not go to the Atlanta Exposition, which was to open the next week, and play. I told her I couldn't ride and it was too far to walk. She advised, she begged, she entreated me to go and see what I could do. No, I had no money to risk, I knew no one in Atlanta, and no one knew me. I could hold the County Fairs, but what could I do with an Atlanta Exposition! The suggestion was an absurdity. I had no business there and I could not go.

The next morning she handed me a round-trip ticket from Charlotte to

Atlanta and said, "Now, you will have to submit to the inevitable and go. I have bought you a ticket; it is a present from me, so pack up and go."

I did pack up and go, with scarcely an idea of what I should do, or how I should start when I got there. (Mind you, this happened in Charlotte too.) I merely folded my hands and drifted with the tide.

I arrived in Atlanta, and again, as "big as life," drove to the Kimball and registered.

I determined to ask the Manager of the Hotel the names of the music Houses, general directions and so on, but anyone who attended that Exposition can appreciate what the word "crowd" means. I could not get near the Manager or Clerk to ask anything.

Feeling as nearly like a nonentity as I ever felt in my life, I sauntered up a principal street, and passed a music House. A small boy came to wait upon me. I asked for the Proprietor, who soon appeared.

I asked, "Is this Mr. Ludden?"

"No, Madam, this is not Mr. Ludden."

"Is it Mr. Bates?"

With a humorous smile he replied, "No, Madam, it is not Mr. Bates either. I flatter myself I am a much better looking man than either Mr. Ludden or Mr. Bates." Then he explained that Ludden & Bates was a Savannah House, whereas I was addressing Mr. Crew, of the firm of Phillips & Crew.

Accepting the amendment, I explained my business, that I wished to play for him, if he had an Exhibition at the Exposition.

He regretted so much he had to disappoint me, but several of his men played, and he really had no need of a performer. No, he did not wish to engage anyone. "But," he courteously added, "you must not leave without going out to the Exposition, and seeing what a display we have," and he reiterated his regret that he could do nothing for me.

I went with them to the Fairgrounds, and a grand Exhibition they did indeed have in their department.

It is not an enviable feeling to go to anyone and offer one's services, and to be told in cold blood that you are not wanted, so when Mr. Phillips invited me to try some of their fine instruments, it was rather with a feeling that courtesy demands courtesy, than any impulse I felt to be musical, that I ran my fingers over the keys of their Concert Grand Knabe.

Then I struck up a waltz and the crowd gathered around.

I went off into some gay dance tune, and the crowd rapidly increased. Then I struck up "Billy in the Low Grounds," and the crowd began to applaud. Then, "I Bet My Money on the Bob-Tail Nag," and the crowd became enthusiastic, and would not have me stop.

"One more piece," I told Mr. Phillips, "and I am done."

I struck up "Dixie," and with what effect anyone can imagine who knows the effect of "Dixie" on a Southern crowd.

Cheer after cheer went up as I stopped.

Mr. Phillips said, "Upon what terms will you play for us, Mrs. Person?"

I told him, "Ten dollars a day."

"Well," said he, "we will pay it."

I could only play for them three days, as I had an engagement to play at the Raleigh Fair the next week.

This was the beginning of my playing at the big Expositions, and was soon followed by engagements in Augusta, Ga., Richmond, Va., Dallas, Texas, and other places.

At the close of my first day's work at Atlanta, Mr. Phillips said that he wished he could show me, in some way, how he appreciated my work, besides paying me for it.

I told him of my Remedy work, and he had a large number of cards printed, with my Remedy advertisement, and distributed them the next two days, and would not allow me to pay a dime on them.

Furthermore, when he handed me the thirty dollars for my three days work he said that it gave him genuine pleasure to do so, and that he had never paid out any money to anyone, with more satisfaction.

What big things little things are, after all!

Fourteen years ago! And yet how vivid is the recollection of the kindness shown me then, again a stranger in a strange land, and working in a new field.

Why will not men more generally recognize the importance of these little acts of courtesy, so grateful to the people's heart, and observe them, and thus settle the disputed question, "Is Life worth living?" Among the most pleasant recollections of my business life are the remembrances connected with my musical engagements.

Surely there must be something about music that softens men's nature, and brings them into closer touch with the humane side of human nature.

My engagements with Messrs. Phillip & Crew, Atlanta, Ga., with Messrs. Thomas & Barton, at two of the Augusta, Ga., Expositions, with Mr. C.H. Edwards, at two of the Dallas, Texas, Expositions, and with Ayland & Lee, at Richmond, Va., are but a series of most pleasant remembrances.

Then came a call for the notes of the old time melodies, as I played them. I published them in '89 and so link was added to link, which strengthened the chain, and I now had three friends to depend upon, instead of one: my Remedy, my playing, my music — each one bringing me nearer the people and at the same time, adding to my income.

In connection with the publication of my music, let me show what man can do, when "looking upward, not downward, Outward, not inward," and living to "Lend a helping hand."

When I determined to publish my melodies, I went to Richmond, Va., to have them written for me.

My friend, Mr. Geo. A. Minor, introduced me to Mr. John Baseler, as one who could serve me well. I asked Mr. Baseler what he would charge to write my music, about twenty pages. He said he did not know and could not tell me until he had finished the work.

"Give me an approximate estimate."

"I cannot even do that. I will tell you when the work is done. I can only promise you that I shall not charge you more than you can pay." I had, by now, acquired a habit of submitting to the inevitable, whenever I couldn't help myself, so I consigned myself to his tender mercies, and, as he did not look like a wolf in sheep's clothing, seeking whom he might devour, I was not much afraid.

We worked hard for more than two days, and the work was done. I then asked him what I owed him; perhaps he would tell me now.

Note his reply: "Mrs. Person, go ahead with your music and have it published. I trust you will make a success of it. I am only too glad it is in my power to help one who has tried so hard to help herself. I know something of your life and its responsibilities, and I am glad to do this for you. I do not wish you to consider it a debt or obligation, for it has been a pleasure to me. I am the debtor, for you have given me the opportunity to work in a good home mission, which I always enjoy," and he made me no charge.

The days of Chivalry are not past, nor its Knights all dead.

When I go to a county now to introduce my Remedy, I make the county seat my headquarters, and hire a double team, requiring them to send a good, reliable white man with me to drive. I go to every country store in the county to advertise and sell my Remedy, stopping at every house on the wayside that has an organ or piano, to sell my music, staying at night among the country people. In that way I suppose I enter more homes, and see more of the home life of the people than any man, or any other woman in the State, has ever had a chance to do.

And do I love the life? Most undoubtedly Yes, though I find many things, many people, that are more than a revelation to me. I find that right here in North Carolina there are scores of people who actually believe that MUSIC is a sin! Think of it! "A sin?" I ask, "How can that be, why do you think it is a sin?"

"Because it makes me feel good, and like I want to pat my foot, and you know that would be a sin!"

And yet we are sending missionaries to China!
Oh, Consistency, what a virtue thou art!

Poor John!

 I carried my music to a lady's house one day to see if I could not sell her a copy. She asked me to play some of the pieces, as she needed some new music and wanted to hear them. Catching glimpse, as I thought, of the almighty dollar, I played the "Italian Waltz."

 "Oh, my," she said, "I wish John was here." I asked her "Who was John?" She said he was her husband, and she wished he could hear that music. I then started on some of the livelier pieces, and I never saw anyone who seemed to enjoy them any more, as she patted her foot to the rhythm of the music. After playing one or two more pieces, I turned to her to accomplish the object of my visit. I asked her if she liked the music.

 "Like it? Why I like it better than any music I ever heard in my life!"

 "Well, wouldn't you like to buy a copy and learn the pieces?" She turned to me in holy horror, and said "<u>I-learn-those-pieces</u>? No, Madam, I wouldn't have that music in my house for anything in this world."

 I told her I understood her to say she liked it. "That's what's the matter. I like it too well; it made me pat my foot, and <u>I am afraid of it</u>. No, Madam, I don't want any of your music. I did wish John was here, but now I am glad he is away. It would have done him more harm than good, for John loves music anyway."

 Let us drop a tear for Poor John.

 I left the house cogitating and meditating, but then I had found something new under the sun, and novelty always interests.

"Sonny"

 On another occasion I went to a preacher's house with my music. I saw his son, a manly little fellow about twelve years old. He said he wanted a copy and asked me to go to his home, and show it to his mother. I did so and played the pieces. The little boy said he must have the pieces and appealed to his mother. She hesitated. He said he had a silver dollar of his own and if she would not buy the music, he would get it himself. The mother told him his father (the minister) was in the study, and to go and see what he said about getting it. The study was in an adjoining room and I could hear the conversation.

 "Sonny," said the Reverend gentleman, "go and ask the lady if she will not take ninety cents for the music; if she will, you can get it. Tell her that is all the change I've got."

I told him, "Yes, as that is all your father has, I would not stand on ten cents. You can have the music, as I had rather have your father's ninety cents than to take your own silver dollar."

So the little boy returned to his father's study for the money, and again the Reverend gentleman spoke:

"Sonny, ask her if she will take eighty five cents for her music; tell her I lack a nickel of having as much as I thought I had." I told him I would not take that. I had rather not make the sale, and made a move to leave. He went into the study to report.

"Ask her if she can change a ten dollar bill."

I told him I could, and he sent me a ten to change. I was counting it out, he called his son and said:

"I don't believe I want that note changed. Here are two fifty cent pieces which I didn't know I had [!] Pay them to her, and <u>be sure to get the ten cents change</u>." So he beat me out of ten cents at last, and the next Sabbath, I suppose, he filled God's pulpit and with raised hands and uplifted eyes, preached about the pomps andvanities of this wicked world!

And yet we are sending missionaries to China!

Not My Daughter, Oh No!

While my music has met with most favorable reception among teachers and judges of music, it is amusing to note the expression of many who really enjoy the pieces, but are afraid of compromising their musical dignity and intelligence by acknowledging it.

A case in point occurs to me, where I submitted my music to a teacher for examination, who had a large class in Spartanburg, S.C., and one who was regarded as one of the leading teachers in the city. She was sick and I could not see her, but she sent me a list of her pupils, with her permission to call on them with my music, as she had seen it before and was familiar with it. I called at the first name given and played the pieces for the pupil's mother. She was aghast with amazement that "my daughter's" teacher should have sent that kind of music here for "my daughter" to play! "<u>She</u> plays classic music and standard music, and I really cannot think that her teacher should have meant for <u>her</u> to play this kind of music! 'The Boatman Dance'! 'Walk-Around'! No, no, there must be some mistake. 'My daughter' wouldn't play that kind of music. Oh no!"

So I came off minus the dollar, but with its worth in something else.

As we journey on we find it is really necessary to have all kinds of people to make up this grand old world of ours. Were it not so, where would the laugh come in?

Contact with diverse people is a good educator, and will revolutionize many an idea one starts the journey with. We are all so apt to yearn for the one thing to us unattainable. We are so apt to feel that if we had the one thing lacking, we would be content.

Are we sick? We want health. Are we poor? We want money. Are we ugly? We want beauty. Are we dull? We want life. Are we old? What would we not give for a backward turn of the wheel for a few years at least.

I have seen the time when I would gladly have sold my health to bring relief to those I loved. Now, I am content, and am convinced it is far better to be as I am, "comfortable," than rich.

There is no truer way on earth to come at the inner inwardness of man or woman than to approach them with something to sell. Ask any canvasser if this is not true. One's true nature then asserts itself. The man shows what manner of man he is, the woman shows herself as she is.

Were I a young person, man or woman, I should never marry anyone until I had, in disguise, gone to my affianced with something to sell.

As a rule, it is far more easy to sell to an average person in moderate circumstances than to sell to an average rich person.

One makes money for the comfort and enjoyment the spending of it brings. The other makes it and keeps it, for the pleasure of having it.

Which, of the two, gets the most out of Life?

Then there is a broader sympathy from those who work and make their own money than there can be from those whose money was made for him, by the work of others.

We cannot judge anything unless we have tried it ourselves.

Can we pronounce a thing good or bad, because someone else has tasted it? No, we will have to taste for ourselves.

In that way, I think injustice is oft times done the rich. Many of them do not feel, because they do not know.

They do not respond, because they do not feel.

One dear old woman gave me a hearty "Goodbye, may God bless you, I wish you well. I cannot get your music or your medicine but I do hope you will succeed."

Another woman — a rich one — gave me "No, I do not wish any music. I have no time for music, and do not care for it. My time is all taken up with my family and my church work, so I do not need it."

Poor creature. How could she know?

What Is Happiness?

I stopped in a little town in Eastern Carolina once and there was a travelling wagon in a vacant lot, next to the Hotel. The landlady expressed a wish that I could know its occupants, as they were so nice, she said. I did see them and from them I learned a lesson that has done me good. There were only two—man and wife—and for ten years they had worked together. The man gave Stereoptican Exhibitions. They were only wayside musicians, singing, performing tricks, working together always, but—they were the happiest people I have ever met. Their little wagon was their Kingdom. They had no other home, but that was enough they said, as long as they were spared each other.

I asked them if such a life was not terrible in cold weather. "Terrible? Why in cold weather we have our happiest time. Our little stove is the best I ever saw, our little room the cosiest; we have it all to ourselves, and we enjoy it, don't we, Jack? We are both well, and we make money enough to get along on and be comfortable. Come over, and let me show you our little home."

I did go—into their home on wheels—and went into one of the daintiest, most homelike and inviting nests I have ever seen, and she was as proud as a Queen of her palace.

I could but sigh as I left.

After all, it is not one's surroundings that bring happiness, but something else. Let those wiser than I say what.

I have often thought of my little wagon acquaintance, for every one who saw her looked upon her as a Sunbeam, and wished there were more like her.

I have been in the home of the rich, where there was everything to make life bright and beautiful, but there was one thing lacking: the Sunbeam. The mistress of it all was a walking monument to Discontent. With no Power behind, forcing her out of herself, she had no thought except for self. Her aches, her pains! Her head, her back, her knees, they were always "aching." She was always "tired." When she got up, she was "tired." When she lay down, she was "tired." She had more "trouble" than anyone else ever had, and yet she had none, save that she loved self too well, and "ached" too badly to know it. She looked so well and ate so heartily that when she burdened the air with her complaints, I chafed under the infliction, but it did me good.

I firmly resolved that <u>never</u>, so long as I lived, would I ever plead guilty to a headache, or a back ache, or ever say I was "tired."

Wherein lay the difference between the two homes?

In one there was a Sunbeam. In the other, a Shadow.

There are things too manifold to mention that we never think of in the light of appreciation, but enjoy them as a matter of course. Our beaten biscuit, our delicious steak, our broiled chicken, our country hams, our homemade sausage, our buckwheat cakes, our hot waffles, our good butter, our unskimmed milk, our fragrant coffee, with sugar and cream, because we have never entered homes where such a bill of fare is an unknown quantity.

There are scores, in our own State, who never know what it is to partake of a meal properly cooked, and I do believe that one-half of all the physical and mental ailments which distress mankind come from the lack of nutritious food, properly prepared.

Starting the day with a good substantial breakfast starts the man a better man and when I see one now irritable and cross, I jump right straight to the conclusion "poor fellow," he couldn't have had a good dinner. Traced back that would be found to be the source of a large proportion of the discontent, the nervousness, the unreasonableness of man and womankind.

What man can sit down to a good dinner and not feel his heart swell with charity for his fellow man?

And then we do not appreciate the luxury of a good bed, when so many never know what it is to go to bed between two sheets, and a great many crawl in on one — and that a colored one!

And then we do not half appreciate our bowl and pitcher as we should. I stopped at a house not long ago, and the next morning (a cold December morning it was, too) I called for a bowl of water. They "'lowed" I'd have to go out into the yard to the bench. I opened the door and viewed the prospect. The "old man" went to the bench and washed in the tin basin. (As the "old 'oman" was getting breakfast, I hoped she had done the same.) Then "the boys," and it was my turn next, and right manfully did I march to the rack.

I poured some water into the pan to rinse it out, but they cautioned me not to waste the water, as it was "low," so with closed eyes and clinched lips, I performed my morning ablutions. All the family wiped on a towel that had hung there Heaven only knows how long, but I had to draw the line there, and went to my grip and availed myself of the provision made against emergencies. I had to "bunk" that night in the room with "the gals" but was fortunate enough to secure a bed to myself. A girl of about fourteen looked on in wonder and amazement as I disrobed, but when I took off my braid, made of my own hair, it was too much for her and she called out, "Oh Ma, come here, the lady's taking off her hair — come quick!"

Traveling in one of the lower counties of the State, it was a source of wonder to me how the working people obtained water to drink. I went miles and miles, consumed by thirst. Plenty of wells did we pass, but not a bucket or any available way to get at the water.

At last we came to an old farm house where we saw a darkie standing by the well. I asked him to be kind enough to hand me a drink of water, as I was very thirsty. "There's plenty o' water here," he said, "but we all drink out o' the bucket. There's nothin' to hand any in."

An old man came out (the owner of the place) and after exchanging the customary greetings, I asked him if I could not get a drink of water, as I was so thirsty. He said, "Lor' bless your soul, honey, there's plenty of water here, but nothing to hand it in, but I've got plenty of good grape juice, and you'll find that monstrous good to lay thirst when you can't get water." He went and brought the grape juice and I found it as he said, "monstrous good," brought in a gourd, colored with the accumulated juice of many seasons.

And yet this old man had planted out grapevines, on either side of the road, for a distance of about three hundred yards, and kept them in good condition, well arbored and trained. I expressed my surprise and he said, "I planted them vines with my own hands. When the grapes are ripe, I sit here in my porch and enjoy seeing travelers feast themselves. They are my pets, and have given refreshment to thousands. I've done that much good in my life. When the season lasts nearly all who pass stop and eat grapes, and there's always enough for all, as long as they last."

I reverently shook the old man's hand when I left. A man, so full of love for his fellow man, that he gladly worked to give them pleasure, and yet so regardless of self.

Big, Rich and a Strong Pillar

Many a time have the days been dark and gloomy, many a time did the shadows envelope me until I could see no light beyond. Many a time have I broken my last five dollar bill, and could see naught ahead. Once, when I was in the depths, and felt that God-forsaken, desolate, dreary, hopeless, sinking sensation, which only the "depths" can bring, I stopped in Charlotte, and told my friend of my need. My stock of Remedy was almost exhausted, and I was without means to replenish it, and could see no way.

If I could only borrow one hundred dollars, clear sailing was ahead of me. We put our heads together, and concocted our own sweet plans for testing human nature, humanity and Christianity.

There was a name always before the public, when help in any good cause was publicly needed. One of our big, rich and a strong Pillar, his name headed the many big charitable donations, with the biggest sum. Let an appeal be made in the public prints for aid in any good cause, he was ever on the alert to respond, so I determined to write to him.

I did so, and told him of my great need. I asked him to lend me one hundred dollars, and I would certainly return it in ninety days, but, unfortunately I added: "If you help me, let this be between You and Me. I do not expect it to be a public thing." Consequently, I received the following:

"Dear Madam,

I regret it is out of my power to comply with your request"—and so on and so on.

And thus we sermonize and moralize as we march onward, but that was years ago, before I had jotted down as many "morals" as I can show now, or understood the nature of public charities as I do now.

An Honest Man Is the Noblest Work of God

On one occasion, while in Charlotte, I lost my pocketbook, containing $125. I had it in my hand when I left the drug store, and when I got to the Central, I found I had lost it, had dropped it on the street. It was on a Saturday evening and the town was filled with people. The streets wore their usual Saturday evening aspect, and I felt the uselessness, even of a search. It was carelessness I was ashamed of and did not wish known, so I resolved I would be silent and tell no one of my loss. I would borrow money and return home, and no one should ever be the wiser.

It was an uncomfortable feeling to lose one hundred and twenty five dollars, and to know that it was gone forever. It was hard to make and its loss meant so much to me.

I sat in my room in meditation anything but enviable. In about an hour, there came "A tapping, a tapping at my chamber door." I opened it, found not a Raven, but Mr. John A. Morris—"the only."

"Is this Mrs. Joe Person?"

"It is."

"Mrs. Person, have you lost anything?"

"Thank the good Lord," I said, "You have found my pocketbook!"

"Yes, I found it on the street, and your money is safe."

It is a glorious thing to meet with an honest man, a man, who unseen except by his God, could have done so differently. He handed it to me, and I feel to this day that I did not say half enough or do half enough, for he would not let me say a thing, or do a thing.

Mr. Morris little knew what his find meant to me, for it was my all at that time, and I feel now, when I pass him on the street, I would like to do so, with head uncovered.

A Woman's Opinion

Journeying onward and onward, I stopped at a lady's house, and asked if I could get accommodation for the night.

"Yes, if you will take home fare, you are welcome. Our supper is now ready, walk right into the dining room."

We had good fare and found it quite a pleasant place.

The next morning I asked her how much she charged me.

"Three dollars," she replied.

My inclination was to kick, but I substituted a protest.

"Why, if I could make my living as easy as you do, riding around seeing the country, I wouldn't care what people charged me," and many a time, working in the winter's cold or the summer's heat, have I wished I could attach her to one end of the paste brush for a week and thus give her an idea of what "riding around, seeing the country" meant.

Finale

But I have had many delightful trips and carry with me always most grateful remembrances of the many kindnesses shown me.

For hospitality, commend me to Person County and to Caswell, to Richmond County and her twin sister, Marlboro County, S.C., to Green and Hyde Counties. In these Counties, one meets with people of the olden time, who place no monied estimate on a night's entertainment to a traveler. They throw open their doors, and make one welcome to the best the land affords, and royally do they know how to serve it and entertain. Their hospitality is unbounded, and their only charge is "Come again."

One of the most beautiful as well as enjoyable trips I ever took was through Hyde County. I went in April, when the woods were redolent with the fragrance of the yellow jasmine (called woodbine in Va.) where the spires would contain twenty five and thirty bells.

I wanted to gather it in as I journeyed on. It was far too beautiful to bloom unseen.

And I was loth to leave the grand old pines, mighty monarchs of the forest, measuring ninety and one hundred feet, from base to first limb, so grand that it seemed sacrilege for the woodman's axe ever to be applied, and I felt that surely they must bring a man nearer his God and make him a better man for dwelling among them.

And so I journey on.

I have had other toilers to tell me that my life was an inspiration to them, and a knowledge of what I have overcome had given them strength for the conflict.

I say to them all: There is only one way to win the Fight, by sledge-hammer blows day after day, week after week, month after month, year after year.

THE END

Book II

A Life Out of the Ordinary
Alice's Story in the Words of Others

Part I: The Woman

Chapter 1

Daughter and Sister

Alice Morgan Person was the second child of Samuel Wilson Morgan and Esther Jane Robinson. The Morgans' first child, Joseph, died less than two months before Alice's birth on July 28, 1840.[1] Welcoming their first daughter into the world while still mourning their first son surely resulted in a jumble of mixed emotions for the young couple. The loss of a loved one was not, however, new to Samuel. His first wife, Elizabeth Dorothy Rivers, died shortly after they married.[2] Unfortunately, these sad events served to foreshadow a life of disappointment for Samuel and his family, which later grew to include three more children: Rufus, Lucy Jeanette (or Lou, as Alice called her[3]), and Alfred. Samuel and Esther raised their children in pre–Civil War Petersburg, Virginia, a prosperous, forward-thinking, cultured city that offered much to young families such as theirs. The Petersburg of the 1850s was characterized by a bustling economy, a quality education system (especially for women), and a growing religious community, all of which certainly contributed to making Alice a strong, independent woman capable of overcoming the difficulties life would send her way.

Money Troubles

Petersburg's healthy economy was supported by three banks: the Exchange Bank, the Farmers Bank, and The Bank of Virginia.[4] Early in the life of his family, Samuel Morgan held the office of teller at the Exchange Bank, where he encountered another major disappointment. In January of 1852 he became indebted to the bank for ten thousand dollars. This was a forbidding sum of money in 1852, and repaying it meant Samuel had to mortgage his Walnut Street home, its contents, and his life insurance policy to prominent Petersburg businessman, Samuel Hurt.[5] Fortunately, the sale of the house paid more than half the mortgage and enabled the Morgans to retain their household possessions,[6] which they took with them to their new home on Old Street.[7] Two years after his unfortunate experience at the Exchange Bank, Samuel entered the ice business with two businessmen from Rockport, Maine. The company bore Samuel's name and maintained two ice houses in the city of Petersburg.[8] Either this venture fared poorly or other factors taxed the family finances beyond their limits; in 1856 the Morgans finally had to deed their household possessions in order to pay additional debts totaling nearly fifteen hundred dollars.[9]

The exact cause of the Morgans' financial problems will probably never be known. Were they the result of an innocent record-keeping error that caused the Exchange Bank to lose a large sum of money, or was Samuel embezzling from the bank? Perhaps a desire for easy financial gain led him to take unwise investment risks. Or maybe he had a gambling problem made all the more difficult to control by the fact Virginia was at that time a horse racing hotbed. Indeed, the Petersburg economy was boosted by the presence of the New Market Races, a prestigious race track drawing hundreds of people each year.[10] Unfortunately, some of the establishments that boosted the city's overall economy left some of its citizens in financial ruin.

Whatever the cause of the Morgans' financial downturn, the fact it occurred may explain the conservative approach to financial matters that proved successful for Alice. She expresses her feelings on the matter in an October 22, 1879, letter to her brother Rufus.[11] In the letter, she tells Rufus that though his baby son, Samuel, is a "beautiful boy," she fears "his name may entail on him a heritage of sorrow and trouble." This is a reference to the difficult life of their father, after whom Rufus named his son. Alice goes on to lament her family's ailing economic health, telling Rufus that unlike him she "cannot live on future prospects," but rather must "see something tangible for the present." While this is a direct reference to the fact that earlier in the year Rufus hoped to improve his family's situation by moving to California where the climate and market promised to support a thriving beekeeping business,[12] it may also recall difficulties resulting from their father's penchant for living "on future prospects"— difficulties Alice was determined not to repeat.

Only the Best Will Do

Despite everything, Samuel and Esther somehow provided their children with every possible advantage; hence Alice's statement she knew "aught save of the elegancies and refinements of life."[13] Judging from Alice's musical, writing, and critical thinking skills, one of these refinements was a high-quality education. Exactly how Alice was educated will probably never be known, but mid–nineteenth-century Petersburg offered several options. Prior to the 1850s there was no public school system in Petersburg and only one free school, the Anderson Seminary, founded and funded by David Anderson in 1819 for the purpose of educating poor children.[14] In all likelihood, Alice's early education did not take place at the Anderson Seminary because her family was not plagued by financial troubles until the early 1850s. The other options were home and private schooling. Homeschooling was certainly possible because Esther Morgan was no doubt well-educated by virtue of her lineage, which included paternal and maternal grandfathers who were Revolutionary War captains.[15] If Esther did not feel equal to the task, it would not have been unusual for a relative or friend to serve as tutor to the young Morgans. On the other hand, the national push for improved female education early in the nineteenth century resulted in a thriving cottage industry of small private female schools in Petersburg by the 1840s. Samuel and Esther may have joined the other Virginia parents who spared no expense to educate their daughters at schools such as this.[16]

Even if Alice's earliest education took place at home, she was attending school outside the home by the age of ten in 1850.[17] And because Petersburg had not yet established its public school system,[18] she had to have been enrolled in one of the city's private schools. As Alice entered young adulthood, an important movement in Petersburg's private education system for young women was underway—one which certainly planted the seed of self-reliance in Alice. The push for improved female education earlier in the century moved beyond cottage enterprises teaching reading, writing, and needlework to incorporated institutions emphasizing intellectual toughness. Three such institutions were founded in Petersburg during the 1850s: Petersburg Female College, Leavenworth's Female Seminary, and Davidson Female College. The first of these offered "the cultivation of habits of concentrated attention, and accurate, clear, vigorous and self-relying thought," and the second promised "mental discipline" by "exciting the powers of the pupil herself, and teaching her to THINK— to reason, investigate, compare, methodize, and judge."[19] Even if Alice did not attend one of these institutions she could not help but be influenced by the social environment that brought them about, and that probably pushed the surviving old-style academies— of which there were still a number — to adopt similar philosophies in order to survive.

Petersburg's growing religious community included the major denominations of the day: Baptist, Methodist, Presbyterian, Catholic and Episcopal.[20] Samuel and Esther chose to raise their children in the Episcopal Church, specifically Petersburg's Grace Church. Though early Grace Church records do not indicate the Morgans were members, Alice spoke fondly of sitting "under the loving ministrations" of founding rector C.J. Gibson,[21] and church records indicate she was married there.[22] This early religious training led Alice to include God in her worldview, and could well have instilled the strong sense of honesty that saturates her written record.

Loving Daughter

Also pervasive throughout Alice's written legacy is her emotional attachment and sensitivity toward her family members. Alice overtly refers to this trait in a letter to her son William: "All my life I have been a bundle of sensitive nerves, keenly alive to every impression, reveling in a kind word or attention from those I love, suffering keenly when I looked and found it not."[23] This admission indicates Alice formed and maintained strong bonds with her parents despite little written evidence of such attachments. In the known collections of her papers, Alice writes about her father just once — the incidental mention of his heritage of sorrow and trouble in her October 22, 1879, letter to Rufus. While this reference to Samuel's disappointing life could have included a level of bitterness, its context indicates it was accompanied by compassionate sadness. The dearth of references to Samuel is perhaps due to his premature death on October 1, 1863, when Alice was just twenty-three. Not only did Samuel's early passing deprive Alice of years of memories to which she could have referred later in life, it was probably upstaged by the fact the Civil War was raging and Alice was left to care for her three young children when her husband joined the Confederate troops. In addition, she had to consider the needs of her nearly destitute mother and siblings, two of whom were only slightly older than her own children.

There is more evidence of a close relationship between Alice and her mother — a relationship no doubt strengthened by Esther Morgan's need to rely on the only one of her children in a position to provide assistance after Samuel's death. Several letters from the years directly following Samuel's passing indicate Esther's presence in the Person family household for extended periods of time, as well as the fact Alice missed her when she left. Esther was with the Persons during Joseph's recovery from his debilitating stroke in April of 1864; Alice closes her April 29 letter reporting on Joseph's progress to her brother-in-law, Thomas Arrington Person, by telling him that "ma joins me in [love?] to you all."[24] A few weeks later Esther is no longer with the Person family; on May 9, Alice's niece, Mary E. Montgomery, writes to Thomas' wife, Abiah, and tells her that if she (Mary) was in better health she would go to assist Alice in caring for Joseph because Alice's mother "has left and is missed so much."[25] In August of the following year, Esther is once again with the Persons. Alice writes to niece Mary Temperance Person on August 8 and tells her, "Ma is with me now and says she would be delighted to see Sister Abiah [Mary Temperance's mother]."[26] Alice's strong affection for her mother is compellingly illustrated in a February 1875 letter from Alice to her sister Lucy in Hickory, North Carolina, where a very ill Esther also resided:

> Dear Lou,
>
> I will send Ma's carpet Monday. Please let me hear from Ma as soon as you get this. I am miserable about her. Would go if I possibly [could] and be with her. Let me know if you think she is in any danger, and I will try and get there if possible — date your postals. Brother wrote me she was improving, and I do hope and trust she is now out of danger. I enclose ten cents. Get some postal cards, and write to me <u>every</u> day, as long as she is sick.
>
> Alice[27]

This is the last mention of Esther Morgan in Alice's extant papers. Did Alice ever make the long trip to Hickory to see Esther before she died a year later on March 4, 1876?[28] Quite possibly the demands of a large family — Alice gave birth to her eighth child just months before her mother's death — and the need to nurture her infant remedy business in order to provide for that family, kept Alice from doing so. In any case, this final mention of Esther leaves no doubt Alice loved her mother deeply.

Big Sister

Alice willingly and ably assumed the role of older sister, a role for which she was well-suited by virtue of both her strong commitment to fairness and her belief in her ability to determine right from wrong. Although Alice's commitment to impartiality wouldn't allow her to favor one sibling over another, letters and events indicate she was closer to her oldest siblings Rufus and Lucy. This is not surprising; only six years separated Rufus and Alice, and though twelve years separated Lucy and Alice, Lucy was her only sister. Alice's younger brother, Alfred, was just two years old when Alice married and left home, so it would have been difficult for them to develop strong bonds.

Alice's belief in her ability to distinguish right from wrong is apparent in the fact she had no difficulty voicing her displeasure when she thought one of her siblings— even a close one — made what she believed to be the wrong choice. Such a moment of frustration with Rufus occurred in October of 1879 while Rufus was in California attempting to establish his beekeeping business. Rufus' wife, Mary, and their two children, Samuel and Mary Bayard,[29] lived with the Person family for months at a time while Rufus was gone. During one such interval, Rufus neglected to send money to Mary. Alice had no compunction about writing to Rufus, and when she did, she wasted no time in addressing the problem as she saw it:

> Dear Bro.
>
> What on earth do you mean by not sending Mary some money — she has been here with her children ever since the 12th day of Aug, & not one cent have you sent her — how do you expect her to get along with two children and a nurse, & not a cent of money? The time is now when she wished to return home, & cannot do so, because she cannot pay her way — she has lost her nurse this week because there was no money to pay for her last month, so you may know how bad it is. We are powerless to aid her, or it would be cheerfully rendered. Our crop of corn this year is <u>15</u> barrels, <u>15</u> & no more, & we are actually put up for the <u>necessaries</u> of life — <u>Every mouthful</u> we have to eat, even down to corn bread & bacon, we have to buy & <u>nothing to buy with</u>. I never saw suffering for bread before me before, but I tremble to look in the future, so you may know we have our hands full, with Joe in his situation. Send Mary some money if you have to borrow it or <u>work for it</u>, she is really <u>suffering</u> for it as you are bound to know. I am very sorry for her sorry for us all, but you are young & healthy & can surely raise some money <u>for her</u> (not us)....[30]

Perhaps Alice's impatient opening was due in part to her mounting frustration over the fact Rufus had not been responding to her letters — a frustration Alice freely shared in her written correspondence, particularly that which she sent to the men in her life. In her closing, Alice tells Rufus in no uncertain terms how she feels about his lack of communication. She does, however, soften these sentiments by mixing them with genuine concern that he not feel bad toward her for what she has written — a hallmark of her closing lines in similar letters:

> Write to me, & give me your assurance you do not think hard of my writing this. I am only actuated by <u>the good of all</u> in telling you all of this, & know it is best I should do so. Goodbye. I hope my next can contain more hopeful feelings. I can't see why you don't write to me. You have never answered my last <u>long</u> letter. Your letters cheer me a great deal when I am in trouble, & I would be glad of one from you now. Don't <u>hurt</u> me by <u>silence</u>.
>
> Affectionately
>
> Alice

Alice wrote frank letters to her siblings until late in her life, and, as was the case with a circa 1911 draft letter to her younger brother Alfred,[31] they sometimes dealt with issues that most people would view as beyond the concern of an elderly sister. In this instance, Alice writes to Alfred after hearing he has neglected his two single adult daughters Laura and Anna. Once again, she moves directly to the purpose of her letter:

> Alfred —
>
> I saw Bayard [Alice's niece] in Raleigh last week and I was worried, or perhaps indignant would be a better word, when she told me about Laura. She said Laura was far from being happy or satisfied and had frequent spells of crying, but she did not see how it could be otherwise when a father whom she worshipped had virtually cast her aside, that you never even write to her, anymore than if she was nothing to you. I asked her if you didn't write Christmas "not a line." I told her you did send Anna a belt and some holly and mistletoe and a letter. She said a letter even from you would have made her very happy, but you never even noticed her anyway, and at Christmas time too! I was indignant over the way you treated Anna when I was in Charlotte, for you caused her many a heart ache and many a tear by your neglect and indifference. I have never seen any children who worshipped their father as yours do (or did) you, and you have cast them completely aside, as if they were nothing to you. I cannot understand how you can treat Fanny's [Alfred's first wife] children that way, and it is enough to make them lose faith, not only in mankind but in religion itself. You are doing your children a great harm, and not only them, but in Laura's case, those they are thrown with. There are Anna and Laura, thrown on their own resources to fit themselves to earn their own living and if you have got no money to send them to help them out, leaving this altogether to other people, you could write to them and make them happy by letting them know you loved them and cared for them. Give my love to Ada [Alfred's second wife?], for from what I have heard of her, I admire her greatly.[32]

For some reason unknown to Alice, Alfred had earlier ceased communicating with his daughters. Alice's well-defined sense of right and wrong does not, however, concern itself with the reason for the neglect, but rather only with the fact that a brother of hers would allow it to occur at all. With the exception of the final sentence, the entire letter is a reprimand of the strongest sort. In contrast to her approach in similar letters, Alice neither makes an attempt to spare Alfred's feelings nor seeks his assurance their relationship is not endangered by the letter's contents. On the contrary, Alice uses the last line to add insult to injury by suggesting that Ada must be an exceptional woman in order to endure life with Alfred. Alice no doubt dispensed with expressions of concern for Alfred's feelings because she felt his unfair treatment of his daughters didn't warrant her fair treatment of him.

It is unfortunate this harsh letter is the only known communication between Alice and Alfred, for it gives the impression the relationship was not a good one. Other documents indicate that while such a conclusion is unwarranted, the relationship was probably not close. Though Alice referred to Alfred as "my dear brother" in her will, she left him only one of her possessions, yet left multiple items to her other surviving sibling, Lucy. Shells and a framed Indian picture were among those items left to Lucy—items no doubt full of fond memories of the trips the two sisters took together. Alfred received a less personal gift—a gold fountain pen.[33] In addition, there is only one mention of a visit to or from Alfred in Alice's extant journals,[34] which provide a detailed account of Alice's activities from 1901 to the end of her life.

Alice's relationship with Rufus, though short, was in direct contrast to that with Alfred. Her respect for Rufus is evident in the fact she frequently sought his comfort and advice. When in December of 1874 Alice's daughter Josephine was near death, she wrote a heart-wrenching plea to her older brother:

> Dear Bro,
>
> Josie is very, very ill, exactly in every respect like she was before. I think her time on earth is well nigh ended. Would give anything on earth if I could have the comfort of your presence like I did before. She is always muttering "my doll"—brother can I stand it. When she was in death's clutches before I prayed God to let me keep her one more year, that I might be better to her. He gave her to me two & now I think He claims her—she cannot notice her doll, but I would not take an untold sum for the happiness dear Mary gave her.
>
> Alice[35]

In a November 1878 letter, Alice provides Rufus with a list of recent expenses for her fledgling remedy business and asks whether he thinks she has invested wisely. In the same letter she writes that she "would give anything I own on earth to see you this morning. I feel a talk with you would do me good."[36] Alice echoes this sentiment in her October 22, 1879, letter when she tells Rufus his letters cheer her "a great deal when I am in trouble, and I would be glad of one from you now."[37] The strength of Alice's affection for Rufus is perhaps nowhere more evident than in the depth of her grief over his death in California at the age of thirty-three after eating a meal of poisonous mushrooms.[38] She expresses that sorrow in a rambling letter to Rufus' widow, Mary, in May of 1880:

> Dear, dear Mary,
>
> Don't judge of me in any way by the times I write to you, or you would do me injustice. Mary, I believe I would speak truthfully if I told you there has not been one hour that I have not been thinking of you since I heard bro was dead. I go to sleep every night thinking of you and grieving with and for you. I can hardly believe this is the same world I have been living in all this time. I do know the brightness of life is

forever dead within me — nothing in it can ever look bright and pretty to me again — I feel so more now than when Dr. Person came and knocked "the news" at me — always thank God your blow came through no one — Mary, forgive me, but I prayed for Death to reap you too — no not prayed — I stopped that years ago — but wished for it for you. I didn't see how you could live through it all, to face the naked truth in all its horror, that brother is dead. Mary to me you will ever be something sacred. I cannot tell you how I feel toward you now — but what are words but air — anybody can talk. I only hope I can prove my feelings — now. I am powerless but I hope and believe the time is not far distant when I will be able to act as I feel, to show you that to me you are more than dear Mary, that you are brother's wife. Oh Mary poverty is a hard master, a fearful despot. I would have been willing to work for anyone six months to have gone to see you & could not. I felt like it would be going to brothers grave — Mary tell me something about brother's last letter. Was he suffering when he wrote it. I have so much thought of that fearful Saturday night [illegible] for him. As soon as Dr. Person finished me off, I wrote & told Lou & Alfred, & to Dr Woodson, & begged him to write me everything about brother's life and death — were you ever able to send him Sam's picture? Mary, don't think I am a poor comforter. I know and you know that there is no comfort for you or for me. If Dr Woodson writes I will let you know at once. I never felt before that I lived in a world of graves, that I only moved in a land of tombs — now everything looks ghastly like death to me, even the sunshine and flowers — I don't believe there is anything in the world but sorrow, trouble and death. Mary did brother ever send you any of his fern work,[39] the work of his hands, if he did & you have much of it, give me a piece, be it ever little. Please write to me, write about him, no one knows what you write to me — you know that cruel morbid curiosity of the world to know how we "took" it — Oh how I hate the phrase, & it is a sure thing I give it no gratification. No one but Joe and Gib knows of your dear letter to me, nor shall they know of a single expression of your sorrow — has trouble made me hateful I wonder. I believe there is one person who truly loved brother & grieves, you, I did not know how much until he died, & that is Sis Mary — I took up one of brother's letters to me the other day — he said sister, don't grumble, & stop thinking — "thinking and grumbling do no good — be a philosopher & take life easy & wait patiently until the time comes to lay it down. I have come to believe that the highest type of manhood is he who does his duty to those around him, & trusts the rest to Providence" — Mary he was so good, so noble, so pure. I believe his memory will be as a guardian angel to me. I do try so hard to be like him now. That is my idea of a perfect life — as near perfect as we weak mortals can lead — don't judge of me by my acts, nor by my writings, at least not yet awhile. You are my dear brother's wife, my brother, my spirited brother, and you were so good to him. Don't ever judge anyone unless you know what circumstances control them now, as I said, I am powerless, but I believe not for always—write me a long letter just as soon as you read this. You don't know what a comfort a long letter from you will be. Joe has just come in and asked who I was writing to—he says "give my very best love to Mary, & tell her to let me know how Sam is getting on, & ask her is she most ready to give him to me?" So you must let him know. No one in the world could have sympathized with you more than Joe, he kept on saying poor Mary, I am so sorry for her, she will miss Rufus so much. Goodbye, dear Mary. I will write again soon — goodbye.

Truly yours,

Sister[40]

Perhaps the greatest testament to Alice's affection for Rufus was the fact that twenty-eight years after his death she traveled to California with Lucy to retrace his steps and locate his grave. A trip of this distance was quite an undertaking in 1908, and it was made all the more difficult by the fact the sisters did not know the exact location of Rufus' grave. With the assistance of the *San Diego Sun* and *San Diego Union* newspapers, Alice and Lucy located a couple who where Rufus' neighbors in Bernardo (a mountainous area northeast of San Diego), and knew where he was buried. Though the area could only be accessed by narrow, precipitous roadways, the undaunted women engaged the services of a driver and six-horse team. On their way through the mountains, a close call with an automobile resulted in a week's delay in order for Alice and Lucy to receive medical treatment for injuries sustained when they jumped from the wagon to escape even greater harm. The two did, however, eventually locate the grave and make a belated final tribute to their beloved brother.[41]

This late–June to mid–October journey was not the only trip the sisters made together to the western United States. They traveled there again in 1911, and were in the middle of their third excursion when Alice passed away in 1913. Their first trip took them to Knoxville, Tennessee; St. Louis and Springfield, Missouri; Laguna, New Mexico; the Petrified Forest and Grand Canyon; San Diego, Bernardo, Los Angeles, Long Beach, San Jose, and San Francisco, California; Yellowstone Park; Salt Lake City, Utah; Colorado Springs and Denver, Colorado; Chicago, Illinois; and Cincinnati, Ohio.[42] Their 1911 late–June to late–August junket involved a similar route. Though this trip was shorter, the women were able to add some additional sightseeing destinations because they were neither seeking their brother's grave nor taking a week to recuperate from a near-fatal collision. Additional stops on this trip included Albuquerque, New Mexico; Mount Shasta, California; and Portland, Oregon.[43] The sisters embarked on their third trip to the West in early June of 1913 with plans to expand their itinerary to include Alaska, but

Alice at the California grave of her brother Rufus in 1908 (courtesy of the North Carolina Office of Archives and History, Raleigh, North Carolina).

Alice's sudden death in Santa Fe, New Mexico, on June 12 put an end to their shared explorations.[44]

The power of the bond between the sisters was such that it took Lucy more than a month to gather the emotional fortitude to record in her diary the events of the day on which Alice died. She finally did so on July 28, the first anniversary of Alice's birthday following her death:

> My dear, lost sister's birthday, the lost one, dearer to me than all else put together: the one spot of sunshine in my life. How can I live without her!
>
> This, her dear birthday, seems to warn me that I've never fully told about the day she left me so desolate. I have never found heart to do so, but I'll try now, so that others can know the little that I know.
>
> Yes she was feeling bad that morning. When I asked her how she felt, she said, "I am constipated. Weren't you ever constipated? Well, you know how you feel when you are constipated — that is the way I feel. That's all." She wanted me to go & locate the curios, thinking she would go after dinner. I proposed her writing to Mrs. Candler that we were coming & I remember her saying something about that being work. All this was not enough to warn me. Mrs. Cameron & I went out, took our time, & returned, probably about twelve. I even took a kodak of a Mexican dwelling.
>
> When I came back, I opened the door & saw my loved one lying on the floor at my feet. I tried to rouse her, never thinking, even then that she had left me. A dark purpling place was on her right temple & under her eyes & at her finger. We rubbed her and the purple got so dark I thought she was reviving. The doctor came & it was not long before he told me the worst. I think I was benumbed. I remember calling my sister over & over, & then the next I remember the doctor told me I must go to the undertaker's. I think now he did this to get me away, for when I came back they had removed my loved one. Mrs. Hisch, our landlady, said that after we went out that morning after awhile my sister came into the dining room, told her she felt so well & wanted her to make some butter cakes for dinner like the ones she had had for breakfast. She had eaten an egg & some cakes for breakfast. The evening before was the first time she had let me know she was constipated & for the first time in my life I heard her say she was tired. As soon as we reached Santa [Fe] I went to the drug store and got her some medicine. All this was in Santa Fe, New Mexico.
>
> I slept down at the undertakers that night with my Sister. I felt that I didn't want to leave her alone, by herself. Mr. Rising fixed a reclining chair, but I put the coverlids on the floor & slept there. This is the note book I took along for our trip. I have the addresses at home of the many so kind to me in Santa Fe. Mrs. Kanen took me to her house for luncheon. I spent all the time with my sister that I could. I started the next day—Friday, June 13—for Charlotte. Mrs. Paul (Mason) went

Alice posing with a Native American interpreter in Laguna, New Mexico, during her 1908 trip to California (courtesy of the North Carolina Office of Archives and History, Raleigh, North Carolina).

with me to Lamy and waited there two hours to put me on the Santa Fe train. Took me in to dinner at the Fred Harvey house at Lamy. When I offered to pay, smiled & said, "That would destroy the pleasure." That was Friday afternoon. I reached Charlotte Monday night. I changed cars five times — Lamy, Kansas City, St. Louis, Knoxville, and Statesville. I saw each time that my dear one was on. How it hurt me to see the word "baggage" where she was put! The word yet, when I see it, brings it to me. I look back & it seems to me that ages are crowded into each of those three days. My loss has changed the world, & even eternity, to me. Josie and I stayed in Charlotte until Friday & then went to Hickory. Monday night, in Charlotte, I slept again in the room with my sister at Mrs. Constable's. They took us all in & had the funeral at 11 next day from their house — just as my Sister wanted it. She was laid to rest on Tuesday, June 17th.[45]

In closing this entry Lucy gives a detailed account of her last interaction with Alice — one which perfectly illustrates the fact Alice never stopped being a devoted older sister, and Lucy never stopped loving her for doing so:

There is another thing I forgot to tell. In traveling, the handle of my hand bag had ripped off. When I was ready to start down the street that morning my Sister was sewing it back for me. She was using a double thread and the needle broke. She asked Mrs. Cameron did she ever have the needle to break just in the midst of such a job — or something to that effect. She then handed me the bag saying it would do until I came back and she would then finish it; so this was probably about the last thing she ever said to me: the last work she ever did, unless it was the handkerchief she had washed out and pressed so beautifully in the window. I have the bag put away and we are saving the handkerchiefs. It so often seems that the sweetest thing in the world would be to lie down and be with her through eternity.[46]

Chapter 2

Wife and Mother

Alice met her husband-to-be, Joseph Arrington Person, when her family traveled to Franklin County, North Carolina, in 1856 to attend the wedding of one of her mother's relatives to one of Joseph's brothers.[1] Joseph was the son of Presley Carter Person, a prominent and wealthy early nineteenth-century Franklin County citizen who served as the county's high sheriff for a number of years.[2] By virtue of his inheritance, Joseph was a wealthy, established forty-two-year-old bachelor farmer when he met the sixteen-year-old Alice.[3] While Alice's parents may have been concerned about the difference in the couple's ages, their financial problems probably overshadowed such concerns and left them pleased and relieved the marriage would provide their daughter with a comfortable life while also leaving them with one less child to feed and clothe. The couple married the next year on December 17, 1857, at Grace Church in Petersburg, Virginia,[4] and moved immediately to Greenwood,[5] Joseph's 466-acre country estate featuring a two-story Georgian-style house overlooking the Tar River just a few miles north of Franklinton, North Carolina.[6]

The couple's union was blessed with nine children—three girls and six boys—born over a period of nineteen years from 1859 to 1878. Their first-born daughter was named Alice Gibson and was called Gibson, or "Gib," in order to avoid confusing mother and daughter. Their second daughter, Esther Morgan, was born two years later in 1861 and was named after Alice's mother. Their first-born son, Wiley Mangum, was born the next year; he went on to distinguish himself politically at both the local and state levels. Josephine Arrington, or "Josie," born in 1864, was named after her father, and was the child who was near death when a neighbor offered the remedy to Alice. Robert Lee followed in 1866. Rufus Morgan, born in 1871, was named after Alice's brother and grew up to become manager of her remedy company. Henry Harris was born in 1873, and Levin King in 1875. The couple's last child, William

Montgomery, or "Willie," was named after a close family friend, William (Billy) Montgomery, who came to the Person family's rescue on numerous occasions and was married to the couple's niece, Mary Temperance (Tempie) Person.

Devoted Wife

In her autobiography, Alice writes fondly of her husband as "one of the handsomest men I ever saw," and also of the fact they were "very happy."[7] Young Alice's love for Joseph is evident in her distraught state of mind when he organized a company of volunteers and headed off to war in 1863.[8] Her devotion is further evident in the way she cared for him after his stroke the following spring. In a letter to her brother-in-law Thomas, Alice tells of faithfully washing Joseph's feet three times a day in mustard water during his recovery.[9] Years later, however, the stress of financial difficulties, chronic disability, and a large family appear to have taken an understandable toll on the relationship.

In November of 1878 a frustrated and bitter Alice scribbled a note on the back of one of her remedy advertisement leaflets and sent it to her brother Rufus, who was then living in Goldsboro, North Carolina:[10]

> Dear Bro,
>
> The check came all right wait until you come, I want to have a talk with you — my heart is sore. I cannot write — will enter into everything fully when you come & until then wait — I did not expect you to charge <u>me</u> interest on Mr. Person's notes when I promised to take them as part payment of what was coming to me. I thought they would be on a par with the other notes in which no calculation of interest was made, am sorry I took them & wish now I had let you and Mr. Person settle, & you settled direct with me. Bro, I feel as if I have been <u>badly</u> treated, <u>not by you</u> however, <u>nor anything you could help</u>. I hope time will even reconcile me. I wish so much you could come <u>now</u>. I would give anything I own on earth to see you this morning. I feel a talk with you would do me good. I sent 45 $ to Cooper for whiskey, 10 $ to Baker Bros for bottles & 5 $ for revenue stamps. <u>Did I invest wisely</u>? But trouble & troubling matters aside, I've a favor to ask of you — could you not contrive to substitute some wash powders I will send you in place of those I sent Dr. Kirby. I think I have just learned how to dry them perfectly. What I have now are as <u>green</u> as when growing — those heretofore were brown. These <u>I know</u> are best, & would like so much to put them in place of those sent but hate for anyone to think I have not had them right all the time. Please tear this up & show or tell to no one — even Mary [Rufus' wife] — & come before Xmas if you can. I feel badly — bitter — & must stop. Please tear this up <u>just as soon</u> as <u>you</u> read it.
>
> Alice[11]

When Alice opens her diatribe, she initially points to Rufus as the cause of her frustration because he charged her interest on loans her husband owed him and which she had earlier agreed to assume as partial payment for a loan Rufus owed her. However, the true source of her perturbation (i.e., Joseph) becomes apparent when she writes: "[I] am sorry I took them & wish now I had let you and Mr. Person settle, & you settled direct with me. Bro, I feel as if I have been <u>badly</u> treated. <u>Not by you</u> however, <u>nor anything you could help</u>. I hope time will even reconcile me." Though she feels bad toward Joseph, Alice feels the need to ensure he will not learn of those feelings when she writes: "I feel badly — bitter — & must stop. Please tear this up <u>just as soon</u> as <u>you</u> read it." The exact circumstances that caused Alice's bitterness are not clear, but her displeasure over becoming involved with her husband's debts is. This desire to separate their debts indicates a schism of sorts between the two — one that would not easily be rejoined.

With time, the remedy broadened the schism; as Alice's obsession with her medicine grew, so did the separation of sentiments between husband and wife. Joseph pushed Alice to assume the traditional role of housekeeper despite the fact her work with the remedy provided a reliable source of income for the family. Alice confides in her sister-in-law Mary in a March 1880 letter: "I <u>can't</u> write to anyone except on 'business.' Joe says I'm going crazy on the subject of medicine and he wishes I had never had anything to do with it. I know better and so does he, he just tells me so, trying to keep me from thinking so much about it, and to get me to think of family affairs more, but Mary I am so anxious to make something. Money is so scarce, and we have so many looking to us."[12] Joseph's actions are not surprising, because the paralysis resulting from his 1864 stroke left him physically unable to work and provide for his family.[13] This must have left the patriarch with feelings of inadequacy and frustration over the fact Alice could take on a responsibility he felt should be his alone. These feelings led Joseph to scoff at Alice's aspirations on at least two occasions. The first occurred shortly after Alice witnessed the medicine's ability to save their daughter from a disease considered to be incurable. When Alice told her husband she thought the remedy was the long-awaited cure for both scrofula and their ailing finances, Joseph "laughed and said, 'Surely you are not going to turn Scrofula-doctor, are you?'"[14] Later, in 1882, as Alice was making plans to take her remedy to the Raleigh medical community, Joseph called her "a poor little fool" and attempted to discourage her from going forward with her plans.[15] Perhaps resigned to the fact there was no chance of reconciling their thoughts regarding the medicine, Alice ignored Joseph's reproaches and forged on with her mission.

At some point, however, Joseph changed his way of thinking. On January 24, 1884, just two and a half months before his death, Joseph signed an agreement allowing Alice to become a "free trader."[16] In the 1880s, North Carolina state law did not allow married women to enter into contracts affecting their real or personal estate without the written consent of their husbands. If, however, a woman was over twenty-one years of age and her husband gave his consent in writing in the county register of deeds, she became a free trader (i.e., was free to conduct her personal business in any way she so desired).[17] The day after registering herself as a free trader, Alice entered into a five-year partnership agreement with Charlotte businessman Charles R. Jones,[18] the second businessman who offered the financial backing Alice needed to speed the expansion of the business.[19] Alice could not afford to turn him down because the Persons had a year earlier mortgaged what was left of their farm to Franklin County businessman Wyatt L. McGhee, and McGhee was now expecting payment.[20]

Joseph's change of heart was no doubt inspired by two realizations. First, he could no longer deny the fact Alice had indeed turned "Scrofula-doctor." By this time, the remedy was well-established in Charlotte, and Alice was fielding inquiries about it from elsewhere in North Carolina. This popularity and the fact a second businessman was interested in associating himself with the remedy meant Alice had accomplished what Joseph had thought was impossible. Second, Joseph turned seventy the day before signing the free trader agreement and he had nothing but a mortgaged farm to leave his family, four members of which had not yet reached their teens. The least he could do was give his wife the freedom to conduct business with a partner who might help make the remedy even more profitable, thereby providing a better life for his family after his death.

Despite their disagreements, an undercurrent of love and respect flowed uninterrupted between Alice and Joseph until his death. When she was away marketing the remedy, Alice wrote home daily; and each day Joseph waited patiently on the porch for the mail carrier. So it was that early in April of 1884 Joseph died of a heart attack while waiting for the mail to arrive. Alice, who was pushing the remedy in Monroe, North Carolina, hurried home to be with her family. She describes just how difficult this time was for her in her autobiography: "I stayed there three days, at the old home, without him; three desolate, wretched, miserable days, and then I felt that any other place was preferable to me now. I could not stay and then there was no need. The living needed me."[21] These words sound selfish — as though Alice hoped to escape painful memories associated with Greenwood by returning to her travels in the interest of her beloved remedy. True, Alice's dedication to the remedy went beyond the financial, but her love for her children surpassed that. If Alice had any chance at all of providing for her first love she had to rededicate herself to her second, and that is what she did. After burying Joseph's body in the meadow behind their home and arranging for the care of her youngest children and the farm, Alice began the next chapter of her life.

Moving On

Alice did not, however, turn the page without first revisiting a paragraph from the previous chapter. A curious note scribbled on the back of a June 1884 University of North Carolina commencement announcement suggests that Alice, perhaps distraught about not being present when Joseph died, sought the aid of a medium in order to communicate with her husband one last time:

> Dear friends
>
> The spirits were quite anxious to get suitable conditions to communicate with you all. They are happy when they have the opportunity to do so. I want to say to my wife Alice that I am much pleased with her efforts and that bright lights are around her. She will succeed and God shall bless you all. Oh, do influence my children too.
>
> Good bye
> Joseph[22]

Such a message would surely have bolstered Alice's courage — something she and her family desperately needed. In May of 1884 Alice wrote to Mary Bayard Clarke (mother-in-law of her deceased brother, Rufus, and respected nineteenth-century author and editor[23]) concerning Joseph's death and its aftermath. Alice related her uneasy feelings about her youngest children being scattered, and also about leaving her second-oldest son, seventeen-year-old Robert, to manage Greenwood on his own. In her response, Mary Clarke echoes Alice's feelings with regard to her "home being broken up," empathizes with the fact that "poor Robert must surely feel the change," and expresses her belief that "you will before long gather your children together in one family."[24] Unfortunately, Mary's prediction could not have been further from the reality that followed.

One by one, the events that unfolded over the next several years conspired to keep Alice from realizing her dream of having her dependent children with her under one roof. In December of 1884, less than a year after joining forces with Charles Jones, Alice had to force the dissolution of the partnership when she discovered Jones had embezzled the business into bankruptcy.[25] A few months later, another partnership (this time with Tarboro, North Carolina, businessman E.B. Hodges) brought Alice to a location closer to her children, but it too failed within a year.[26] Worse yet, as the Tarboro partnership began to crumble, the situation with Alice's twice-mortgaged farm reached a crisis point. The November 1884 default date for Alice's second mortgage had come and gone,[27] but mortgagee Wyatt McGhee refrained

The impressive Victorian front added to Alice's Georgian-style Franklin County home by Wyatt McGhee in the early 1890s (photograph by David Hursh).

from taking action, no doubt out of consideration for the plight of the widowed Alice. By November of 1885, however, the task of keeping the farm in working order had, understandably, become too great for Alice's teenage son Robert. The farm's land had depreciated to the point that McGhee would take a large loss if he did not foreclose.[28] On November 24, 1885, the roof under which Alice had hoped to gather her children was sold at public auction to Franklinton businessman E.B. Clegg in order to pay the mortgages. Alice's son-in-law William Henry Harris made a valiant attempt to purchase the farm, but a misunderstanding on the part of the auctioneer resulted in Clegg being declared the high bidder.[29] Two weeks later, Clegg, unable to secure the necessary cash down payment, sold the property to Wyatt McGhee.[30] Greenwood's house, now known as the McGhee-Person House, still stands along U.S. 1 South between the Tar River and Franklinton. It is owned and occupied by Wyatt McGhee's great-grandson, Wyatt L. McGhee III, and his wife, Libby. The original Georgian structure is now fronted by an impressive Victorian one, which was added by McGhee in the early 1890s.[31]

Juggling the Demands of Career and Motherhood

After the failure of the Tarboro business in April of 1886, Alice established her base of operations in the small town of Kittrell, North Carolina, just a few miles north of the farm she once owned and in close proximity to her family and friends. Even though Alice was no longer limited by the location of her business partners, her dependent children did not live with her. In a January 1887 letter to her niece Tempie Montgomery, Alice tells of joining her youngest children at the Franklin County home of her daughter Gibson during her customary two-month holiday break from pushing the remedy:

> We came to spend Christmas with Gibson, and Tuesday Willie broke out with measles, then Levin, then Henry, Billy, Mona and Hal, all six sick at a time — what a siege Gib and I had nursing! Henry was very ill, as the disease settled on his bowels, producing intense inflammation — all are now well — the children all went down in the woods today to get some light wood, and you don't know what a treat it is to look at the beds and see them vacated — we will return to Kittrells [sic] the first of next week, at least I will send the children to their respective headquarters, while I will remain with Gib a few days longer.[32]

This particular break must have been a disappointment for Alice; she spent a good deal of it nursing her children rather than getting to know them better, an activity that would have been crucial to the relationship between a mother and three young sons who saw each other so infrequently. Unfortunately, the children were no sooner well than they had to return "to their respective headquarters" (i.e., the homes of generous relatives and friends in the central North Carolina area). As much as Alice surely hated to disperse her dependent children, living arrangements such as this were necessary even when she was in Kittrell because her time there was consumed by manufacturing the remedy in preparation for her selling trips — an activity that would have been impossible while attending to three young boys.

Perhaps in an attempt to make such arrangements unnecessary, Alice's sixteen-year-old son, Rufus, joined her in the remedy business early in 1887.[33] This effort was, however, in vain; Alice's familial dreams were shattered on March 17, 1887, with the death of her penultimate child, Levin.[34] The cause of Levin's death is not known. Did he die of complications from the measles he and his brothers contracted just two months earlier? In any case, Wyatt McGhee kindly allowed Alice to bury Levin next to his father in the meadow behind her former home.

Unfortunately, three more of Alice's children would precede her in death. Thirteen months after Levin's death, Alice's married daughter Esther Blacknall passed away just a few days after her twenty-seventh birthday.[35] As with Levin, the cause of Esther's death is not known. In June of 1904, shortly after Alice relocated to Charlotte, North Carolina, her thirty-year-old son, Henry, died of lung congestion in a Jacksonville, Florida, hospital. Alice rushed to his side and was able to have a day with him before he died. The day after Henry's death, Alice brought his body back to Charlotte and buried him in the city's Elmwood Cemetery in the family plot she purchased, and in which she herself would be buried nine years later.[36] Henry's older brother, Robert, died just a year and a half later at the age of thirty-nine of a concussion resulting from being thrown from a carriage not far from his home in Macon, Georgia.[37]

Mention of Henry's and Robert's deaths in Alice's journals serves only to mark the dates of these sad occasions, giving no hint of Alice's dedication to them when they were alive. Such an intimation is, however, provided by two small groups of notes and letters, one group dealing with Robert, and the other (actually just a pair of letters) with Henry. The first group consists of several 1889 communications from Alice to Billy Montgomery regarding Robert, who was then twenty-two and living in Richmond, Virginia. It begins with a promissory note from Alice for two equal payments of thirty dollars to Billy for his early January 1889 loan of sixty dollars.[38] This is followed by a late–January letter in which Alice tells Billy the money they gave Robert to pay debts incurred as the result of a serious illness was for naught:

> I would have written to you, but wanted to wait until I could tell you something definite about Robert, which I cannot yet do. When he paid the money to Lithgow, the Constable, that we gave him, Lithgow did not tell him the garnishment had been served against him — when an employee's wages are garnished, the rules of the company demand their discharge, so when Robert went to work Monday morning, he found that he was discharged. After hard work, with the officials, for more than a week, I succeeded in getting an application from Capt. Gentry for his reinstatement, then I got it endorsed by Capt. Ryder, Gen'l Superintendent of the R & D.R.R., and they forwarded the application to the authorities at Washington City, for their action. I waited in Richmond a week to see the result, but Robert wrote me Friday there was no news from the papers yet, but with Capt. Gentry's application, endorsed by Capt. Ryder, I do not think there is any doubt of his getting his place back. It was much more serious than I had any idea of when I went there. The execution cost me $8.40, then I paid off all Robert owed everywhere, before I could do a thing — drug account of $9.70 doctors bill $6 — it is all paid now, and I have done everything in my power for him. There was only record against Robert of this debt, and of lost time. Mr. Bailey, Capt. Gentry and Capt. Ryder all gave him a good character — said he was steady, kept no bad company, and they considered him a boy of good moral character, which will go far towards his reinstatement.[39]

Many parents would not go to such lengths for their adult children, but then Robert was not like many adult children. It was he who so valiantly gave up his last few teenage years to keep the Person farm afloat after his father's death. Certainly, Alice felt the lengths to which she went were the least she could do now that the tables were turned. This saga of heroic love and motherly dedication ends with a September 1889 letter from Alice to Billy in which she tells him of the relief she felt upon hearing from Robert the day before that he had been reinstated to his job.[40]

The pair of 1897 letters from Alice to twenty-three-year-old Henry paint a picture of nonjudgmental love towards the family's black sheep. Henry never married and settled down as did his siblings who had the capacity to do so.[41] Instead, as these letters indicate, his professional activities took him far from home, and he and his older brother Rufus were at odds. In the first letter, a concerned Alice skillfully communicates with her wayward lamb:

> Dear Henry,
> I never was so glad to get a letter in my life as I was to get yours today. I didn't write my boy because I had no idea where you were. I have not had one line from you. Gibson got a postal mailed from Ocracoke saying you would soon be at home, and we have been looking for you every day. I have watched the papers daily to see if I could see anything about your playing, so until your letter came, I was in the dark. You know I am not mad with my boy — I only feared you were in bad luck and wouldn't let me know because I couldn't do anything the last time you asked me. I looked forward to having you with me [on?] my birthday, and did look for a letter if you couldn't come home, but I never got a line, so I thought, well maybe Henry is sick or in bad luck and can't write, so you may know I was glad of your letter, and to know you were doing well. I never like to say "do this" or "don't do that" — I had rather let my boys decide these things for themselves, but I did hope you could get a place where I could see you sometimes. Will you go on the steamer, and if so when, and if so where. Dr. Hal Harris and his wife were down for my birthday, Jack, Bro Presley, Miss Addie, Rufus & Jessie, Willie & Josie — & Wiley — his wife cameth not. So you see I had all with me except you and Robert. Gibson wrote & invited Robert and I wrote and asked him to come, but not a line did I get. I did want you so much, and do want to see you so bad I don't know what to do. Wherever you are, write to me once a week — write here & mark it <u>personal</u> & no one will read it but me. I am sorry you feel you have been badly treated. Rufus is rough, but I believe he does what he thinks is right. I will be here next week, so write to me again, and tell me all about your steamer plans, and all about yourself. Your letters are sacred to me, and there is nothing on earth I would not do for my dear boy. I would have written long ago, had I known where you were.
>
> With fond love —
> Alice Person[42]

In typical fashion, Alice initially scolds Henry because she has "not had one line from him." However, she quickly pulls back — as though not to chase him off — by saying, "You know I am not mad with my boy — I only feared you were in bad luck," and later reinforcing this statement with "I never like to say 'do this' or 'don't do that.' I had rather let my boys decide these things for themselves." Near the end of the letter, Alice draws on the strong sense of fairness that served her so well in her relationships with her siblings, impartially addressing the schism between Henry and Rufus by telling Henry that, though his older brother's actions towards him seem hurtful, the motivation behind them is not. Alice's closing lines pulse with both the guilt of having spent so much time away from Henry when he was a boy and the hope that she can somehow make it up to him now.

In the second letter, Alice seems ready to come to Henry's rescue just as she did ten years earlier for Robert. She opens a two-sentence inquiry by asking Henry to "please tell me who Mr. Caleb Allen is and what claim has he on you and for what," and ends it with "This is of importance to me." Alice closes this letter by again acting as peacemaker between Henry and Rufus, telling Henry not to visit her if she is not in town because Rufus will be there.[43]

You Had Better Write to Me

Though Alice may not have liked telling her sons what she thought they should do, her strong convictions would not allow her to refrain from occasionally doing so. Alice was a letter writer; her sons were not. Just as she did in the first of her 1897 letters to Henry, Alice would from time to time gently scold her other sons for not writing. In 1903, however, she decided stronger action was necessary in order to curtail their neglect. This action came in the form of the following sarcastic masterpiece to her youngest son, twenty-five-year-old William.

> Dear Willie,
> Your dispatch just received and I was truly glad to hear you were well, and getting along nicely. That closes that issue. Never again do I expect to ask one of my boys to write to me, for I am fast attaining a chronically safe condition mentally, where it's "all right." If they write to me it's "all right." If they accord me silence, hereafter, it shall be "all right" too. So you see I am in a peculiarly contented frame of mind, that I hardly think an earthquake could affect now. I have always cared so much. It is so much better to care not at all. Think of the soul satisfaction of not caring! It seems like a precious flower I have just found, and I think by cultivation, it will bring me content I never knew before. I am hugging it to my heart as a precious possession. I imagine the feeling is something akin to just being "converted." All my life I have been

a bundle of sensitive nerves, keenly alive to every impression, reveling in a kind word or attention from those I love, suffering keenly when I looked and found it not. And only to think of my armor of protection now, steel clad against it all! Isn't it grand and glorious to have lived to find this peace? No more looking for what never comes, no more expecting what never is shown! After all Life is worth living and it's "all right." Do you not congratulate me?
Lovingly,
Your Mother[44]

Though Alice made William the target of her frustration in this instance, her papers indicate he was otherwise an ideal son, later writing her detailed letters telling of his activities,[45] visiting more than once for her birthday, and assisting with her move to Charlotte in March of 1904.[46]

Such was not the case with oldest son Wiley, who perhaps had the distinction of being Alice's greatest source of parental pride while also being her greatest source of parental frustration. Like any parent, Alice took great pride in the fact her son graduated from a prestigious institution of higher education (in this case the University of North Carolina) and became a lawyer. On the other hand, Wiley required monitoring throughout the course of his life in order to remain on the straight and narrow. As a child, he was strong-willed and refused to listen to his mother. During one of her stays in the Person household, Alice's sister-in-law, Mary Morgan, wrote to her husband about the situation: "I would not live like sister does for untold gold. It is one continual row & fuss from morning till night. Her children don't pretend to mind from the youngest to the oldest. She tells Wiley to do a thing & he does not notice her any more than if she had not spoken. She whips him which seems very wrong to me." [47] Mary also reported on Alice's loss of patience with Wiley: "Sister does not mind saying she wishes Wiley would go away, if he were to what do you reckon she would do?"[48]

As a young adult, Wiley's attraction to the drinking and card playing crowd led Alice to write him a frank letter in April of 1890 begging him to "cut loose from it all in toto":

Dear Wiley,
I was in a company of ladies and gentlemen not long since, and a gentleman came to me and said, "Mrs. Person, I have got the most unbounded respect for you and feel an interest in all your family, let me speak a word to you as a friend — do you know the danger your son Wiley is in, a danger that he is blind to. See him and talk to him and tell him for God's sake to let whiskey alone. He is a smart boy and a good one. He can make anything of himself if he will try. He does not get drunk I know, but he drinks too much for his good." Wiley, these were the words of a true friend, a man of wealth and influence, and no

connection <u>whatever</u> to the family. And I know he was right. You are on the threshold of life, and it lays with you to be what you will. You drink too much, you play cards too much, cut loose from it all <u>in toto</u>, draw back while you can and touch not another card, drink not another drop, and there is no power that can keep you from being a success. Come out of that Whist Club, it is no place for you, you do not belong there and I tell you these things which you can see no harm in are weakening you every day that you are connected with them. I do not believe there is any hope for your future unless you make up your mind to turn your back on them. They are not your friends who will invite you to drink or to a game. Stop spending your nights among the young men of the town, it can certainly do you no good and is certainly doing you great harm, and weakening your influence. For my sake as well as your own, you ought to listen to me. I have nothing on earth to live for but my dear children, and I want them to be all my heart craves for them. When I was with you, it hurt me to see you looking so seedy, not like a young, promising lawyer ought to look, but these things naturally follow. You will be poor as long as you follow your present habits, for it divides your interest and keeps you from self improvement. How gratifying it would be to you to take a leading stand in your profession, and you can do it if you will. Will you listen to my words, my boy. Write to me here, and with fond love, I am,

Alice Person.[49]

In the end, Wiley must have heeded Alice's words; he went on to become the mayor of Louisburg, North Carolina, a member of the University of North Carolina board of trustees, and a Franklin County representative in the North Carolina State Senate.[50] Nevertheless, more than ten years after her 1890 letter, Alice saw the need to at least contemplate once again writing to him to express great concern about his conduct. An undated copy of a letter to Wiley found among the pages of one of Alice's 1901–1913 journals provides the basis for Alice's concern. In this case, Alice had heard Wiley was planning to involve himself in legal proceedings against long-time family friend Billy Montgomery. The letter does not provide a complete explanation of the circumstances surrounding the lawsuit, but it does provide a clear picture of the injustice Wiley would perpetrate should he choose to become involved:

Dear Wiley,
I have been told that you are going to bring suit against Billy Montgomery for that home place that Mrs. Dr. Person left him. I write to beg of you <u>not to do it</u>, either for yourself or anyone else, for such an act by one of my children would subject me to deep humiliation and regret. Life is too short — and uncertain — for spite work, and I want my children to hold themselves above anything so petty. Years ago, I was virtually in the depths, yea of despair, situated so that I could not

have bought a pair of shoes or a piece of meat for myself or little ones. Billy Montgomery heard of it, and without a request or a wish he put his hand in his pocket and handed $200 to your father to relieve his extremity. Not one dollar of it was ever returned. True, you are not called upon to pay your father's debts, nor do I expect or want you to do it, but I do want you to remember the kindness, and not by any act of yours do anything that would cause him trouble or worry.

True, you have lost money by him, but that is nothing — a little money is nothing — God has blessed you — and me — now let us do our part, and not oppress one we can befriend. If anyone else wants you to bring suit for that place, or in any way try to wrest it from him, for my sake, for your manhood's sake, for God's sake, refuse positively to have anything to do with it. <u>No one</u> knows of this letter, nor shall anyone ever know it, should you respect my appeal, for I want it to be your act, not mine. May God's blessing be upon my boy, and may he be strong enough to be right. With love, I am —

Fondly — Your Mother[51]

In this letter, Alice resorts to manipulation in order to ensure Wiley chooses what she believes to be the only acceptable option. In the closing lines, she appears to give Wiley the freedom to make his own decision, but closer examination reveals she is threatening him with mild retaliation in the form of exposure if he disregards her advice: "<u>No one</u> knows of this letter, nor shall anyone ever know it, should you respect my appeal, for I want it to be your act, not mine." A manipulative maneuver indeed, yet one Alice felt justified in making given the gravity of the situation.

Such devious tactics were never necessary in Alice's relationship with the son she named after her brother Rufus. When Alice memorialized her sibling in this way, little did she know his namesake would take his place as her confidant and later become her right-hand man in the remedy business. Alice owed much to Rufus because the remedy would not have been as successful as it was without his help. After being wronged by three different partners, Alice was loath to trust another and resigned herself to accepting the limitations imposed by being the sole employee of her company. Rufus' desire to become her partner — one she could finally trust without reservation — was a godsend. Alice recognizes this fact in her will when she writes, "I gave the most to Rufus because it was by his faithful attention to my business that I am able to give anyone anything."[52]

Only one letter between Alice and Rufus exists among Alice's known papers. This was perhaps because there was seldom any need to write; when Alice was not traveling on behalf of the remedy, she lived with Rufus from the time he joined her in business until 1911.[53] This letter, which Alice wrote in 1911 from Rocky Mount, North Carolina, while on a remedy selling trip, centers on the fact Rufus is planning to sell his Charlotte home and move to the country:

> Dear Rufus,
>   There is nothing to write about except the weather. I went to Nashville [North Carolina] yesterday, but could not get out to do a thing after I got there, as the snow commenced soon after I left R. Mt. I stayed last night with Mrs. Spruill, who has an elegant house. What are you going to do with my things when you sell your home and go to the country? I think I had better rent a room with Mrs. Ross if I can get one, so that you could move them when you gave up your house. If Mrs. Ross' rooms are taken, perhaps I could get one with Mrs. Stutz. I leave it in your hands, and whatever arrangement you make will be all right with me. I sent you a copy of the letter I wrote Will when I returned his note, but I cannot get his answer until I get to Whitaker's. You are right about no one aught to give away their possessions in their life time. I can see it now as plain as you have always seen, but the thought I have ever had has been to help my children along. If you have to give up your house at once, just rent a room somewhere for me, and move my things, if you see it as I do, that it is the only thing left me to do, and the best, so do what you think best in the matter, and it will be all right with me. I shall go to Spring Hope tomorrow, then to Whitaker's, then Enfield, and one day out to the country stores, then Weldon. You had better write to me at Whitaker's.
>
> Your Mother[54]

In this letter, Alice provides an example of the complete trust she placed in Rufus—the same trust that made them a winning team in the remedy business—when she tells him to "do what you think best in the matter, and it will be all right with me." She also provides an example of the fact that she looked to son Rufus for advice just as she did brother Rufus when she writes "You are right about no one aught to give away their possessions in their life time. I can see it now as plain as you have always seen, but the thought I have ever had has been to help my children along." And, of course, this would not be a letter from Alice to one of her sons if it did not close with her signature exhortation: "You had better write to me."

The Mother-Daughter Bond

If Rufus was Alice's right-hand man, her oldest daughter, Gibson, was her right-hand woman. As Alice's oldest daughter, the task of caring for the four youngest children (Rufus, Henry, Levin, and William) after Joseph's death fell to twenty-four-year-old Gibson and her husband, William Harris.[55] Even after the growth of her own family forced Gibson to relinquish this responsibility, Alice relied on her to provide a place for family gatherings during the holiday season, such as the one during which both Alice's and Gibson's children contracted measles. Alice's extant journals also indicate she spent a great deal of time at Gibson's home at times other than her winter holidays. As with Rufus, only one letter between Alice and Gibson is present in Alice's known papers. Alice wrote this long letter on November 7, 1912, just seven months before her death. In it, she simultaneously addresses Gibson as adult confidante and selfish child. Alice's general purpose for the letter is to inform Gibson she will no longer be able to shower her grandchildren with gifts; she must in her old age keep more money to spend on herself if she is to have a retirement worth living. In the following excerpt, Alice justifies her decision by confiding in Gibson about an offense of which she considers Gibson herself to be guilty:

> Dear Gibson,
> There are times in life when we are called upon to decide important issues, and all we can do is to do what we think is right. Now let me present my side of the case to you and leave you to say if I am not right. For years I have been making money, and for years I have been spending it and giving it away as fast as I made it. I love to give those I love the things they need and aught to have and could not get without me. I have always loved to buy the Sunday and evening dresses for the girls that they could not otherwise have had, and it gave me so much pleasure as it did them. <u>But</u>, time brings changes. I am now in my 73rd year, and I cannot imagine a more trying life than old age would be to me without money to spend. I would be wretched and miserable. Suppose I wanted a hundred dollars, or two hundred or five hundred to take a trip, say out West, have I got a child that <u>could</u> give it to me. No, not one. Those that were able wouldn't want to do it, and those that wanted to do it would not be able, and even if they were, I doubt very much if they would feel able to sign a check for <u>my pleasure</u> as gladly as I have always signed for them. Not one of them would let me lack for something to eat and some sort of clothes to wear, but have I got one who would feel able to pay $3 a yard for dresses for me to wear, and buy three at a time? No.[56]

Alice clearly feels the family for which she has given so much has taken her for granted, and she is so certain of her estimation of the situation that she closes by insisting Gibson agree with her: "I want you to answer this and tell me if you do not know that I am <u>right</u>— 73 years old, don't forget that."

Alice excluded her youngest daughter, Josie, from any responsibility for providing her aging mother with pleasure money. Unfortunately, Josie was not even capable of supporting herself. Her extant letters exhibit barely legible handwriting that appears to have been produced with great effort. In addition, even though she was in her late twenties and early thirties when she wrote some of these letters, their content is more typical of a young teenage writer:

> Dear Cousin Tempie,
> Here I am — mother and I — at Southern Pines. Are you surprised? We are having a good time with the Yankees, at least I am & Mother seems to enjoy seeing me enjoy myself. I like the Clarks very much. Mrs. C. is an elegant lady & the Capt. is the "easiest," funniest man I ever saw. Mother will leave in few days — I going will [sic] stay a month. I will not stay any longer. May return at any time, so you may look out for me. I think I will get enough fun at [the?] end of the month. The ground was covered with snow when we left K. & [when?] we got here the snow had all disappeared & we have had lovely weather all the time & I am having a delightful time. But what a time I had of it in Jan.! Did you ever see such weather? I never [did?] & hope I never will again, mother was so sorry she could not go to see you again, but never mind I am going to give you another "<u>dose</u>." It seems to me that I never wanted to see you and Cousin Billy as bad in my life. I must say Good-bye. I don't have time to write or do anything else. It is always something up to do. I am beating everybody at whist. Play every day & night with Dr. Campbell & play against mother and Mrs. C. or Capt. C. and against Mrs. C. and Mother. Write me when you feel like it. I got your kind note was received [sic], with a heart <u>full of</u> sincere love for you you [sic] and Cousin Billy. Write to me here.
> J—[57]

For most of her life, Josie divided her time between four different North Carolina locations (Franklin County, Hickory, Southern Pines, and Charlotte) and lived with the same people in each of these locations. In Franklin County she lived with Tempie and Billy Montgomery, in Hickory with her aunt Lucy Beard, in Southern Pines with the Clarks (mentioned in the preceding letter from Josie), and in Charlotte with her brother Rufus and his family.[58] This systematic rotation indicates Josie was not able to live on her own, and also that, in order to avoid overburdening those with whom she lived, Alice had her shift between several locations. Alice's journals indicate she paid board for Josie throughout her life, and also that she bought her a house in Hickory, North Carolina, in 1910.[59] In addition, Josie received special attention in Alice's will — a generous bequest of stock holdings and a monthly stipend from the profits of the remedy company for the remainder of her life. Alice was so concerned with Josie's care in her will that she stated she wished "Josie's bequest to have precedence over all," and provided a contingency plan in the event her stock holdings became worthless.[60]

Alice's papers contain no indication of the cause of Josie's need for life-long assistance, though family members recognized it would be necessary early on. Mary Morgan wrote to her husband about it in 1879 when Josie was fourteen: "There is an awfully disappointed set here to day. They got every thing ready to go to 'Ebonezia' to the big meeting & it rained. Gib is especially cut up, as I think she was to meet Mr. Ellis there. Sister would not let Josey [sic] go & she is very much rejoiced that it is raining. Poor child she surely makes herself unhappy. I don't know what will become of her when sister dies."[61]

It is possible the very illness that provided Alice with her livelihood resulted in Josie being incapable of earning hers. Alice's doctor "pronounced the trouble Scrofula,"[62] but it could actually have been any number of other serious maladies capable of doing irreparable damage. In addition, though Alice's written account indicates Josie survived a single bout of serious illness, her December 1874 letter to her brother Rufus indicates the child withstood two, and also that the second was perhaps worse than the first. In this letter, Alice tells her brother that "Josie is very, very ill, exactly in every respect

The graves of Alice and her daughter Josie in Charlotte's Elmwood Cemetery (photograph by David Hursh).

like she was before," and also that "when she was in death's clutches before, I prayed God to let me keep her one more year that I might be better to her. He gave her to me <u>two</u>, and now I think He claims her."[63] The 1872 bout had to have been the one during which Alice's neighbor offered her the remedy, because later in that same year Alice used it to cure a large open sore on her husband's face.[64] Though she surely administered the medicine again in 1874, Alice's gloomy prognosis in her letter to Rufus suggests it was having a more difficult time fighting the ailment the second time around. In the end, the remedy may have been responsible for two miraculous recoveries, but it probably was not capable of completely reversing the harmful effects of such severe episodes— effects that could have manifested themselves in permanent mental and emotional disabilities.

While Josie's mental and emotional conditions were no doubt the main reasons Alice provided her with special care throughout her life, two other factors could also have been involved. First, four of Alice's children preceded her in death. With the passing of each, Alice's appreciation for the fact Josie survived two near-death experiences no doubt intensified, motivating her to do all she could to ensure Josie a long and comfortable life. Second, Josie's first brush with death served as Alice's introduction to the remedy. Though Alice would certainly have preferred Josie not endure such an illness, she could probably not help but be thankful it provided her with a good life — one she in return freely shared with her daughter. Josie lived until the age of seventy, at which time she was buried next to Alice in the Person family plot in Charlotte's Elmwood cemetery, a fitting resting place for one who played a leading role in shaping her mother's life.

Chapter 3
Medicine Maker and Musician

Alice's medicinal and musical careers did not involve extensive educational preparation, meticulous market analysis, or elaborate strategic planning. On the contrary, they were based largely on serendipity, and were guided by Alice's rare combination of emotional sensitivity and shrewd analytical ability — a union that enabled her to effectively read and assess events and make positives out of negatives.

The beginning of Alice's medicine-making career provides an excellent example of her business model: fate brought the medicine to Alice, her empathy with the pain of mothers in similar situations (and with all who suffered from the previously incurable scrofula) developed into an obsession with the medicine, and her analytical skills converted this obsession into a three-year period of product evaluation. Alice's method of evaluating the remedy entailed sharing it free of charge whenever she heard of someone with scrofula, or scrofula-like illnesses, and asking them "to give it a trial and report the result."[1] These reports not only provided Alice with a number of testimonials, they also established the medicine's effectiveness with conditions other than scrofula.[2] The first indication the remedy might be suitable for broader application resulted from a problem Alice's own husband was having. She tells the story in one of her advertisements:

> I receive numerous letters asking if my Remedy will cure cancer. I can only cite the following case, which is the only one I have ever cured, the only one upon which I have had an opportunity of testing it in its incipient stage. When we were married in 1857, my husband had a small wart-looking place on his left cheek bone, which he told me then he thought would eventually terminate in cancer. We paid no attention to it, though we could see with advancing years that it was increasing in size. Then it commenced to form a scab, something similar to a piece of dry bran, which would shed every few days, another form, and so it continued until March, 1872, when it broke out into a regular

running, eating sore, which continued to spread with most alarming rapidity throughout the spring and summer. The sore had eaten in considerably, was about the size of a silver quarter, had the appearance of a honeycomb, with the cells distinctly marked, bled considerably, had a smarting, irritating sensation, as if needles were pricking the surface, with occasional sharp, darting pains, which extended to the eye and weakened it. Everybody who saw it considered it a case of well developed cancer. The physicians advised him to have it cut out, whereas I advised treatment at a cancer infirmary. At last one of the physicians suggested that I try my Remedy, and said he believed it would cure it. The thought of using it had never occurred to me, as I then only knew it to be good for Scrofula. I commenced its use on the sore the 1st day of October and discontinued it the 7th day of November, as it was perfectly cured. It had been a running sore for six months. It broke out again for four consecutive years, in the spring, each time more severely, and requiring much longer to cure. It broke out last in 1876, when it required four month's treatment to effect a cure, since which time it has been and is now perfectly well.[3]

Near the end of the assessment process, fate once again intervened, this time in the form of a man from South Carolina who had been desperately seeking a cure for "a scrofulous affection on the heel." He sent Alice a letter requesting some of the medicine and promised a five hundred dollar payment if it cured him. Alice's empathic nature led her to fill his request and limit his payment to just twenty five dollars.[4] On receipt of the South Carolinian's monetary gratitude (the first payment Alice received for the remedy), Alice realized her mission to assuage suffering could also provide relief to her family's ailing finances. To that end, she spent a generous portion — two-thirds — of her first profits on advertisements for the remedy,[5] a business strategy she strove to maintain for the remainder of her career.

Onward and Upward

With a renewed vision for her product, Alice developed a trademark and set about to establish it as her property by filing an application with the United States Patent and Trademark Office in January of 1878. By August of the same year her trademark was registered. The trademark, "an Indian warrior in a kneeling posture on a bank or cliff overlooking a waterfall,"[6] appeared on paper labels affixed to most of Alice's remedy bottles and packages for the remainder of the remedy's life. With this registration Alice also established the official name of the medicine as Mrs. Joe Person's Remedy, a name she claimed "she did not bother about," because "the name came."[7] While serendipity may have indeed provided the name, Alice's acumen certainly would not have allowed her to overlook the fact it would commend her product to a broad range of customers. Use of the title "Mrs." indicated she was a respectable married woman, and use of her husband's forename moniker indicated she was down-to-earth and a friend to people from all walks of life. With time, Alice identified so closely with this name that, with the exception of letters to family and friends, she used it almost exclusively in both business and personal documents.

The recipe given to Alice by her neighbor was a bitters (i.e., a mixture of herbs and alcohol) and contained the following ingredients: 20 percent alcohol, pipsissewa, queen's root, Mexican sarsaparilla, prickly ash bark, star grass, helonias, and trillium.[8] This bitters was not the only product manufactured and marketed by Alice; as early as 1878 she was also developing and selling a wash. In her bitter November 1878 letter to her brother Rufus, Alice mentions her "wash powders" and the fact she "just learned how to dry them perfectly." She tells him they "are as green as when growing" unlike those she previously produced, which were brown.[9] In an extensive, forty-one-page advertising booklet issued in 1884, Alice told potential customers how to properly combine the bitters and the wash: "When used in cases of Scrofula or Cancer, in which there are external sores, the Bitters must be used to purify the blood, and the Wash to cleanse and heal the sores. In such cases the use of the Wash is of as much importance as the Bitters. It is perfectly painless to the worst sore or the eye, and is very soothing and healing. In cases of Scrofula, in which there are no sores, and for the other diseases for which it is recommended, the Tonic Bitters alone is necessary."[10] The combination of internal and external medications brought healing in the following way: "The Bitters WILL EXPEL the disease from the system. Where there are no sores, this is done frequently by causing an eruption, varying in intensity according to the severity of the disease, frequently by PRODUCING sores as outlets for the impurity of the blood. Where sores already exist it causes a largely increased discharge from them, and often the formation of new ones; these are cleansed and healed by the means of the Wash, and a cure is soon effected."[11]

With regard to the amount of each medication necessary to effect a cure, the 1884 booklet recommended the following: "A bottle of the Bitters will last a man able to take a full dose a little more than a week. One package of the Wash is sufficient to last in ordinary cases several days. I advise all persons, in ordering, to procure enough medicine to give it a 'fair test,' when I am confident they will not be disappointed in the result. To those who can conveniently order enough to do this, I advise to get one-half dozen bottles Bitters, and one-half dozen Wash packages—any quantity, may, however be ordered."[12]

In addition to the preceding general facts about the remedy, the 1884 booklet provided detailed instructions on how to prepare and apply the wash:

To prepare the WASH, boil the contents of one package in a pint and a half of water, about 15 minutes, let it settle, strain, bottle, and in warm weather keep in a cool place.

Pour enough of the WASH to use once in a basin, wet a soft rag in it, and with it thoroughly wash the sore, then instead of returning that rag to the basin, as in the ordinary method of washing, *throw it away* and get a fresh one and continue to wash in that manner each time until the sore is *thoroughly cleansed*, always recollecting, after the rag has touched the sore, it must by *no means* be returned to the WASH, as the Scrofulous corruption which adheres to the rag would poison the WASH, and completely destroy its effects. It will of course take a good many rags each time the sore is washed, which must be at least three times a day. If the sore is of such a nature that every part of it cannot be reached with a rag, use a small syringe, being careful not to let any of the WASH fall from the sore into the vessel containing it. The WASH may be warmed before using or applied cold, as may be most pleasant. It is best however to be warmed in cold weather.[13]

Finally, detailed instructions for the use of the bitters were also included in the booklet: "In regulating the dose of Bitters, I find some require more than others. I think it advisable for a grown person to begin with one tablespoonful, and gradually increase to the prescribed quantity; half a wine glassful I think a good, full dose for a lady. Enough must never be taken to feel the effects of it in the head.[14]

Several additional products were eventually added to the company's product line: Red Indian Brand Liver Pills, Red Indian Brand Blood Pills, Red Indian Brand Kidney Pills, Red Indian Brand Diuretic Pills, Red Indian Brand Cathartic Pills, and Rub-It-On — Ezit. These products were added sometime after Alice and Rufus moved the company to Charlotte in 1904, and perhaps not even until after Alice's death in 1913. The letterhead, order form, and memo stationary on which these products were touted indicate the company's location as Charlotte and also sport a name change for the original bitters from Mrs. Joe Person's Remedy to Mrs. Joe Person's Old Time Medicine. The addition of "old time" indicates a later attempt to appeal to those customers who valued the tried-and-true over the latest twentieth-century pharmaceutical creations. In addition, replacing the word "remedy" with "medicine" was no doubt an attempt to change the image of the product from that of a hillbilly concoction to a legitimate medicinal preparation in response to increased turn-of-the-century governmental scrutiny of proprietary products.

While Red Indian Brand Blood Pills contained the same active ingredients as Alice's liquid remedy, they also contained other ingredients that could not easily be prepared in liquid form, and were offered for those who preferred pills over liquids. They were to be taken four times a day and caused

3. Medicine Maker and Musician

Two Mrs. Joe Person's Remedy bottles. The empty bottle on the right (from the private collection of Thilbert Pearce) dates to circa 1906, and the unopened bottle on the left (from the private collection of Wyatt and Libby McGhee III) was produced after 1939 (photograph by David Hursh).

the urine of those who ingested them to turn blue — an intentional side effect that served to indicate when the medication reached a patient's bladder. Red Indian Brand Kidney Pills served to "tone up" kidneys weakened by "over-eating, strong drink, over-work, lack of rest, and exposure to cold or dampness," and were to be taken three times a day. Red Indian Brand Liver Pills were cathartics and intended for use once or twice a week while taking the kidney pills, the liver pills, or the bitters in order to ensure the best results from those medicines.[15]

From the start, Alice practiced the conservative business model she urged her ill-fated Tarboro partner to adopt when she told him it was "so much better to begin small and work up big."[16] From 1878 to 1884, Alice produced the remedy in her home with the help of her children, even though they loathed the activity because it stained their hands.[17] Alice's early patrons were the country folk in the area immediately surrounding Greenwood, a customer base vulnerable to the fickle agricultural economy. In a letter to her brother Rufus in the autumn of 1879, Alice bemoaned the fact that "the cotton crop everywhere is short, and my business is prostrated."[18] This market limitation, along with Alice's desire to share her healing discovery with more people, resulted in her trips to the metropolitan areas of Raleigh and Charlotte in 1882, and also in her partnerships with businessmen who offered the financial backing necessary to launch the venture in a way Alice could only dream of doing. As Alice so beautifully recounts in "The Chivalry of Man," the city of Charlotte was the only one of her attempts to "work up big" that resulted in lasting benefit. Raleigh turned her away, and all three of her early partnership ventures ended in ruin.

In customary fashion, Alice turned these negatives into positives. Rather than continue to seek the elusive trustworthy partner with the capital necessary to produce the remedy on a larger scale, Alice made the personalized production and sale of the remedy her hallmark. To facilitate this, she settled in the small town of Kittrell, North Carolina, in 1886. This was an ideal location for several reasons. First, the fact that Kittrell was a small town complemented the remedy's "down home" image. Second, Kittrell was unique among small towns in that the existence of mineral springs and two large hotels made it a tourist destination that each year attracted hundreds of visitors seeking the health benefits of the springs.[19] These visitors would certainly have been attracted to Alice's remedy, and if satisfied with its healing abilities would have told others about it when they returned home. Third, not only was Kittrell located near Alice's scattered children, it also was in central North Carolina, nearly equidistant from all the marketing destinations Alice visited personally. Last, one of Kittrell's two hotels (the one known as the Glass House) provided Alice with additional income from regular piano playing engagements in the hotel's large entertainment hall[20] — engagements that also provided Alice with the opportunity to acquaint her listeners with the remedy.[21]

A year after Alice relocated to Kittrell, her son Rufus joined her in business. Although Rufus was not able to meet Alice's need for a well-heeled partner, he more than sufficed for a trustworthy one. Over the course of the next eighteen years, the duo purchased property in the downtown section of Kittrell,[22] established a laboratory on that property for the production of the remedy,[23] and expanded their operation to include wholesale agents in Richmond, Virginia, and Baltimore, Maryland.[24]

Three's Company

During this same period of time, Alice made the acquaintance of what she considered to be her third friend in the battle of life — her published music.[25] By the time Alice issued her arrangements of southern folk tunes in 1889, her other friends (her remedy and her piano playing) had been her close companions for some time — the remedy for fifteen years and her music making for nearly her entire half-century existence. Alice's parents owned both a piano and a violin,[26] and because of this she no doubt learned to play at an early age. With the assistance of this, her oldest friend, fate introduced Alice to her newest friend by providing her with the opportunity to demonstrate pianos at county fairs and state expositions all over the South beginning in the mid–1880s.[27] Visitors to the exhibits at which Alice played enjoyed her heart-felt renditions of music from a bygone era so much they asked her to publish her arrangements so they could revel in nostalgia without having to wait for the next exposition. Alice, all too ready to oblige, called on George Minor, one of the owners of Hume, Minor & Co., a Richmond piano manufacturer for which she demonstrated pianos.[28] Minor probably shared Alice's love of old Southern melodies because he was a Confederate veteran of the Civil War who taught vocal music and led singing schools and music conventions— activities which provided him with ready access to all of the resources necessary to publish music.[29] Minor assisted Alice with music transcription,[30] copyright research,[31] and printing,[32] and by so doing successfully launched Alice's third professional venture.

Though Alice's performing repertoire consisted of at least fifty tunes,[33] she chose just eighteen of them for inclusion in her published repertoire. These were divided between two collections, one containing fifteen tunes and the other just three. In its first edition, the larger anthology bore the title *A Collection of Popular Airs as Arranged and Played Only by Mrs. Joe Person at the Southern Expositions*. This edition's cover featured a picture of a middle-aged Alice and included a list of the collection's contents (see photograph on following page).

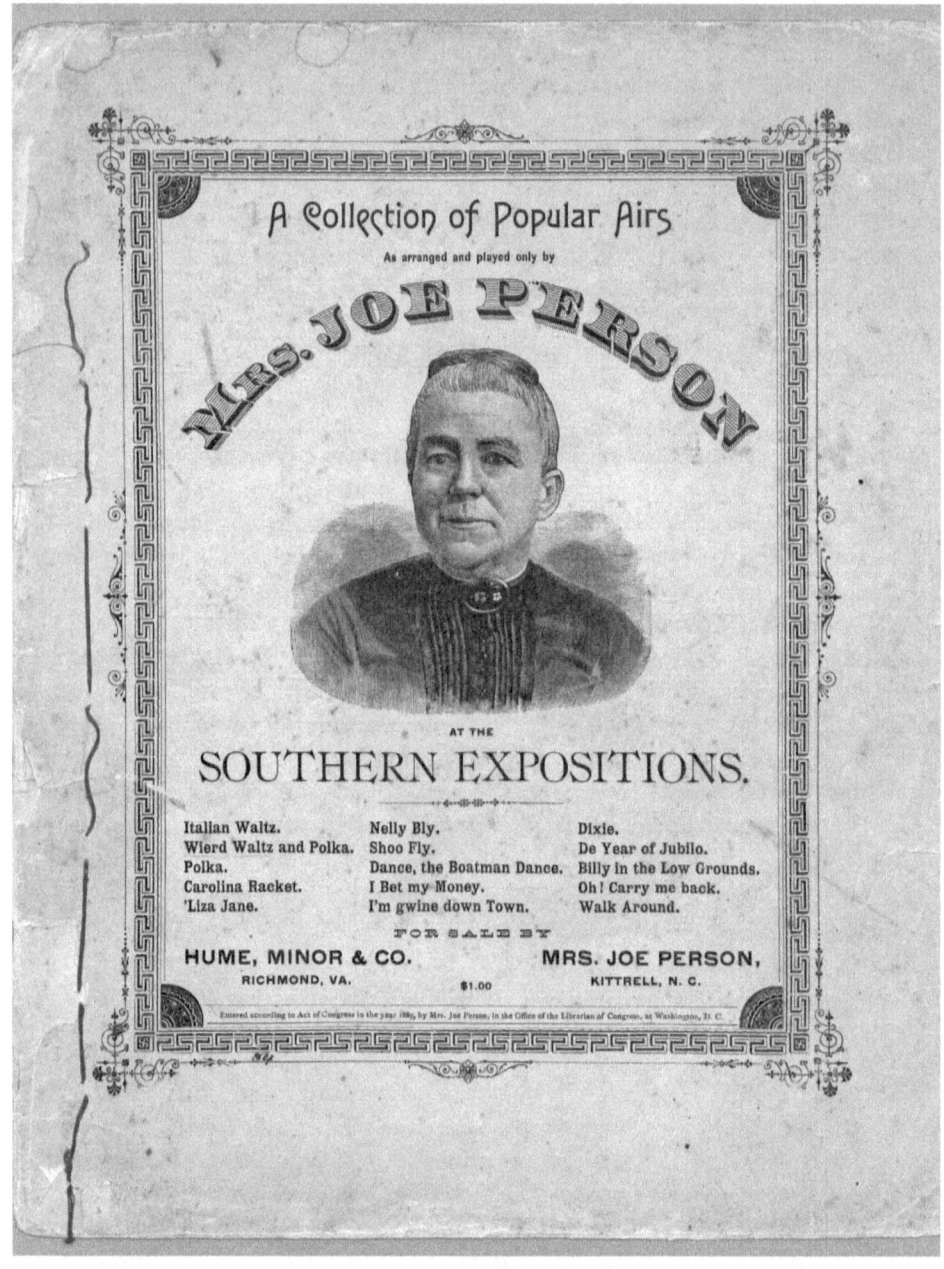

The cover of the first edition of *A Collection of Popular Airs* (Alice Morgan Person Collection, East Carolina University).

Two known editions, one reprint, and three cover design variants (one for each edition or reprint) of *Popular Airs* exist. Alice published the second edition of this collection sometime after relocating to Charlotte in 1904,[34] at which point her supply probably needed replenishing. The first edition contained a glaring spelling error — the second and third letters in the word "weird" in the title of the second piece were transposed on both the cover and in the music. Alice no doubt took advantage of the need to correct this error on the printing plates by making some additional refinements, two of which appeared on the cover. First, Alice lengthened the title to *A Collection of Popular Airs and Plantation Melodies as Arranged and Played Only by Mrs. Joe Person at the Southern Expositions*. Second, she removed her picture. Additional revisions in the second edition included the following: (1) relocating "Dance, the Boatman Dance" to the end of the collection; (2) altering some of the individual song titles; and (3) adding song texts above the music for some selections (perhaps to increase the nostalgic pleasure of potential customers). Alice must have been pleased with her edits in the second edition because the next time her supply dwindled she simply reprinted it with minor cover design changes.

Alice first published her trio anthology titled *A Transcription of the Beautiful Song Blue Alsatian Mountains! Also "Down-Town Girls" and "Boatman Dance" as Arranged and Played by Mrs. Joe Person* in 1889 after the *Popular Airs* collection.[35] As with *Popular Airs*, three known versions of *Blue Alsatian Mountains* exist. Unlike *Popular Airs*, there is only one edition; the two later versions are simply reprints of the original music plates with varying cover designs.

Alice did not copyright all of her published arrangements. The only Library of Congress copyrights registered in her name are those filed on April 10, 1889, for each of the fifteen *Popular Airs* tunes.[36] Unfortunately, George Minor's assistance with preregistration copyright research did not prevent the specter of infringement from haunting Alice during the summer and fall of 1889. Motivated by her penchant for "solid facts,"[37] Alice wrote to Boston-based music publisher Oliver Ditson early in the summer of 1889, telling him that if she "had unwittingly been infringing on his copyright" she "would of course comply with his terms."[38] She told him she would, however, have to see a copy of his music before she did so. Rather than provide that copy, Ditson responded with a strong letter demanding "immediate attention" in the form of monetary compensation and new printing plates:

> Mrs. Joe Person
> Dear Madam:
> Your favor received. We do not care to have our name used on music we do not publish, we notice in your collection of Popular Airs that

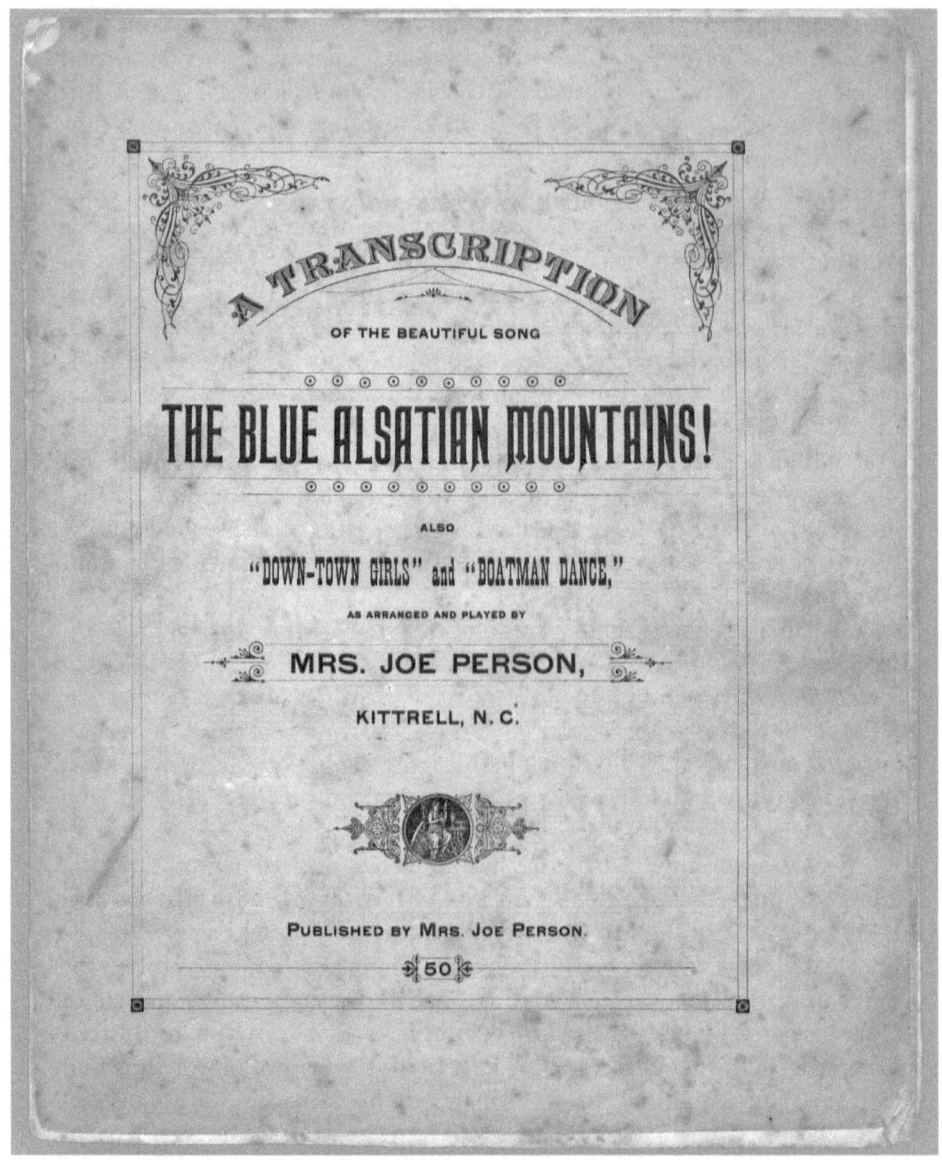

The cover of the first printing of *Blue Alsatian Mountains* (Alice Morgan Person Collection, East Carolina University).

you have used some of our copyright melodies viz: "Dixie" and "Nelly Bly" we cannot grant you permission to use these without compensation and must charge for the first named $10.00 and the other $5.00 and shall require you to put on the plates of each the words, Used by

permission of Oliver Ditson Company owners of the copyright, and send us plate proofs at once, also that you have a rubber stamp with the above words put on and stamp the same on all copies with each tune that you have on hand, if this is not satisfactory send us the plates at once with all copies you have. Please give this matter your immediate attention.
Your truly
Oliver Ditson Company
Send us a copy showing how you use rubber stamp.[39]

Alice once again requested the copies of the Ditson publications, and this time she received them, along with another strong letter and a bill:

Mrs. Joe Person
Dear Madam:
Your favor received and we send you copies of the songs in question which are our copyright property and any instrumental arrangements made from these are infringements we enclose bill and have marked the acct. to be settled in 90 days, please send us as soon as possible a copy showing permission notice also plate proof showing that they have been corrected for next edition.
Yours truly
Oliver Ditson Company[40]

Perturbed, Alice had nowhere to turn but her lawyer son Wiley. In September of 1889 she sent Wiley a letter accompanied by the music she received from Ditson:

Dear Wiley—
Of course you have seen my piece of music I had published — if not, you can see it at Joe's store in Louisburg. I wrote Ditson word that if I had unwittingly been infringing on his copyright, I would, of course comply with his terms, but before doing so, I must see a copy of his music, upon which he claimed the infringement. As I had had the matter examined into, in Richmond, before I had mine published, & Hume and Minor, also the gentleman who wrote the music had assured me, upon examination, they found I was entitled to the copyright. No instrumental arrangement of Dixie was on the market, & the copyright even of the vocal piece was expired. I requested a copy that I might see my infringement, & they sent me the piece of music I send you, registered, by which you see that Firth Pond & Co. were copyrightests [sic] in 1860 — but if an instrumental piece can be an infringement of a vocal — which I do not believe — there might be some claim liable from Msrs. Foster & Co.— see 3rd page. I had a stamp made in St. Louis in case they should have right on their side —"By permission of Oliver Ditson Co. Owners of Copyright." Write me here by return mail, & let me know if there is any ground whatever for their claim, &

what must I do about it — they are a reliable House, but I cannot see the justice of their claim. What shall I write them?[41]

Unfortunately, the outcome of this disagreement will probably never be known because no further correspondence between Alice, Wiley, and Ditson exists. It does, however, seem likely that Wiley was successful in freeing his mother from the need to credit Ditson in her music; none of the half dozen known copies of *Popular Airs* does so.

More Trials and Tribulations

The summer and fall of 1889 were not only trying for Alice with regard to her music, they were also difficult with regard to her medicine. The September letter to Wiley in which Alice asks for copyright advice also includes discussion of another legal matter — the "'great' Davidson case."[42] This case was a remnant of Alice's failed 1883 partnership with George Davidson, which she describes in great detail in "The Chivalry of Man." After Davidson defaulted on his agreement, Alice sued him with the help of Raleigh lawyers Fuller and Snow. At each term of the court after Alice brought suit against Davidson, her case was continued to the next term because Fuller and Snow failed to appear on her behalf, the result (according to Alice) of Davidson having bribed the partners. Two letters to Wiley (the September one already discussed and another a few days later in October) and one to Billy Montgomery (sent two days before the first letter to Wiley) provide details about Alice's battle with Davidson which she does not include in "The Chivalry of Man."

In her letter to Montgomery, Alice indicates she is concerned Davidson may attempt to use her trademark on another product.[43] The 1883 contract between Alice and Davidson stipulated that after Davidson paid Alice twenty thousand dollars she was to transfer the remedy trademark to him.[44] Though Davidson never paid the money, he had a document containing Alice's signature — a document he could use to claim he had paid her. In typical fashion, Alice attempted to make this negative situation into a positive one by using it to advance Wiley's nascent law career. In the first of her two letters to Wiley, Alice encourages her son to become associate counsel to a seasoned lawyer with whom she had been making plans regarding the Davidson case:[45]

> Suppose you have a talk with Mr. Gulley — perhaps show him my other letter & see what you can do — he has all my proofs, & I have today sent him a letter I have just received from Dr. Carmer, Balt — the weakest letter you ever read. I wish very much you were associated with Mr. Gulley, and hope you can so arrange it — he will expect ½ of the damages. Suppose you propose to join him, for such a part as you may agree upon with him, say he to have ⅔ and you ⅓, or would you advise

me to write him my wishes in the matter. Which would be best? I think 'twould be best for you to show him my letter & let him see my wishes, which I think he would be guided by. I believe it will be a big thing for both of you.[46]

In her second letter, Alice makes plans with Wiley for her big court appearance:

> Dear Wiley,
> I have not entered into any written agreement with Mr. Gulley, nor have we had any specific understanding about the matter. It is my wish for you to appear with him as associate counsel, but I suppose I will have to attend court as witness, and we can then arrange the minutiae. Do you spell "attorneys" correctly "attornies"—which is right? I have no dictionary, but always use the first. I enclose an order on Fuller & Snow for some papers, please get them. Davidson's father, who was worth three million, is now dead. Davidson himself was worth ½ million. I would like to know how much he paid Fuller to drop it—at least a thousand I reckon. Get the papers any how by when I come in Nov.
> Alice Person.[47]

Unfortunately, the outcome for Wiley and Alice was not what she hoped it would be. The case never came to trial, and the court awarded her just $1,250 in order to clear it from the docket.[48]

Nearly ten years passed before Alice met with another major professional hurdle. In December of 1898, a fire originating in Alice's Kittrell laboratory did damage to half of the business section of the town. One of Alice's sons and a friend were sleeping above the laboratory and their only means of escape was a telegraph pole outside one of the upstairs windows. Unfortunately, Alice lost her entire inventory of the remedy and was only insured for half its value.[49] Fortunately, her reputation was so well-established in the state of North Carolina that residents responded to news of the disaster with great empathy:

> Our sympathies with those of the press of the State and every one who knows her go out in words or thoughts of condolence to Mrs. Person, in the loss of her laboratory, during the late fire at Kittrell. She has ever evinced such laudable enterprise, such untiring energy, coupled with so gentle and amiable a disposition, so affable and pleasant in all business relations—we have known and admired her every bearing so much that when the news of her loss reached us, we received it as if it were a personal concern.
> We are pleased to learn that this loss will only occasion a temporary suspension of her manufacture of her famous "Remedy." She will reestablish her business, and rather than being disheartened at disas-

ter, we shall expect to see her business take on new life, and greater adaptation to the demands of her constantly increasing volume of trade.[50]

This esteem for Alice and her remedy kept demand high and swiftly placed her back on solid financial ground. Beginning just a few days after the fire and continuing for the next five years, Alice and Rufus purchased multiple adjoining properties in Kittrell — acquisitions that would appear to indicate they were gradually expanding their business and pushing deep roots into the central North Carolina soil.[51] Alice even made two of these purchases within days of each other in November of 1903, an action that would certainly seem to indicate that a significant laboratory expansion was imminent. Nevertheless, Alice, Rufus, his wife, Jessie, and their four children relocated to Charlotte just four months later.[52]

Working Up Big

On March 9, 1904, Rufus, his youngest brother, William, and "Uncle Jim Harris" arrived at 805 North Church Street in Charlotte's fourth ward for the purpose of adding a laboratory to the rear of the existing home. Jessie and the children followed two days later.[53] Alice delayed her arrival until March 22 because she was recovering from an illness at Gibson's home.[54] A picture of the vine-clad, ginger bread-adorned Church Street cottage and laboratory appeared in a 1907 brochure promoting the city of Charlotte. Information regarding the increase of remedy sales in this brochure indicates that relocating to the Queen City was a wise move. Sales of the remedy nearly doubled — from eight thousand packages a year to fifteen thousand — by the end of the Person family's third year in their new location.[55] An uncomplicated plan of evenly divided responsibility governed the success of the Charlotte enterprise. Rufus owned the home.[56] Alice owned the laboratory.[57] Rufus (with the assistance of his nephew William Harris) managed the day-to-day activities of the company's headquarters.[58] Alice promoted the remedy throughout North Carolina and in parts of Virginia and South Carolina,[59] boarding with Rufus and his family when she was not on the road.[60] The duo's financial plan was a simple one. They paid all expenses involved in the production and promotion of the remedy with the proceeds from the sale of Alice's sheet music. This meant all income from the sale of the remedy was "clear profit."[61]

On the surface, the company's marketing plan was also simple — a two-pronged approach consisting of print advertising and personal visits by the company's founder. At its core, however, the plan was expensive, complex, and time-intensive. Though the mother-son team did not spend two-thirds

Rufus and Alice's Charlotte home and laboratory from a 1907 brochure promoting the city of Charlotte (Alice Morgan Person Collection, East Carolina University).

of their profits on print advertising as Alice did with her first remedy profits, they were committed to spending thousands of dollars annually to spread the word in this way.[62] These funds paid for two types of advertisements: (1) circulars ranging from one-piece leaflets and trade cards to elaborate multi-page booklets containing remedy facts (such as the preparation instructions in the 1884 booklet discussed earlier), personal testimonials, and scenarios; and (2) strategically placed, themed newspaper ads.

Alice's one-piece circulars were greatly abbreviated versions of her extensive advertising booklets. The first of these compact advertising tools was probably the leaflet on which Alice scribbled her November 1878 note to her brother. Alice must have been pleased with this first attempt at writing marketing literature, because she based the instructional portions of her 1884 booklet on the text of that leaflet:

> My remedy is in two forms: *Bitters*, which I give three times a day to purify the blood, and which will expel the disease from the system, and a healing *Wash*, to cleanse and heal the sores. I sell the Bitters at $2 per quart bottle; ingredients for making the Wash $1 per package, $10 per dozen, $5 per half dozen. A bottle of the Bitters will last a man able to take a full dose a little more than two weeks. One package of Wash ingredients will make a pint of Wash, sufficient to last in ordinary cases, several days. I advise all persons, in ordering, to procure enough medicine to give it a *"fair test,"* when I am confident they will not be disappointed in the result. To those who can conveniently order

enough to last a month at one time, I advise to get two quarts of bitters and one dozen packages Wash, if their sores are very numerous or extreme, if not, one half that quantity of Wash is sufficient to [illegible] out with two quarts of Bitters—any quantity may, however, be ordered. In regulating the dose of Bitters, I find some require much more than others. I think it advisable for a grown person to begin with one tablespoonful and gradually increase to the prescribed quantity, half wine glassful I think a good, full dose for a lady. Enough must never be taken to feel the effects of the whiskey in the head. While I do not recommend my remedy in cases of *true cancer,* I find no difficulty in curing up old sores, pronounced by physicians to be cancerous in their nature, and I have even cured one cancer, which, although it breaks out again every Spring, always readily yields to my treatment, and is *now* perfectly well. I do not believe there is an old ulcer or sore that will not yield to my Remedy, properly applied. Where there are no sores, only a tumor or enlargement, I direct the affected places to be bathed with the Wash. In ordering medicine, 25 cents must always be added, to cover cost of boxing, &c.[63]

Trade cards required an even greater economy of scale. One such card from Alice's Kittrell days reads as follows:

Mrs. Joe Person's Remedy Is a Specific for all Blood Diseases.

As a **Tonic** and **Alterative** it is unequalled. As a **Purifier of the Blood** it is indorsed by all who have used it. It will cure Muscular Rheumatism. Cancer in its early stages, Heart Disease, Erysipelas, Tetter, Eruptions and Skin Diseases. Infallible for Bilious Colic. Infallible for Scrofula. Infallible for Indigestion. Price $1 per bottle.

The Wash is all-important in cases in which there are external sores or eruptions. Price 50 cents per package.

Send for pamphlet, containing testimonials of wonderful cures among our home people, and indorsements by the druggists and prominent men of North Carolina.

Wholesale Agents:— The Owens & Minor Drug Co., Purcell, Ladd & Co., Powers & Taylor, Richmond, Va.; Boykin, Carmer & Co., Wm. H. Brown & Bros., Gilpin, Langdon & Co., Baltimore, Md.

Address all communications to MRS. JOE PERSON, Kittrell, N.C.[64]

Testimonials were the backbone of Alice's advertising scheme, and as such comprised the greater portion of her advertising booklets. In fact, one booklet published about 1901 consisted of nothing but testimonials—ninety in all. Two testimonials from this thirty-one-page collection are of particular interest. The first claims the remedy cured tonsillitis, and did so by using the wash as a gargle, something Alice did not include in her instructions for its use: "For a long time my son was troubled with bronchial trouble, which, every time he took cold, settled in his throat and produced something like tonsillitis. The tonsils would enlarge and swell so that he had great trouble to swallow anything and could take no solid food. Last spring he took one-half dozen bottles of Mrs. Joe Person's Remedy, and gargled with the Wash, and it cured him. He has not had a spell since."[65] The second testimonial is from a woman, Mrs. I.G. Guthrie of Bethel Hill, North Carolina, who found relief from a chronic skin problem that was so severe it kept her from restful sleep for years. Mrs. Guthrie's gratitude was such that she penned a poem in honor of Alice:

> I live for Mrs. Person,
> > For her who knows me true,
> For the heaven that shines above me,
> > And awaits my coming too;
> For the cause that lacks assistance,
> For the wrongs that need resistance,
> > And the good that I can do.[66]

Of the dozens of original testimonial letters that Alice received, only one remains among her known papers. This letter is particularly touching because it deals with a nine-year-old girl who was critically ill and made a dramatic recovery after taking the remedy. This testimonial perhaps received pride of place in one of Alice's journals because the child was the same age as her daughter Josie when the remedy precipitated an equally dramatic recovery from an equally bleak condition:

Dear Mrs. Person:

I have a little girl 9 years of age, who has had white swelling for 6 years, has been in the Hospital in Charleston S.C. & in Richmond Va. In all we have had 4 operations performed on her. We thought she was well, till about two months ago. The trouble returned, her leg inflamed & bursted in four different places. We called the doctor in he treated her for about two weeks, she growing steadily worse all the time, having high fever all the time, had one hemorrhage, wounds would discharge about a pint per day, was in bed <u>all</u> the time could not walk a step. Pieces of bone would work out, as before, the doctor said the leg would have to be amputated. I would not consent. My wife had been taking your medicine & prevailed on me to try it on the little girl. Up to the present time she has taken 9 bottles. She is now out of her bed. In about two weeks after we commenced using your medicine, she got up out of her bed and could walk with crutches. About a week ago she discarded her crutches. At this writing her leg is not swelled at all, discharges have almost ceased. She has gained about 35 lbs. in weight. Just as hearty as she can be. If there is any information you can give me on this case, or any suggestions you may offer us will be appreciated.

Yours very respectfully,
E.F. Kelly[67]

Though Alice's advertising tours de force featured testimonials she received after the remedy had proven itself, Alice also received letters from desperate individuals hoping to find the cure they sought. Like the lone testimonial letter, three of these cries for help ended up among the pages of Alice's journals. These letters provide a representative cross section of the remedy queries to which Alice refers in her booklets. The writer of one of the letters had already tried the remedy for her self-diagnosed "change of life" problems, but writes to be sure she is using it properly:

Mrs. Joe Person
Dear friend, I will try and write you a few lines to see if you will write and give me a little direction how to use your remedy. I am 46 years old. I have had good health till this year and have been sick most of the time. I never was married. I reckon it is the change of life. I have been regular all my life and am yet, but it gives my head fits. I have taken your remedy — think it has done me some good. It helped my legs — they ache all the time. Please write and let me know if I am to take your remedy when I am sick or not. That's all that I am afraid of. Write soon.
Fernshale Saville Griffithe[68]

Another woman writes to inquire as to whether Alice has a "specific" for her severe case of physician-diagnosed facial eczema:

Dear Madam:
I have been advised by friends to try your remedies for "Eczema" on the face, and I write to ask if you have a special treatment for it, and to beg your advice in the matter. The eruption began nearly seven years ago, and tho' I have tried several physicians and various remedies, it has steadily grown worse, til now I am quite disfigured; and annoyed by curious people's questions. The "M.D's." tell me it is caused by uric acid poison, and must be reached thro' the blood, which I have vainly tried to do. Your remedies are sold in our town, but I thought perhaps you had a specific for this peculiar form of Eczema, and if so, I shall be pleased to try it. Enclosed please find a stamp for reply at your earliest convenience, and oblige.
Yours very respectfully,
Mrs. M. Sue John[69]

The remaining letter is from a worried husband who has just read about Alice's remedy in the newspaper and wants to know if it will be effective in removing a lump from his wife's breast:

Dear Madam:
Enclosed you will find a clipping of your remedy from the *News & Observer*. My wife has a hard lump under her right breast something like a tumor. Hers pains her at times, especially when she exerts her-

self much. If you feel your remedy can remove her lump please let me hear from you and your terms. I have been thinking of sending her to Richmond, but much prefer it being carried away without the use of the knife. Please let me hear from you and kindly oblige.
Very respectfully,
Jno S. Powell[70]

Alice peppered her pages of testimonials with inventive scenarios, several of which appear in the 1884 booklet. The first of these is titled "An Interesting Comedy in Five Chapters." Alice probably considered this to be a comedy because it is the story of a physician — like those that earlier pushed the remedy aside — who moves from cautiously trialing it to wholeheartedly recommending it to others. The first three chapters feature communications between Alice and Marion, North Carolina, doctor J.H. Gilkey, who reports success and orders more of both the bitters and the wash as the chapters progress. The fourth chapter is a letter from a man to whom Dr. Gilkey recommended the remedy:

> Madam:
> Dr. Gilkey, of this place told me you were here sometime ago and — **told him you could cure Scrofula** — and he advised me to write to you for some of your circulars. I have a sore on my leg and hip. It will cure up and break out just below where it cures up. I have been treated by several physicians. Some say it is Scrofula, others say it is Lupus and Salt Rheum. It is just skin deep; it never gets deep; is very painful; don't rest at night. I want you to send me your circular and prices of your medicine, and if I think, after reading them, that it will do me any good, I will order some of the medicine at once. I have had the sores for 18 months, and have paid out a great deal of money to parties that have done me no good. Hoping to hear from you soon, I remain,
> Respectfully,
> S.C. Dale.[71]

The fifth chapter is simply a clever opening remark followed by a quote from the local newspaper announcement of Dale's miraculous recovery:

> The following, cut from the *Marion Lamp Post*, makes a fit ending of the comedy, and speaks for itself:
> Mr. S.C. Dale, of this place, who for years, had been suffering from aggravated Scrofula, has in three months use of this medicine entirely recovered. His case was almost hopeless, being scarcely able to get about on crutches. He is now in active business. Six bottles effected a cure.[72]

A serendipitous public tout such as this was the best kind of advertisement, and Alice was sure to include it in her formal solicitations.

Alice delighted in the irony of physicians prescribing her remedy, and she used the theme in another scenario in the 1884 publication. In this three chapter scenario, the first chapter is a letter from Triangle, North Carolina, druggists Kincaid & Linebarger:

> Madam:
> A circular advertising your Remedy for Scrofula was handed us by a highly respectable physician a few days ago, who said it had been recommended to him by such medical authority that he desired to give it a trial in his practicie, and desired us to keep it in stock. Please give us terms.
> Yours,
> Kincaid & Linebarger.[73]

The second chapter, titled "Significant Testimony," is a follow-up letter from Kincaid & Linebarger:

> Dear Madam:
> Please send three dozen more of your valuable Remedy, as the lot you shipped us last is all sold except one bottle. We have sold four and a half dozen of your Remedy since April, and all save one bottle *have been on physician's prescriptions*. With best wishes for your success, we are,
> Yours truly,
> Kincaid & Linebarger[74]

Alice introduces an additional comedic element to the third chapter — one which, in addition to being amusing, is undeniable testimony to the effectiveness of the remedy:

> A month or so later Messrs. Kincaid & Linebarger ordered six dozen more, and on the 21st of June, 1883, wrote the following significant letter:
> Your card of the 18th inst. Received to-day. Our "silence" means that we still have "Remedy" in stock. Don't grow impatient; remember what a quantity we bought at the last "haul." There is one unfortunate circumstance connected with the sale of your "Remedy" which we cannot obviate: *When a patient has taken it till he is cured he immediately stops buying it!* Then as sales have to await the development of new cases, we are "silent," and you seem to be puzzled over that "silence." Is not silence a virtue when we have nothing to say? You'll hear from us when our stock, like the "judiciary" of North Carolina on one occasion, is "*exhausted*."
> Yours truly,
> T.J. Linebarger.[75]

Alice's ability with strategically placed, themed publicity is evident in any number of Person Remedy newspaper ads, but two show it to best advantage. The first appeared in the government pages and carried the clever title "Democratic Rule for Good Government and Mrs. Joe Person's Remedy for the Blood."[76] The second features two heart-shaped figures, one above the other. The upper one is upside down — a mirror image of the lower. The upper heart contains the phrase "IT TAKES PURE BLOOD FOR GOOD HEALTH," and the lower one the phrase "FOR PURE BLOOD IT TAKES MRS. JOE PERSON'S REMEDY." The heart images dovetail perfectly with the witty phrases about pure blood. Alice must have been proud of this creation because she clipped and pressed it between the pages of one of her journals. In so doing, she separated the ad from its publication information, but surely it appeared on or near Valentine's Day.[77] In addition to ads like this, the company would occasionally sponsor contests in search of the best advertisement for the remedy. With these contests, Alice and Rufus not only acquired new advertisements, they introduced the remedy to potential customers by offering product information to contestants unfamiliar with it. The *Raleigh News and Observer* reported on the outcome of one of these contests:

> On the 14th day of October the following advertisement appeared in the *News and Observer*:
>
> $10 GIVE AWAY!
>
> I will give Ten Dollars to the person sending me by November 15th, 1899, the best written 5-inch advertisement of Mrs. Joe Person's Remedy. Those who do not know about the Remedy can get reading matter by applying for the same.
>
> Hon. John Nichols and Mr. E.M. Uzzell, of Raleigh, acting with Mr. T.R. Manning, of Henderson, will be the committee to decide who sends the best written 5-inch advertisement of the Remedy.
>
> MRS. JOE PERSON
> Kittrell, N.C.
> October 15, 1899
>
> In response to it scores of answers competing for the prize were received, one from Boston and others out of the State as well as a large number from points in North Carolina.
>
> Yesterday Mr. R.M. Person came to Raleigh and brought with him all the advertisements of all the competitors. The committee, composed of Messrs. Thad R. Manning, John Nichols and E.M. Uzzell, met yesterday afternoon and gave a careful examination to all the advertisements written by the competitors and awarded the prize to Miss Ruth McCraw, of Littleton, N.C. She is a daughter of Mr. J.C. McCraw, of that place. Mrs. Person will send Miss McCraw the $10 today, and will have her prize advertisement electrotyped. It will appear shortly in the *News and Observer*.[78]

The second prong of the company's marketing plan was the most time-consuming, and resulted in Alice taking to the road for weeks at a time to spread the good news of the remedy to druggists and individuals alike. Alice made the majority of her marketing trips to cities and towns in the central North Carolina area between Charlotte and Raleigh, with less frequent trips extending to Lenoir in the west and Greenville in the east, and only occasional ones to extreme western and eastern parts of the state such as Madison and Dare counties, respectively. The northern and southern boundaries of Alice's marketing territory spilled over into Virginia and South Carolina. It was not unusual for Alice to peddle her wares in the south-central Virginia towns of South Boston and Christie, and she even made the occasional journey as far east as Portsmouth. Alice's selling trips to South Carolina were confined to the north-central part of the state between Spartanburg in the west and Mullins in the east. Though Alice did not shun larger cities, she tended to concentrate her efforts on the hamlet-studded North Carolina countryside, no doubt to fill the advertising gap where there were no newspapers, and where a good portion of the population could not read a newspaper even if there was one. Small North Carolina villages such as Marshall, Morven, and Elrod comprised a large portion of Alice's direct marketing demographic.[79]

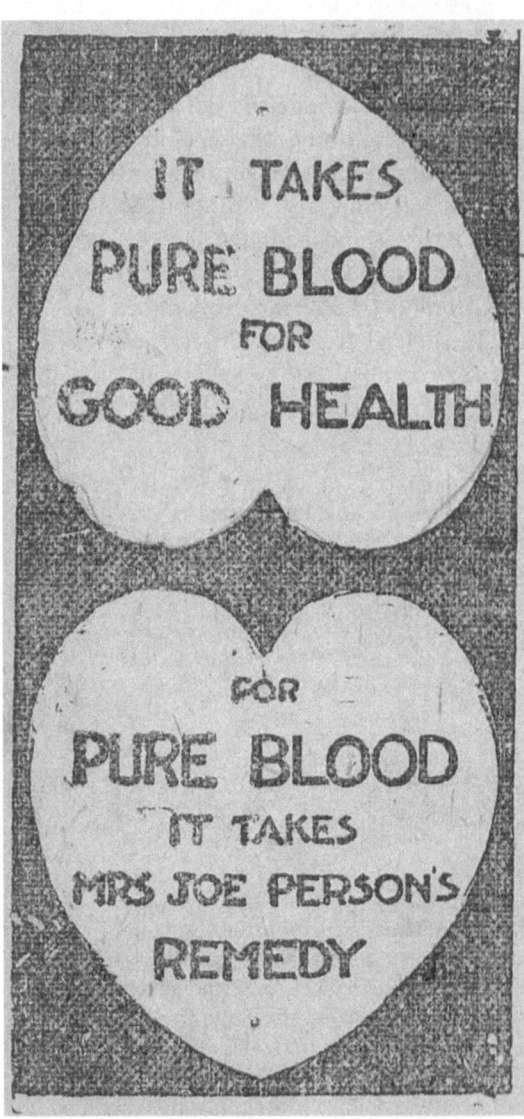

One of Alice's clever newspaper advertisements for the remedy (Alice Morgan Person Collection, East Carolina University).

Extended trips such as this resulted in Alice spending the better portion of her nights in a wide-ranging assortment of accommodations, from hotels to boardinghouses to private residences. As a memory aid, Alice ranked her accommodations in her journals. These ratings range from a low of "never again" to a high of "none better," with an array of graduated ratings between. Alice used "terrible" or "horrible" most frequently to indicate an unacceptable place for a return visit. Perhaps only slightly better were those marked "bad" and "fair." Alice decided to give one of those she rated "fair" another try, but the second visit resulted in a rating of "never again." Acceptable lodgings were those receiving at least a "good," and "No. 1" indicated a certain return visit the next time Alice was in the area. In addition, Alice would append qualifiers such as "tip top" and "the very best" to exceptional "No.1" accommodations.

Time to Say Good-bye

For six years Rufus and Alice operated a successful business from their Church Street headquarters, during which time Alice owned the company's formula and trademark. However, as she approached her seventieth birthday, Alice decided it was time to reverse that arrangement. On March 25, 1910, she sold Rufus "all right, title, interest and estate in and to the formula and trademark known as Mrs. Joe Person's Remedy and Mrs. Joe Person's Wash" for a one-time cash payment of five thousand dollars and a $125 monthly payment for the remainder of her life.[80] Just five days later, Guy V. Barnes of Kittrell and Dr. Thomas M. Jordan and F.P. Ward of Raleigh purchased stock in the company, incorporated it under the name Mrs. Joe Person's Remedy Company, and returned its headquarters to Kittrell.[81] The first-named stock holder, Guy Barnes, was a close family friend of the Persons from their Kittrell days who visited frequently after they moved to Charlotte.[82] Exactly two months after buying the formula and trademark, Rufus subleased them to Barnes for a period of ten years subject to the terms and conditions set forth in the original agreement with Alice.[83] Though Alice worked as a traveling saleswoman for the fledgling corporation when they needed her and her schedule of retirement travel allowed,[84] circulation of the remedy expanded beyond her established territory to states as far away as Texas, Florida, and Connecticut.[85] Rufus' sublease served to sever his ties with the company he had spent the last quarter of a century building. A year later, he sold his home and its obsolete laboratory and relocated his family to the country outside Charlotte.[86] Alice, perhaps wishing to spend her free time with her downtown Charlotte friends, boarded with one of her neighbors at 802 North Church Street until her fateful trip to the West in 1913.[87]

Alice sang the swan song of her musical career in the autumn of 1912. Hers was a two-verse song, with the first being a performance at a fiddler's convention where "the audience went wild with appreciation."[88] The second verse was her recording session with the Victor Talking Machine Company at its Camden, New Jersey, factory on October 4, 1912. She recorded ten pieces in all, seven of which were from *Popular Airs*: "Dixie," "Year of the Jubilee," "Italian Waltz," "I'll Bet My Money on the Bob-Tail Nag," "I'se Gwuine Down-Town," "Liza Jane," and "Walk-Around." From *Blue Alsatian Mountains* she recorded "Boatman Dance" and "Down-Town Girls." The tenth piece was one Alice did not include in her published repertoire—"Yankee Doodle." All required two takes with the exception of the *Blue Alsatian Mountains* duo, which required only one.[89] Reportedly, Alice was paid five dollars for each minute of playing time, and the results were exceptionally clear.[90] However, Victor Talking Machine Company files indicate the recordings were "personal," and, therefore, never pressed and marketed. Unfortunately, the master recordings almost certainly no longer exist.[91]

Unlike her musical legacy, Alice's medicinal legacy continued to be commercially viable for decades after her death. When Guy Barnes died in February of 1916, Rufus dutifully took the wheel and steered the company on in honor of his mother. This new direction initially involved reincorporating the company under the abbreviated name Person Remedy Company, enlisting the financial support of three new stockholders, and returning the company's headquarters to Charlotte in April of 1916.[92] A year later, however, Rufus proudly announced the remedy had "come back home:"

> I am now sole owner and proprietor of Mrs. Joe Person's Remedy and the Person Remedy Company. I am going to live up to the principles and policies of my mother, the late Mrs. Joe Person, and give everybody a square deal, as my mother and I did when we worked together for twenty-five years. I feel that our old and new friends alike will be glad to learn that Mrs. Joe Person's Remedy has "COME BACK HOME" and will be handled in the old-time way which proved so satisfactory and made so many friends from 1878 to 1910.[93]

Such an announcement implies there were disagreements between Rufus and his stockholders with regard to how business should be conducted, and also that these disagreements had a negative effect on the public's perception of the company, no doubt resulting in disgruntled customers and reduced sales. Once again, Alice's business weathered the woes that attend ill-fated partnerships and returned to the safe harbor of family ownership. Rufus' wife, Jessie, and his daughter, Alice, served as the company's president and vice president, respectively, and Rufus served as secretary and treasurer.[94]

Rufus carried his mother's gauntlet for an impressive thirty-year run, renewing the remedy's trademark in 1929,[95] while simultaneously ceasing to actively market it.[96] This was probably due to the fact Jessie died in 1926, leaving the fifty-eight-year-old Rufus to juggle the majority of the business's activities on his own. Even without promotion, demand for the remedy continued (though on a reduced basis) via word-of-mouth recommendations from satisfied customers.[97] In 1939, weary of carrying on by himself, Rufus began seeking buyers for the dying business in the hope they might breathe new life into it. Interested parties ranged from individuals in and around Charlotte to corporate entities including Bissette Laboratories in Wilson, North Carolina, and W.H. King Drug Company in Raleigh.[98] Rufus went as far as drawing up the following contract with one potential buyer in November of 1940, but the deal was never finalized:

> I do agree to sell to Paul Chatham the business known as Person Remedy Co. and Trade Mark formula known as Mrs. Joe Person's Remedy free of debt for the sum of five thousand ($5000.00) dollars. This agreement is good for six months from Nov. 1, 1940. I reserve the right if I have the opportunity to sell to some other party I can do so, but will take the matter up with Mr. Chatham. If Mr. Chatham closes the deal I am to pay him five hundred ($500.00) dollars.
>
> R.M. Person[99]

Of the corporate entities that showed interest, the W.H. King Drug Company held the greatest promise for a successful sale. Rufus sent the following letter in response to their request for more information on the remedy company's assets and volume of trade:

> Att. Mr. Starling
> Dear Sir,
> In reply to your letter of the 28th. The Trade Mark and Formula is the principal thing we have to sell. I am enclosing the Trade Mark so you can [see?] for yourself. I have not done any advertising in 10 or 12 years have not called on any of the trade or asked anyone to buy a bottle. I fill what orders come in by mail, if they don't come I don't get them. My inventory is about 4 or 5 hundred dollars in stock fixtures and [illegible]. All my fixtures are old and out of date. The possibility for this business under proper management is great. It is a money maker. It has a good record. No dissatisfied customers. Wonderful care has been made by this medicine. 65 years is a long time for a business like this. I am selling between 5 and 6 hundred dollars each year. I am 71 years old, have to quit. If you have a proposition, make it to me and I will consider it. Hoping to hear from you soon.
>
> Yours truly,
> R.M. Person[100]

Unfortunately, the product's shrinking customer base proved to be a major deal breaker, and Rufus was left in December of 1941 without a buyer:

Dear Mr. Person:

We wish to thank you for your letter of December 3 and the information given us concerning Mrs. Joe Person's Remedy.

We realize you have a good product, but in view of the small amount [of?] business you are doing, we do not think we would be interested in buying you out.

We are returning herewith the papers which you sent us and if we become interested later, we shall be glad to let you hear from us.

Yours very truly,
W.H. King Drug Co.
By H.C. Starling[101]

By 1943 the corporation had begun to unravel and the end was imminent. The company's officers were now located in three different states: president and treasurer, Rufus, in Florida; his son and vice president, Allen, in Kentucky; and his daughter and secretary, Alice Person Sparrow, in North Carolina. In addition, World War II was raging and the country's tightened purse strings prompted the trio to temporarily cease operations.[102] When the war ended in 1945, the task of reconnecting with customers was no doubt beyond the capabilities of the aging president and his scattered assistants. There being no business to speak of, they probably saw no need to pay their annual franchise taxes— an infraction that resulted in the suspension of the company's certificate of incorporation in January of 1947.[103] With this suspension, Alice's precious cure returned to its seventy-year-old roots, relegated for a time to home production and distribution among friends and family before dying altogether along with Rufus and his children.[104]

Chapter 4
Public and Private

Alice artfully parceled and blended feminine sensitivity and what were then considered masculine traits (i.e., shrewdness and assertiveness) as situations dictated. Not only did this mixture of characteristics make her a curiosity in the public arena, it also prompted one of the many newspaper reporters who interviewed her to state she was "more than two parts man":

> There is a strange feeling when talking to Mrs. Person that she is more than two parts man. And this impression comes queerly enough at the same moment that you are thinking what a motherly woman she looks. It is clear that in a business transaction with Mrs. Person, it would be "man to man" with the odds in favor of the woman. It is equally patent that in a moment of distress or at a call for pity, the Mrs. Joe Person of "Remedy" fame and drumming success would vanish instantly into the character of a very round, ordinary and wholly sympathetic old lady, with the foolishness of mother-love and tenderness her characteristic trait. After all, it was this very mixture of the love of an everyday mother and the prowess and determination of a hustling young man which worked together for the establishment of a unique business, and made something more than a man out of Mrs. Joe Person.[1]

The same reporter provides a description of Alice's physical appearance and mannerisms—a description that perfectly complements his estimation of her personality:

> There was no missing Mrs. Person. I walked up to her without hesitation as an old friend. As she sat straight on the seat in the station, herself and her packages overflowing from the confining arms of the bench, she was a figure that would have instantly attracted attention anywhere. Under a self-assertive bonnet her grey hair protruded in willful wisps while her head held itself erect upon her shoulders, and her keen, twinkling eyes roamed the station with the unconcern of a constant traveler and the sympathy of a kind hearted woman....

> Mrs. Person extended a fat hand, chubby and a little red and a little bit work-marked. She laughed with a gurgle that came as she talked, quickly, emphatically, a little under her breath as though that were a commodity that was to be preserved. One feels that Mrs. Person will spend herself in effort, will talk as much as she pleases—and that is a good deal—but that she will do it on a modicum of breath.[2]

With time, the press's interest in Alice moved beyond curiosity to infatuation, resulting in a constant flow of adulation. Here the *Raleigh News and Observer* echoes the *Roxboro Courier*'s declared affection for Alice:

> We were glad to have a call from Mrs. Joe Person yesterday evening. Though the weather was dark and stormy she came in like a ray of sunlight. Happy indeed is the person who possesses her disposition. -*Roxboro Courier.*
>
> Yes, indeed! Not long ago she came into the business office of *The Observer*, bringing the sunlight of her life with her. The writer arose from the desk and went to the counter to greet her. "How are you, Mrs. Person?" "I am just as well, sir, and as happy as I can be. I haven't an ache nor a pain and not a trouble. I haven't much money but enough to pay my debts, so why shouldn't I be happy?" Bless her soul! May she never be less well nor less happy! But think of it! As well and happy as could be, not an ache nor a pain nor a trouble and enough money to meet the demands of the collector. Not many people can say it [at?] all: few deserve as much as she does to be able to say it.[3]

At times, this adulation resulted in inadvertent free advertising for the remedy: "Mrs. Joe Person of Charlotte, than whom a nobler woman ever lived, has been on a visit to her daughter, Mrs. Billie Harris. Mrs. Person is more widely known and has more friends to shake her hand than any woman in any State. She is as lively as when we first knew her some forty years ago and says that no one need complain or get sick that takes her remedy."[4]

Alice's achievements were held in such high regard that the press considered her to be an "industrial force in the State."[5] Her activities, from the minor to the monumental, were reported in the newspapers of the day; her confinement to a hotel with a "deep cold"[6] was as newsworthy as her 1908 trip to the West in search of her brother's grave.[7] Alice's performances at piano vendors' exhibits at the various southern expositions were of particular interest to reporters. When she demonstrated pianos for Dallas, Texas, piano dealer C.H. Edwards, the press reported that the popularity of Edwards' exhibit was due in large part to Alice: "As an evidence of his enterprise he has secured the services of Mrs. Joe Person of Charlotte, N.C., a lady who has quite a reputation as a performer on the piano, who will daily delight visitors by the artistic manner in which she manipulates the keys of the best instruments on the market. Mrs. Person held audiences spellbound yesterday and as long as she remained at the piano thousands congregated to hear her play."[8]

Another report of Alice's Dallas visit declared her "queen of the Wheelock," and indicated her reputation as a performer preceded her:

> The readers of THE NEWS are familiar with the biblical story of the visit of the queen of Sheba to Solomon in his temple, being influenced by stories of his greatness that had reached her ears. While it is not the intention of THE NEWS man to liken Mrs. Joe Person with the queen of Sheba in all respects, it is a fact that hearing of the greatness of the Wheelock piano, she left "old North Caliny" and traveled into the empire of Texas to see and hear for herself. But like the Wheelock, her reputation had gone beyond the borders and when she reached Texas, lo! there was a reception awaiting her. Mr. C.H. Edwards, the piano dealer of Dallas, he who was awarded the first premium for the best display of pianos, immediately sought her and before she had yet rested from the fatigue of the trip, the populace had proclaimed her the "queen" of the Wheelock. Thus the readers of THE NEWS have a story of two queens. Mrs. Person was especially good in her manipulation of the keys yesterday, and the Edwards space, as usual, was the center of attraction all day. She beats the life out of "Old Bob Ridley" and sails down the "Sewanee [sic] River" at the same time, not forgetting the ever popular "Orleans Town" as an encore. Mrs. Person's rendition of old southern melodies just beats the world. The justly celebrated Wheelock pianos upon which she performs are still going as fast as sandwiches at a free lunch, and last night recorded several new placards placed on sold instruments.[9]

The *Knoxville Sentinel* dubbed Alice "a unique musical genius," and provided the following description of her playing and the personality that added to its appeal:

> Her style of performance is extremely novel, her touch being remarkably vigorous and exact, heavy yet sympathetic: her repertoire is composed almost exclusively of old ante-wartime melodies and songs. A *Sentinel* reporter listened with delight to several irresistibly captivating airs which she kindly gave for his benefit on a sweet-toned Kurtzman in McArthur's music store yesterday afternoon. The numbers were executed with an earnestness of expression which rendered them all the more fascinating. Mrs. Person, whose manner is charmingly unaffected and cordial, made quite a number of friends during her brief visit to this city.[10]

Private Places

Of course, even celebrities have private sides, and jottings in Alice's journals dating from 1901 to 1913 provide a glimpse into that side of the great lady. This is a view she thought no one else would ever have; she provides no explanation of her words, leaving prying eyes with little understanding of the meaning behind them. Offenders may, however, draw two conclusions from Alice's journal scribblings: (1) she had an almost child-like fascination with Christmas; (2) she harbored a degree of bitterness toward the opposite sex.

Alice's fascination with Christmas is evident in the fact she labeled every December 25 from 1901 to 1912 "Christmas," while rarely labeling other holidays. Her yuletide enthusiasm is further evident in the addition of exclamation points after most of these labels, as well as words or sentences after nine of them:

> 1901—Christmas!
> 1902—Christmas again!
> 1903—Christmas! I wonder—Oh my, yes, you'll be here. Turn over, and see.
> 1904—Christmas! And Echo answers where? And What? And When?
> 1905—Christmas! "Men may come and men may go but I go on forever."
> 1906—Christmas.
> 1907—Christmas—and still its so.
> 1908—Christmas! And don't you forget it.
> 1909—Christmas! And I am still I!
> 1910—Christmas!
> 1911—Christmas—Alice, where art thou?
> 1912—Christmas! Rocky Mt. Mar. 6, 1911.[11]

The addition of the word "again" to the 1902 label communicates Alice's gleeful attitude toward this holiday, but the other additions hint at a vulnerable side she did not reveal to others. Though the exact meaning and correlation of these holiday messages are virtually indiscernible, all but two (1905 and 1912) connote doubt and disbelief.

The 1912 message "Rocky Mt. Mar. 6, 1911" is a curious one. The entry for this date in Alice's journal indicates nothing beyond the fact she was indeed in Rocky Mount, and that she paid one dollar for room and board to Mrs. Lillie Powell. Alice did, however, write a letter to Rufus on March 8 while still in Rocky Mount. This is the letter in which Alice told Rufus to rent her a room with a Church Street neighbor if his Charlotte home sold while she was gone. In this letter Alice also shares with Rufus the realization that he was "right about no one aught to give away their possessions in their life time." She continues: "I can see it now as plain as you have always seen, but the thought I have ever had has been to help my children along."[12] Perhaps this epiphany occurred two days earlier on March 6, and Alice viewed it as a major point of arrival in her personal life—one so important she needed to revisit it on Christmas day nearly two years later in an attempt to bolster her sagging resolve. Alice's mention of her possessions and children in her letter to Rufus certainly resonates in her strong November 7, 1912, letter to Gibson in which she refused to continue showering her grandchildren with gifts in order to ensure herself a comfortable retirement. The tie to the 1912 Christmas holiday is certain when Alice closes her letter to Gibson with: "No, you will not need me Christmas. You will have a house chock full and running over, Lou and Josie will have only me."[13] Though Alice's journals do indeed indicate she spent the Christmas of 1912 in Hickory, North Carolina (the home of both her sister and her youngest daughter), she was no doubt plagued by motherly guilt — guilt that prompted her to make a reminder of her March 6, 1911, resolution part of her Christmas day journal entry ritual.

Alice's 1905 Christmas day message joins another journal message in echoing the theme of bitterness toward the opposite sex that sounds forth elsewhere in her written record. The other message appears between December of 1901 and January of 1902 — as though a New Year's Day resolution — and reads as follows: "Woman can mark it down, but they may be crossed out or left blank. Well, we will wait and see."[14] The 1905 message reads as follows: "Men may come and men may go but I go on forever." The difference in tone between these two messages in combination with their chronological placement suggests a strengthening of resolve much like that of the Rocky Mount message. The first message both laments and challenges the marginalization of women; the second trumpets the victory of women — or at least one woman.

By 1905, Alice had been in the remedy business for twenty-seven years and sales were at an all-time high. Such an accomplishment laughed in the face of at least four men in her life: (1) her husband, who discouraged her from even setting out on her mission; (2) George Davidson, who defaulted on their contract after deciding her product was not worth funding; (3) Charles Jones, who so underestimated Alice's business skills he thought he could successfully embezzle from her; and (4) E.B. Hodges, who only lasted for a year in the remedy business after ignoring Alice's advice regarding the proper way to establish such an enterprise. Her way — a woman's way — had stood the test of time and surpassed those of a number of men in the process. Any doubts Alice had in January of 1902 were gone — she would never again "be crossed out or left blank."

Alice could not, however, have been more consequential in the eyes of her family. Her journals contain a poignant reminder of this fact in the form of a homemade bookmark. This faded purple ribbon with frayed ends was in all likelihood a Christmas gift from one of Alice's grandchildren. In the center of the ribbon, the creator used gold paint to write the word "Banny," a family name for Alice suggesting a young child's corruption of the word "granny."[15] On either side of this moniker the young artist painted holly branches, each adorned with two dark green leaves and two bunches of bright red berries. A gift such as this on Alice's favorite holiday certainly meant much to a grandmother who was "keenly alive to every impression" from those she loved.[16]

Alice's family was foremost in her mind when, in March of 1913, she began making journal entries that foreshadowed the fateful events of the following June. Health problems dominated the month's entries. Alice was "under the weather" and "knocked off from work" for most of the first week of the month, was "low, sick" on the twenty-second, was again "under the weather" on the twenty-ninth, and on the last day of the month she suffered an "aberration of memory."[17] While Alice mentioned no additional health problems in the remaining two months of her journal, she did indicate on April 16 that she visited a doctor who put her on a special diet for six months.[18] Perhaps Alice saw no need to continue writing about her bad days because they occurred more frequently than not. Perhaps, too, she sensed her time on earth was coming to an end. Rather than waste the time she had left reporting on her health, Alice visited her beloved children and grandchildren. Her four oldest surviving children all lived in North Carolina — Gibson in Wake Forest, Wiley in Louisburg, Josephine in Hickory, and Rufus in Charlotte. Her youngest child, William, lived in Corey, Alabama, a suburb of Birmingham.[19] With the exception of Louisburg, Alice visited each of these towns at least once in April and May of 1913. Louisburg is, however, in close proximity to Wake Forest, leaving open the strong possibility she also visited Wiley. Sadly, Alice made her last journal entry on May 31 despite the fact she was planning to begin her third trip to the West in just ten days.[20]

A Woman of Peculiar Force

Of the numerous obituaries that dotted North Carolina newspapers during the days that followed Alice's death on June 12, 1913, one perfectly captured her essence: she was "a woman of peculiar force."[21] Others referred to her as a "heroic, noble, brilliant woman,"[22] "one of the most remarkable women the state has ever known,"[23] and the possessor of "a rare character and dominant traits."[24] These descriptions are all apt, but the first perfectly synthesizes the others. Multiple adjectives such as "brilliant," "remarkable" and "rare" find appropriate representation in the more colorful word "peculiar." Likewise, descriptors such as "heroic," "dominant," and "noble" are combined effectively in the word "force."

Alice's peculiar force was evident in every aspect of her life. From the physical to the emotional to the social, she projected a larger-than-life personality. Her physical vigor manifested itself in the exceptional health she enjoyed until the end of her life despite having endured a great deal of stress. Early twentieth-century modes of travel were not what they are today, yet Alice had the energy at the age of seventy-three to begin an extended trip to the western United States, Canada and Alaska.

Alice's unusual emotional fortitude served her well when confronting the disappointments that began to present themselves when she was just twenty-three years of age. Few nineteenth-century women possessed the self-assurance to become the breadwinner for their families. Fewer still possessed the backbone to stand up to unscrupulous male business partners and begin anew after dissolving ill-fated partnerships. Alice did both, and did so without becoming cynical. Instead, she retained a fresh, positive attitude toward men and women from all walks of life — an attitude that made her a social magnet.

Alice's warm personality quickly endeared her to those with whom she came in contact — from the citizenry of an entire city such as Charlotte to casual acquaintances such as Captain Claud Morrison, conductor of the train on which she began her final trip to the West. Morrison's account of his exchange with Alice days before her death is an example of her genuinely inclusive nature: "When she changed cars at Statesville she ran to Capt. Morrison saying in her quick, business-like way: 'Give me your street number — want to send you some cards from the West.' Capt. Morrison in speaking of her last night said: 'She was the most remarkable woman I have ever known.'"[25] Morrison was not the only person moved by the peculiar force of Alice's social charisma. A group of Santa Fe Masons were affected in much the same way. As soon as word of her death reached Charlotte, Masons in that city contacted their fellow Masons in Santa Fe. These men were so moved by Alice's story, they came to the aid of her sister Lucy by making arrangements for the return of Alice's body to North Carolina. One of the Santa

A portrait of elderly Alice probably taken within a few years of her death in 1913 (Alice Morgan Person Collection, East Carolina University).

Fe Masons even accompanied Lucy to Memphis to assist with a change of car.²⁶

The large number of people who attended Alice's Charlotte funeral — and those who were among them — gave testament to the popularity she enjoyed in her home state. Her surviving siblings and children were present, as was her business associate, Guy Barnes. Six Charlotte druggists served as pallbearers. These men were introduced to Alice by way of the remedy, but they later developed personal friendships with her as evidenced by their willingness to serve in this capacity even though she had been out of the remedy business for three years. The service took place at the home of Alice's Church Street neighbors, the Constables, whose "house and yard were filled with people" who later formed "a long line of carriages" en route to Charlotte's Elmwood Cemetery, Alice's final resting place.²⁷

Epilogue

Alice Morgan Person considered herself a "toiler" who made "sledgehammer blows day after day, week after week, month after month, year after year" to "win the fight."²⁸ Alice's sledgehammer, however, contained extra measures of strength, ingenuity, and spirituality that caused her to rise above other toilers. Her extra measure of strength bolstered her faith in the medicine's potential despite the fact her husband discouraged her from even attempting to market it. With well-placed blows, she successfully distributed it far and wide and used the proceeds to feed, clothe, and educate her family. As though that was not enough, she ingeniously combined this activity with a seemingly disparate one (i.e., music) to form a unique synthesis. While this combination separated Alice from the crowd, her spirituality lifted her above it. She considered her life's work to be a calling not of her choosing — talents thrust on her by a higher power which also made them a mission by leaving her with no other way to support the family she dearly loved. This purposeful resignation is the peculiar force for which Alice has been, and will continue to be, remembered.

Part II — Reflections on the Medicine and the Music

Chapter 5

Snake Oil or Native American Medical Marvel?

Alice Person wrote repeatedly that the formula for her remedy came ultimately from an Indian. How much did she base her own heartfelt belief that her medicine really cured many desperately ill people on its claimed Native American origin? The image of the Indian did connect regularly with the patent medicine world, and did so in two ways. First, European immigrants and their descendants adopted many Indian medicines gradually (that is, they employed native botanical substances, not the spiritual practices that were an indispensable part of Native American healing). Indian botanicals were used regularly over a long period, and, in many cases, over a very broad geographical expanse (that is, wherever the plants that were the sources of the medicines grew). Second, joining with the long-standing use and perceived high value of many Indian medicines was the romanticizing of the image of the Indian late in the nineteenth century, the emergence of the "noble savage" who was believed to possess powerful insights about the natural world in general and herbal remedies in particular. The patent medicine industry exploited this image with skill and vigor. Various companies, the most famous being the Kickapoo Indian Medicine Company, used Indians—or non–Indians dressed as Indians—both in gigantic and well-traveled medicine shows and in public relations. Serious problems tied to this mating of business and popular romantic ideology would eventually surface. However, those problems lay far in the future when Alice commenced selling her medicine. It was certainly a sound business decision at the time for her to let her public know that her remedy had a Native American origin.

Wyatt and Libby McGhee, who now live in the house just north of Franklinton, North Carolina where Alice resided when she began making the remedy, own a bottle of it the label of which, in conformity with the Food and Drug Act of 1906, specifies ingredients. Michael Boyce, one of Alice's great-

great-grandsons, speculates that the list might be incomplete, leaving enough of the total formula secret so that competitors could not counterfeit the remedy. But quite a few ingredients are named, in fact about as many as such medicines contained on the average; perhaps any secrets had to do with proportions and processes rather than ingredients. This description is certainly well worth studying. It prompts the series of questions this chapter is designed to answer. Were these in fact plant materials that Indians in the Person family's part of the United States employed for medical use? And if so, did these Native Americans believe that these specific botanicals cured the same ills that Alice and her customers did? This presents quite a jigsaw puzzle, but a fascinating and worthwhile one.

What Alice Claimed and What Her Customers Believed

The title pages of the booklets with which Alice advertised her remedy most thoroughly during the heyday of patent medicines made a detailed claim for what the remedy could accomplish. The words and how they were typeset combined to show what she felt was most important about her medicine. Near the top of one such booklet in a large font are the words "All Blood Diseases," then "Tonic." Here potential customers are being informed that this is a general remedy that does a broad spectrum of good things, that makes you feel better in a comprehensive way. Then the prose gets down to business, listing specific problems for which the remedy is said to be good. The eye is drawn immediately to the boldest print remaining, words using up plenty of ink: "Infallible for Scrofula" and "It Relieves Catarrh." Last, there is a list of other ailments in smaller print: "Rheumatism, Cancer in its Early Stages, Heart Disease, Erysipelas, Indigestion, Chronic Bilious Colic, Eruptions, and Skin Diseases."[1]

Some of the problems and solutions Alice specified in her booklets are called by the same names today, others are not. In fact, some of these terms are quite mysterious to modern readers! However, the exact words that she employed matter during the first step in this exploration: reading the testimonials that make up the bulk of the brochure in order to learn which ailments her customers believed that the remedy cured. After all, Alice and her public used the same vocabulary, whether or not modern readers are familiar with all of their terms and usages. A tally of how many times and how emphatically certain expressions appear results in some interesting findings. For the most part, the results match the graphics on the title page: the largest words refer to the problems that got the most attention in the testimonials. One set of terms was mentioned between five and ten times each in those letters: "tonic," "alterative," and "purifier of the blood." Again, this constituted general praise: this stuff was good for what ailed you, and was refreshing. Surprisingly, the word "catarrh," also printed in large letters on the title page, didn't come up at all in the testimonials. While catarrh might indicate something as serious as a sinus infection, it would more likely be simply a stuffy nose, an annoying problem you would certainly be eager to fix but not something so grave that curing it would inspire writing a passionate letter. The word mentioned the most was "scrofula," a word we seldom encounter today. It appeared nearly forty times; the writers of these testimonials were amazed and delighted that the remedy had helped them with what apparently was a common and very serious malady back then.

What was scrofula? During that era, the causes of many diseases weren't understood (a fact still true today, but even more prevalent then), and illnesses were often identified solely by the symptoms they produced rather than infective agents or other causes. Scrofula referred to swellings and horrific outbreaks on the skin of the neck and the underside of the chin. Most of these, medical researchers now say, were the result of tuberculosis. It is true that tuberculosis most frequently attacks the lungs— Alice and her contemporaries called this more common form of the disease consumption — but the lymph nodes of the neck were another part of the body that tuberculosis bacteria might colonize and destroy. The resultant swelling would eventually be so bad and so aggressive that it would break through to the surface, creating suppurating wounds (classified as scrofuladerma). Was everything called scrofula in the brochures of Alice and her contemporaries actually this kind of tuberculosis? Probably not, though precise percentages can't be pinned down. Most of Alice's testimonials did not specify a location on the body, so we can't tell if the eruptions were most likely the result of tuberculosis or not. A half dozen descriptions in this brochure mention the neck, so these lesions were probably tubercular, while five mention the legs or other places that are less likely targets for the tuberculosis bacterium.

Two other maladies were mentioned as having been cured by Mrs. Joe Person's Remedy in a half-dozen testimonials each. These were "eruptions" and cancer, meaning skin cancer. Indigestion comes up three times, heart disease and rheumatism twice each, and erysipelas once. Chronic bilious colic didn't appear in this batch of testimonials.

After looking carefully at every problem mentioned in this brochure, we are left with two groups of citations. One is the tonic-alterative-blood purifier group, referring to general health. The other group, scrofula-eruptions (plus similarly described skin problems)-cancer, overlapped in symptoms and probably in diagnosis: a given doctor might call a serious skin affliction of the head or neck by any of those names. What all of this leads to is a simple conclusion: the main array of specific problems that Alice and her customers claimed her remedy cured were serious skin conditions of the neck and lower face, conditions that they usually called scrofula. It is hard to overstate how important it is to keep in mind during this evaluation of possible cures of scrofula that some eruptions called scrofula weren't tubercular, or even distantly related to tuberculosis, and were more likely to have been helped by Alice's remedy. Here is another consideration: adult cases of scrofula were more likely tubercular than were children's cases, such as young Josie Person's. Childhood scrofula, like the adult form, was a bacterial infection, but one caused by a relative of the specific agent whose scientific name is Mycobacterium tuberculosis, not that infective agent itself. As a result, it was less virulent and more curable than adult scrofula. Thus, even if Josie Person had scrofula rather than another, lesser skin problem, it was children's scrofula. It is possible that her case was truly cured — though she seems to have been frail later in life — and possible that the remedy had a hand in her recovery.

The Ingredients of Mrs. Joe Person's Remedy

Before we turn to Native American medicine and the list of ingredients of the remedy, let's consider the liquid in which the active ingredients were often suspended. When the remedy was in the form of pre-bottled bitters, this liquid was a mixture of water and alcohol (probably whiskey, which was extremely common in patent medicines). Having alcohol in the remedy would have had at least two valuable effects. First, it was believed (correctly) that alcohol helped elicit many of the active principles from plant tissues — it helped botanicals work.[2] Also, the whiskey in the bitters would often have had a calming effect. Imagine how many nervous teetotalers this impacted. Today, there are relatively harmless nonnarcotic and nonalcoholic solutions to such tension. But totally innocuous sedatives were not available back then, though nervous ailments and routine sources of stress were certainly not in short supply. Of course, during the Prohibition Era (1920–1933), alcohol-laced cough medicine was especially popular!

What are some good sources of information on Indian herbal remedies? Probably the three most thorough books on the history of the subject all resulted from the study of original letters and manuscripts spanning centuries of contact between Native Americans and Euro-Americans. Arriving whites benefited enormously from Indian knowledge of cures for scurvy right away, and for innumerable other problems over time. These three reference books come from different generations. Alma R. Hutchens' *Indian Herbalogy of North America*, although first published in 1973, is a very old-fashioned "how-to" book, one that recommends various native medicinal plants for specific medical needs.³ Although more enthusiastic than scholarly, it contains considerable information not found elsewhere. Virgil J. Vogel's *American Indian Medicine* is a solid dissertation that was first issued in book form in 1970,⁴ and Daniel E. Moermann's *Native American Ethnobotany*, first written as a truly massive dissertation, was first published in 1998.⁵ These three books are neither rare nor common today. They are not likely to be sold in neighborhood bookstores, but all are in print as of this writing and can be bought through the Internet.

The authors of these three very different books each had something to say about nearly all the ingredients of Mrs. Joe Person's Remedy. The list of ingredients taken from the McGhee's 1939 bottle, consists of common names of plants ("common" here meaning simply that these are names that regular people employ, not the scientific names). These names are as follows: helonias, pipsissewa, prickly ash bark, queen's root, Mexican sarsaparilla (also spelled "sarsparilla" and "sasparilla"), star grass, and trillium. The following chart collates information on each ingredient gleaned from the three books. This collation process was required by an unfortunate but unavoidable problem: the larger the reference book, and the longer the index, the more likely hundreds of errors are to creep in! Websites posted by the U.S. Department of Agriculture reveal that absolutely all of these plants were native to the area surrounding Alice's various North Carolina homes. If a common name referred to several species, the range of each species helped narrow down which one Alice must have been calling by that common name. In addition, the Indian population nearest to Alice's North Carolina homes whose herbal medicines have been studied closely, is the Cherokee. Since their uses of botanicals might be especially relevant, these uses are underlined in the chart.

The Ingredients of Mrs. Joe Person's Remedy and How They Were Used in Native America

Name (and Scientific Name)	Other Common Names for the Same Plant	Native American Uses Matching Those of Mrs. Person	Other Native Uses
helonias (Chamaelirium luteum)	blazing star, false unicorn, Barton's plant, devil's bit, fairywand	skin ulcers, tonic, coughs	gynecological, snakebites
pipsissewa (Chimaphila umbellata or maculata)	pursh, striped prince's pine, lion's tongue, ratsy vein	scrofula,* alterative, rheumatism, cancer, ulcers, tetter, blood purifier, heart disease	gynecological, ringworm, urinary problems, pain, colds, emetic, febrifuge

Name (and Scientific Name)	Other Common Names for the Same Plant	Native American Uses Matching Those of Mrs. Person	Other Native Uses
prickly ash bark (Zanthoxylum americanum)	yellow wood, toothache tree, suterberry, prickly ash berries	scrofula, skin ulcers, alterative, to purify blood, indigestion, rheumatism	toothache, sweat, tuberculosis (of lungs), STDs,
queen's root (Stillingia sylvatica)	yaw root, queen's delight, silver leaf	scrofula, alterative, indigestion (esp. diarrhea), tetter	syphilis, jaundice, gynecological
Mexican sarsaparilla (Aralia nudicalis) or	spikenard, spignet, quay, quill	scrofula, rheumatism, dermatological/sores, blood purifier, tonic, pulmonary, cancer	gynecological consumption
(Smilax herbacea), (if not S.medica!)	smooth carrionflower	rheumatism, skin problems, digestion, ulcers	gynecological, pain, kidney problems
star grass (Aletris farinosa)	ague root, crow corn, true unicorn root, colic root, love plant	scrofula, sores, indigestion, dysentary, coughs	gynecological (to prevent miscarriages), fever
trillium (Trillium erectum)	bath root, beth root, birth root, Indian balm, squaw-flower, wake robin	ulcers (skin), tumors, indigestion, coughs, tonic, alterative	gynecological
alcohol		rare use for infusion; shows white influence	

*A use documented among the North Carolina Cherokee

The row in the chart dealing with Mexican sarsaparilla presents a taxonomic problem that turns out not to be very serious for our purposes. What plant was Mrs. Person indicating? The truly Mexican type of sarsaparilla, having the scientific name Smilax medica (the same species sometimes called Smilax aristolochiaefolia), is the type we would normally assume was meant here. It grows in Mexico and nearby parts of Latin America, not in North Carolina. This is the species of sarsaparilla sent home by the conquistadors and their descendents and that remained the main European and North American type of medical sarsaparilla. However, other species in the genus Smilax, such as Smilax herbacea, are native to North Carolina, were often called sarsaparilla, and were used by the Cherokee for the medical needs listed on the chart. Another plant used medically by these same groups of Indians, one that Euro-Americans called wild sarsaparilla, was the plant with the scientific name Aralia nudicalis. It acquired its common name because it has roots that look like those of the true sarsaparilla species. It grows well near the locations of Alice's various homes, and is the most likely of the various plants called sarsaparilla to have been in her remedy if she was still harvesting all of her herbs locally. In the end, the fact that we cannot be sure which sarsaparilla was in the remedy may not matter much, because Aralia nudicalis was used by Indians for pretty much the same purposes as were the various species of Smilax.

What does the information summarized in this chart teach us? First, absolutely all of the ingredients of Mrs. Joe Person's Remedy (other than alcohol) were indeed venerable Native American botanicals. Second, nearly every ingredient was used by either the Cherokee or other Eastern U.S. Native American populations to cope with major skin problems (often specified as scrofula in the reference books). Third, all of these ingredients were actually multiuse cures among Indians at the turn of the twentieth century, and the uses to which they were put matched up well with the problems cited in Alice's assertions and in the testimonials in her advertising brochures. Further, since these are all plants widespread in North Carolina (assuming her sarsaparilla was Aralia nudicalis), we can take Alice's testimony that she gathered the ingredients locally quite literally. This matches family oral tradition: Michael Boyce remembered that his grandfather and great-aunt — Alice's grandchildren — would spend whole days gathering these raw materials. In sum, her remedy was as on target to support her claims as any patent medicine of her day could have been. She genuinely believed in the efficacy of her remedy, and the historical Native American uses of the individual ingredients strongly support her faith.

Towards the Present: Did Mrs. Joe Person's Remedy Work?

The next few paragraphs in this chapter deal with recent Native American uses of the remedy ingredients. While the three reference works discussed earlier do yield the most complete and reliable information for Native American uses of herbal remedies as employed back when Mrs. Joe Person's Remedy was in production, sources concerning current Native American herbal remedies in North Carolina are also helpful. The two best such books concern botanicals used by the western North Carolina Cherokee and the southeastern North Carolina Lumbee. J.T. Garrett's *The Cherokee Herbal: Native Plant Medicine from the Four Directions* divides Cherokee botanical medicines into four groups based on an insider classification taking into account both practical applications and spiritual meanings.[6] Each of the four groups is also associated with a compass direction. A medicine used for many purposes is associated with more than one direction. Indeed, those Cherokee botanicals matching most of the ingredients of Mrs. Joe Person's Remedy are relatively versatile: star grass, pipsissewa, and prickly ash all figure in three of the four directions. Helonias (Chamaelirium luteum) is also listed in this book on modern Cherokee cures. Helonias appears only in Hutchens among the three broad historical reference works on Indian botanicals. Since Hutchens is the least carefully researched of those three supposedly comprehensive sources, this citing by Garrett is valuable confirmation of helonias' Native American medical use.

The only one of Alice's botanicals that Garrett does not describe as being in use among the Cherokee, queen's root (Stillingia sylvatica), was numbered among the *Herbal Remedies of the Lumbee Indians* by compilers Arvis Locklear Boughman and Loretta O. Oxendine.[7] This unique published Lumbee list of botanicals is relatively short. However, it does include, in addition to queen's root, both star grass and pipsissewa, which were also used extensively by the Cherokee. In summary, not only was every one of Mrs. Person's botanical ingredients both available for harvest in North Carolina during her lifetime and employed historically for the same uses she and her customers cited, each ingredient also remains in active use among one or both of the largest Native American populations in the state.

How have these botanicals been used in modern times by Indian tribes located nearer to Alice's central North Carolina homes than the Cherokee and Lumbee? The nearest of today's substantial Native American populations is the Haliwa-Saponi, a community of about 4,000 centered in Halifax and Warren counties. Of course, the Native American populations of North Carolina have moved around a bit over time, and some groups have broken up or consolidated. And there are smaller Indian communities even closer to Alice's Vance County home, notably the ethnically mixed population of that county whose collective skin color resulted in their being referred to locally as "Cubans." They are among the many tiny Indian populations who had, following a verbal formula ubiquitous among North Carolina Indians, "hidden in plain sight" for decades. They minimized public display of their ethnicity to dodge deportation during the Trail of Tears and to avoid becoming the targets of miscellaneous acts of prejudice later,[8] and they retain less traditional folklore than do the larger populations. In the end, the best way to learn about herbal remedies from Indians living closer to the Person homes remains the Haliwa-Saponi. Maxella Richardson, mother of Haliwa-Saponi chief, Arnold Richardson, remembers the use of only two of Alice's ingredients— pipsissewa and sarsaparilla. While she recalls these being used for skin problems— though not for scrofula, since this has not been a problem in living memory in Native American populations in North Carolina — they have not been the principal remedies for this. Two salves have been used instead. One is Vicks—yes, the over-the-counter commercial Vicks—and the other is not herbal, but rather a mixture of boiled pork fat and sulphur. Also, her verbal list of botanicals was much shorter than the historical individual lists combined in the three big reference works on Native American herbal remedies. This should not surprise us for two reasons. One is that during this population's own decades of "hiding in plain sight" in central North Carolina, much traditional lore must have been forgotten (although the Haliwa-Saponi retained much more than did the Vance County "Cubans"). But also, and more important, Native American medicine has continued to develop during the last century, readily incorporating inexpensive new products such as Vicks.

How effective was the remedy? It did not contain conventional antibiotics, and so could not have directly attacked infectious agents such as the tuberculosis bacterium responsible for scrofula. However, that criticism is anachronistic: Alice's customers could not travel into the future and be treated with streptomycin along with supplements (the standard treatment for tuberculosis today). Their options in their own day were limited; they could take a patent medicine, consult a physician (a chancy option at the time), or do nothing. We must judge her remedy in comparison with options available in her day, not in ours. It is true that testimonials were part of the advertising of many a patent medicine, and often should be taken with a grain of salt. Nevertheless, the letters Alice published were from real people—a few of the original letters still exist—from customers who were genuinely grateful that they felt better after employing the remedy. How much each recovery depended on natural healing over time, how much on the actual medicinal value of the remedy, and how much simply on their confidence in the power of the remedy as such, or in Alice's assurances, is impossible to know.

How much real, verifiable medical value (apart from building sufferers' confidence) did the remedy have? The short answer is that we don't know, and probably never will. Nevertheless, tantalizing details are emerging in current research. Some background information is necessary before explaining those details. It is undeniable that most patent medicines, since they contained relatively low doses of anything, rarely produced dramatic changes—for the better or for the worse. On the positive side, that means that taking a patent medicine in recommended dosages would not have set a patient back the way that late-nineteenth-century doctors' stronger prescriptions often did, and this was a true advantage, since the medical maxim "first, do no harm" was observed more often in the breach back then. Working with physical herbs and other botanicals has broad advantages and disadvantages, naturally. The strength of solutions is hard to calculate since plants experience variable growing conditions affecting potency, (e.g., variations in rainfall, soil chemistry, amount of shade, etc.). Since dilutions were mild, modifications of strength due to these factors may not have mattered very much. More important, raw herbs are much more complex than are their laboratory-refined parallels. This has a negative potential in that there can be active parts of a botanical that are undesirable, but there exists a stronger positive side: they often contain several allied substances working in complementary ways. For instance, digitalis, the heart medicine present in the foxglove family of plants, actually is represented in the raw leafy herbs by "some thirty different closely related glucosides, all of which possess cardiotin properties but which, due to small structural differences have different speeds of onset of action and different durations of their effects."[9] This offers a chance for relatively nuanced, delicately layered therapy.

Few of the exact species of plants used in Mrs. Joe Person's Remedy have been subjected to modern rigorous double-blind clinical trials. This is a matter of limited time and money. There is plenty of such research going on, but there are many thousands of botanicals to evaluate. Just two of her ingredients are mentioned in modern medical literature written for laymen. Varro Tyler, the most skeptical evaluator of cures among the most highly qualified students of botanicals, confirmed that prickly ash bark does indeed help with toothaches, and noted that the various Latin American plants called sarsaparilla (genus Smilax) neither helped cure syphilis nor offered a source of testosterone, thus debunking two common claims for sarsaparilla.[10] But research has proliferated since he published in 1994. One can type scientific names of plants (or ailments, etc.) into a simple online search engine at www.pubmed.gov or www.ncbi.nlm.gov/sites/entrez and access abstracts of literally hundreds of very short, very specialized articles on plants in the same genus as those employed in Mrs. Joe Person's Remedy.

Such searches result in interesting conclusions. Pipsissewa has antioxidant and antifungal properties. Prickly ash bark (or close relatives) seems to have potential in antifungal, antibacterial, and some gynecological uses (also an area of potential use for a relative of star grass). Sarsaparilla (in its various species) has anticancer potential (as does Aralia nudicalis, wild sarsaparilla), helps with psoriasis, may help attenuate inflammation caused by autoimmune conditions such as rheumatoid arthritis and a kind of gout, might even help with AIDS, and (drum roll please) has some modest but real effect against some mycobacteria, such as the one which causes tuberculosis. It does this by binding with the wall of an individual bacterium, which flushes that bacterium out of the blood; it is indeed a "blood purifier." The studies on which these summary remarks are based were all tightly circumscribed in aims and procedures, generally they were done with lab rodents rather than human subjects, and their results are couched in carefully guarded phrases. Nevertheless, there is significant promise in this recent research, portending a fair amount of vindication for botanicals such as those employed in Alice's remedy. Taking the remedy regularly clearly would have done some good, even if it was not quite "infallible for scrofula."

Postlude: The Survival of Patent Medicines: A Few Bottles and Plenty of Attitudes

The previous paragraphs are proof that many of the ingredients of Mrs. Joe Person's Remedy have verifiable medicinal value, and either already have a role in formal medicine or will likely assume such a role when continuing research confirms their efficacy and safety. While this goes a good way towards vindicating Alice's claims for her remedy, it is far from constituting the whole story. The remedy was more than a mixture of North Carolina herbs. It helped people feel better partly in response to how it fit into late nineteenth- and early twentieth-century culture, that is, because of beliefs about health and because of ways of expressing those feelings that Alice and her customers shared.

The impulse to seek out natural, botanical medicines as alternatives or supplements to formal, official medical treatment certainly survives in modern America. In every pharmacy, strong medicines prescribed by physicians repose in a segregated area and are dispensed with an efficient but slightly daunting recipe of paperwork, ritual (the white smocks, the packaging), and damnable expense. However, more floor space in each store is assigned to self-medication, both to packages of relatively low dosages of common medicines and, in a separate section, the direct heirs of the patent medicine world, organic nostrums and health food supplements.

Also, a few people continue to assert some degree of very personal control over health issues by making their own medicines following local oral tradition. George Cecil McLeod, a dairyman and retired state senator living in southern Mississippi, is one such person. Some home remedies in use in his family during his youth in the 1930s and 1940s were: Lane's Liver Pills, castor oil (a good purge was still thought to fix many health problems), and Vick's for respiratory ailments. The word "scrofula" is not familiar to him, but he remembers, as a cure for skin problems of all sorts, "ichthyol" (or "ichthammol," common names for ammonium bituminosulfonate, which is distilled from sulfur-rich shale oil; remember that Maxella Richardson recalled a cure for skin ailments that included sulphur). A brochure published in 1913 by the gigantic pharmaceutical concern Merck and Company, stated that this "black drawing salve" helped attenuate the effects of many manifestations of tuberculosis, including both pulmonary tuberculosis and the kind called scrofula.[11]

Senator McLeod also remembers one botanical remedy that his family employed quite recently. Both his wife, Elaine, and adult son, George, were bitten by brown recluse spiders. Elaine went to a doctor and received a prescription that did little or no good. George employed instead a remembered botanical formula, a poultice made by combining ground up portions of the cambium layer just beneath the bark of white oak, of yellow pine, and of bay tree. This worked well for young George and then also cured his mother, after she abandoned the doctor's failed prescription in favor of the home remedy. This cure takes us not just back to Alice's day, but to her daughter Josie's bedside: a family member had a serious medical problem, the doctor failed to cure it, then a homemade cure based on local knowledge did a better job. Botanicals that were harvested in the neighborhood and combined following oral tradition saved Josie Person, and, well over a century later, cured Elaine McLeod. In addition, Mr. McLeod's story resembles those of many testimonials in Alice's advertising brochures!

Returning to the pharmacy, many of the old Indian herbals remain in use, but incognito, that is to say, a fair number of ingredients of both modern prescription medicines and contemporary over-the-counter cures and dietary supplements were indeed initially used by Native Americans— including many of the herbs ubiquitous in the old patent medicines— but that connection is seldom mentioned today. In some cases, the link may simply have been forgotten, but, more important, manufacturers have become progressively more reluctant to use the word "Indian" in situations in which that reference might be interpreted as a caricature, or otherwise offensive. Indeed, several of the herbs in Mrs. Joe Person's Remedy, all of which were employed in Native medicine, appear in the ingredients lists of modern herbal products for sale in organic sections of pharmacies and in health food stores. Helonias (false unicorn) is part of the formula for both Nature's Cure Yeast Control Capsules and NatraBio Candida Yeast Relief Products (both for vaginal yeast infections; Indians used helonias similarly). A species in the genus Zanthoxylum (another species in that genus is what Alice called prickly ash bark) takes part in Blue-Emu Super Strength Formula, a rub that is said to ease the pain of arthritis, a claim closely paralleling the Native American (and patent medicine) use of prickly ash bark to treat toothaches. Also, sarsaparilla is used today as a general booster of health in tea and in some vitamin supplements. In none of these cases are Alice's herbs' Native American histories mentioned on the packaging of the modern herbals.

A very few other botanicals that were acquired from Native Americans do still have that link mentioned, though there is little consistency in how that is done. For instance, the currently fashionable herb echinacea seldom is advertised as being used by Native Americans. But, in a rare acknowledgement, the following sentences appear on the packaging of one product: "Echinacea nutritionally supports healthy immune function.* Native to the United States and used by the Plains Indians more than any other plant, it is also known as purple coneflower. Introduced to settlers as they moved west in the 1800s, it is still used today for its many healthful benefits." The asterisk refers to the following legally required demurral, reproduced on most bottles of herbal supplements: "These statements have not been evaluated by the Food and Drug Administration. This product is not intended to diagnose, treat, cure, or prevent any disease."

Just a handful out of the multitude of other herbs employed today and used first by Native Americans have that association still regularly mentioned. The most common and most extended references are for black cohosh. The prose on perhaps one package in three notes its Native American use, that is, to minimize the symptoms of menopause. Black cohosh, while not part of Alice's remedy, was an ingredient in several patent medicines sold during her day, among them Mrs. Lydia Pinkham's Vegetable Compound, to be discussed at the end of the following chapter. The longest contemporary description appears on the side of a box of Alvita Black Cohosh Root Tea Bags:

> Black cohosh (Cimifuga [sic] racemosa) is a tall, stately plant native to the eastern forests of the United States and Canada. The herb was named black because of its dark roots, and cohosh is Algonquian for "rough," another reference to its roots. Early American settlers found that black cohosh was widely used by American Indian tribes. Specifically, the hard, knotty rootstock or rhizome was used for a variety of health purposes. The Indians used it externally on the skin and internally for the nutritional needs of women. This explains why it was also known as "Squaw Root."

Of the sixty (!) other varieties of Alvita tea for sale in local health food stores, Native American connections are asserted for only a few others. But many of the remaining varieties are, according to the packaging, herbs with ancient, or exotic, connections—fennel to Rome, Eucalyptus to aboriginal Australia, ginseng to the Asia of 3000 years ago, and so on, in most cases with those historic associations celebrated in prose just as lengthy as that quoted from the packaging of Alvita's Black Cohosh Tea.

In Alice's day, many patent medicines with Native American heritages had those historic connections honored — indeed, thoroughly exploited — in the advertising of the botanical remedies. Indians symbolized nature and ancient history and thus medical authority on a track separate from that of formal medicine. Indian connections for botanicals weren't just cited when appropriate, these links were often claimed even when false just to help make sales. Today, we lean the other direction. Native American associations for the many herbs with real histories as Native American cures are sometimes mentioned, but often not. Instead, we celebrate nature more broadly — bottles of herbal supplements show pictures of flowers, leaves, and stalks of plants — and widen our attention to history. One bottle sporting a claim for the contained herb's long-standing connection with Native Americans sits next to another citing ancient Greeks such as Pliny or Hippocrates, another ancient India, and so on. Asserted quality still relies on the wisdom of history, but we now seek more variety in that endorsement through citing many different ancient associations.

The old Native American botanicals in general, and Mrs. Joe Person's Remedy in particular, are certainly still with the health conscious among us, even if we seldom fully understand or acknowledge our profound debt in this area. Each morning, when I eat a piece of toast (whole wheat — lots of fiber) and drink some grape juice (replete with antioxidants), I also swallow two pills, one of glucosamine, on the vigorous advice of my father, and one of a Seminole specific, saw palmetto, on the hesitantly proffered recommendation of an open-minded doctor. Then, each evening, during dinner, I welcome the cleansing effect of a capsule or two of sarsaparilla, on the advice of Alice Morgan Person.

Chapter 6

The Remedy and the Turn-of-the-Century Patent Medicine Trade

For centuries, the process of seeking medical help was guided by belief more than by knowledge or logic, by respect for historically sanctioned authority and time-honored cures, or by confidence in the veracity of specific individuals like Alice Person. Physicians of her time were more often certain in their beliefs than they were right; even today, the best doctors agree that it is easy to overestimate how much they know and how much they can do. So many patients have problems that are more psychological than physical, though doctors' training emphasizes physical causes and physical cures, as medical education always has. In addition, many medicines work for reasons that remain poorly understood. Given the much, much greater shortcomings of turn-of-the-twentieth-century formal medical treatment, should we wonder if patent medicines really did offer a valuable alternative to doctors' care? Were they usually "snake oil," or a series of mixtures of what might be useful with what was surely fanciful? In short, what was the relationship of the medical establishment to the patent medicine world during Alice's lifetime? How can her remedy and her career selling it help us to better understand that relationship?

The broad outline of how she became involved in the patent medicine business is clear. She acquired a formula for a combination of medicinal herbs based on Native American traditional practice. She tried to get doctors — individually and collectively — to witness her remedy's virtues and to endorse it, but failed. Instead, she marketed her remedy through face-to-face sales, through word of mouth, and through local print advertising. She buttressed her sales through playing the piano and marketing her sheet music. Her business eventually succeeded on a regional level, despite her lack of formal training in how to run a business. Her advertising changed with the times. Sales of the remedy slowly declined after her death, with what became her son's company ceasing to function by the mid 1940s.

Three stories will offer us points of departure for the chapter: two versions of the discovery of her medicine, plus her outraged narration of her attempt to gain the medical establishment's endorsement. One publicly distributed version of the origin of Alice's remedy came out in a Raleigh newspaper, then was reprinted on the back cover of an advertising booklet for her medicine (the line between news and advertising was quite thin during the nineteenth century). I quote this article without change, following the published capitalization, spelling, and usage (for instance, still employing the antiquated use of the word "receipt" for "recipe"):

> Years ago an old Indian left a receipt for curing Scrofula with Mrs. Joe Person's father. Mrs. Person lives in Franklinton, or in that section. A child was born to Mrs. Person, and it had the Scrofula. The doctors gave it up to die. She thought of the receipt, that was now old and musty and hid away in an up-stairs drawer. She concluded that if the child was bound to die it wouldn't hurt to follow that receipt. She went out and gathered the herb, got the whiskey, and did as directed to the child. Her child now lives well and hearty. More than this: only a few months since a South Carolinian, whose name has slipped us, was suffering from some scrofulous affection on the heel. He had been to the Hot Springs in Arkansas, and from there he went to Kittrell's Springs. Nothing did him any good. At Kittrell they told him of Mrs. Person's receipt, and Dr._____ wrote to Mrs. Person if she cured that South Carolinian her receipt was worth money. And the South Carolinian sent her word if she cured him he would give her five hundred dollars. She sent him directions what to do, and added if they cured him he could send her twenty-five dollars; she would not ask five hundred. The South Carolinian went home, and shortly afterwards sent Mrs. Person a check for twenty-five dollars, and wrote the most grateful letter he knew how. Bless these old Indians! We would like to have one for a neighbor.

Alice's own testimony concerning the origin of her medicine matches up fairly well with the above, but contains a few telling differences. She relates that story in full in the first chapter of "The Chivalry of Man." In brief, a doctor diagnosed young Josie Person with scrofula and gave up on her. A neighbor lady (Alice's father doesn't appear in this more authoritative version) offered to cure Josie with a formula that had been given to the neighbor's father by an Indian. Alice and the neighbor gathered the ingredients in the local woods. Josie recovered. That formula became Mrs. Joe Person's Remedy.

As a last bit of preparation for the substance of this chapter, here is a summary of Alice's dramatic and angry story of how she tried to obtain an endorsement of her medicine from several doctors in Raleigh, which she related in full as the second chapter of "The Chivalry of Man." She decided to confront the city's medical establishment, offering to cure "any case of scrofula or blood impurity" for free in exchange for public endorsement. The first doctor she contacted said that "a sense of professional duty and etiquette would compel him to decline to witness any of those wonderful cures I claimed I could make." Other doctors were initially more welcoming. One promised several times to meet with her and an array of scrofulus test subjects. He stood the group up each time and finally wrote her as follows: "After careful deliberation on the propriety of examining the subjects sent you for treatment, I am convinced that it would be wrong, and must therefore decline. In the first place, a public test of a secret patent medicine is not feasible. Second you are pursuing a course just adversely to the admonition extended to you by two other physicians. If I examine anybody for you now, I, of course, connive at the effort to enrich the owner of a patent secret remedy." That is, he didn't want to break ranks with his colleagues. Her request to address a meeting of doctors was also denied.[1]

Why did the doctors refuse to help her? Were they simply protecting their own profits? That is what her husband suggested. More importantly, was the gap between proprietary medicine and the medical establishment impossible to bridge? What was the nature of the difference between what happened to you when you visited a physician and when you instead chose to employ a patent medicine? Alice Person's experience exemplifies many aspects of the world of informal medicine of her day. It is an open door into the way in which many people then thought about illness and cures.

The Medical Establishment at the Turn of the 20th Century: What Doctors Could Do

This was a transitional period in the history of formal medicine. Doctors had inherited some of their abiding central attitudes from Galen, the Greek who, in the second century A.D., fully expounded the theory of humours (a theory already far from new). According to that school of thought, good health depended on the humours—yellow bile, black bile, phlegm, and blood—being in balance. Each humour was associated with a season, an element, a combination of temperature and humidity, and with certain illnesses, which then could be treated by reversing the general effects of the humour. It is worth taking a look at how these factors line up, because several critical aspects of nineteenth-century American medical treatments really did hark back to this ancient theory. Here is a chart of the humours and their associations:

Humour	Season	Element	Effect
yellow bile	summer	fire	hot and dry
black bile	autumn	earth	cold and dry
phlegm	winter	water	cold and moist
blood	spring	air	hot and moist

If a body's complement of humours got out of balance, exercise and diet were encouraged. If that didn't fix the problem, a good purge might eliminate the excess of the offending humour: harsh emetics and diuretics were still essential to nineteenth-century formal medicine (emetics caused vomiting and diuretics copious urination — either way, you might get rid of your surplus of a humour). Cooling might help the choleric effects of too much yellow bile, and warming the excesses of black bile or of phlegm. A favorite way to modify temperature and perhaps also be purged was to visit mineral springs. A person could drink certain mineral waters as an emetic there and lie in hot or cold baths. "Taking the waters" both internally and externally remained a healing recreational activity for those who could afford it throughout the nineteenth century. Kittrell had springs, and there was a pair of hotels for the patrons of those springs. Alice often played piano at Kittrell's large Davis Hotel (also called the Glass House), which tended to be filled with health-conscious Northerners. Music also helped them heal (especially the melancholic victims of an excess of black bile), and this offered yet another chance for Alice to sell her remedy.

Unfortunately, the most frequently diagnosed form of humor imbalance for centuries was excess blood, for which the therapy included surgical incisions (called bleeding), or the application of leeches. In addition to bleeding (which had largely died out by Alice's day) and exhaustive, exhausting purging (which had not!), nasty mineral medicines such as calomel, a compound of mercury, were prescribed. The general theory behind these heroic methods of treatment was that serious illnesses required parallel responses. Testimonials for the efficacy of patent medicines often criticized doctors' drastic methods, stating that a given parent just couldn't subject their child to any more doctors' medicines, or that taking a patent medicine to address a serious leg infection was a successful way around a doctor's insistence that amputation was the only solution. About a fourth of the published testimonials for Mrs. Joe Person's Remedy include such critical references to doctors' treatments, though she also took care to mention any instance when a doctor admitted that her remedy had helped a patient. This illustrates an enduring ambivalence in the patent medicine business; physicians' endorsements were valuable, but, physicians were the competition, and their treatments were far from perfect.

There were many insightful doctors, of course, though it was professionally perilous to break ranks against inherited doctrine. James Le Fanu, in his *Rise and Fall of Modern Medicine*, pointed out that as early as the 1830s, "a few courageous physicians acknowledged that virtually everything they did— bleeding, purging, prescribing complicated diets—was useless."[2] But steady progress was made during the century; by the time Alice was selling her remedy, doctors vaccinated for smallpox, did some kinds of surgery effectively, set broken bones, alleviated some pain through drugs, and dealt reasonably effectively with indigestion, constipation, and some kinds of poisoning. Quinine was available to prevent malaria, and some antiseptic procedures were in place.[3] Also, the germ theory of infection was gradually gaining acceptance. Nevertheless, most progress in the decades flanking the turn of the century was in diagnosis rather than treatment. In fact, more people were getting infectious diseases towards the end of the nineteenth century than early in that century, due to deteriorating work conditions and increasingly crowded living.

It is true that when physicians condemned patent medicines, there was plenty of fodder for their criticism. However, they couldn't do any better at the time outside of the few areas specified in the previous paragraph, and often they did worse. Their aggressive treatments often lessened the ability of a patient's body to heal itself. While formal medicine was an upwardly mobile profession, the struggle between formal and informal medical treatment was eventually won by the doctors due to their collective professional image, solid organization, and the expectation of successful therapy rather than being able to actually cure sick people. Antibiotics would not be readily available until World War II, decades after formal medicine had largely pushed informal medicine aside. It is impossible to overemphasize this point: the medical establishment's victory drew on ideology, rhetoric, publicity, and consequent status in society much more than on contemporary accomplishment.

The Often Wild World of Alternative Medical Treatment: Where Did Alice Fit?

Medical treatment outside of the doctor's office has always been characterized by luxuriant variety in techniques, in medicines, and in the relative sincerity of claims for the efficacy of treatments. American informal medicine inherited the English model and employed English products for some time; then gradually it incorporated local herbs, drawing on contact with Native Americans. The fact that competition between proprietary medicines was a governing principle of the industry meant that extravagant and deliberately deceptive advertisements sat beside more honest ones in newspapers. An ad for Mrs. Joe Person's Remedy, however brash its claims might seem today, was restrained in comparison to a printed pitch for Dr. Clark Johnson's Indian Blood Syrup, the ads for which claimed it was "the best remedy known to man," and that it would cure ague, biliousness, bowel problems, dropsy, dyspepsia, erysipelas, fever, heart disease, impure blood, indigestion, kidney problems, liver diseases, nervous debility, rheumatism, skin diseases, scrofula, and so on.[4] Even more comprehensive was the rainbow of virtues claimed for the Magnetic Money Belt, one of dozens of devices briefly in vogue late in the nineteenth century that succeeded by claiming association with real advances in the physical sciences. The Money Belt was advertised in the paper Alice's first customers would have read, the *Henderson Gold Leaf* (Henderson is just ten miles north of Kittrell). It was said to cure the following problems that men might have: "pain in the back, hips, head, and limbs, nervous debility, lumbago, general debility, rheumatism, paralysis, neuralgia, sciatica, diseases of the kidneys, spinal diseases, torrid liver, gout, seminal emissions, impotency [nice to have both of those complementary problems fixed], asthma, heart disease, dyspepsia, constipation, erysipelas, indigestion, hernia, rupture, catarrh, piles, epilepsy, dumb ague, etc." What problems were left to be considered part of "etc."? Perhaps scrofula. For the ladies, the belt was claimed to fix an excruciatingly detailed laundry list of gynecological problems.[5]

Ads that targeted fewer maladies probably represented more sincere belief. Even these will seem improbably broad by modern standards, but we have to remember that each medicine had many ingredients, and that versatility was a virtue, even when universality was clearly a hoax. For instance, an ad for Tutt's Pills (one appeared on the same page of the *Henderson Gold Leaf* as the lengthier ad for the Magnetic Money Belt) restricted its effects to "Torpid Bowels, Disordered Liver, and Malaria" in bold print, then elaborated in the fine print that it would cure "loss of appetite, bowels costive, sick headache, fullness after eating, aversion to exertion of body or mind, eructation of food, irritability of temper, low spirits, a feeling of having neglected some duty [!], dizziness, fluttering of the heart, highly colored urine, constipation," plus kidney problems and skin conditions that resulted from impure blood. Thus, this medicine concentrated on liver, digestion, and nerve conditions, just as Mrs. Joe Person's Remedy emphasized serious skin problems along with ubiquitous "tonic" qualities, though again citing cleansing the blood as important (an emphasis replacing the historical emphasis on bleeding as therapy). In another strategy, a company could cover all illnesses—and thus all bases in terms of sales—by offering several different nostrums. The Ayers Company did that, offering Ayers Sarsaparilla for problems of liver and skin, and a complementary product, Ayers Cherry Pectoral, for throat and lung diseases.

6. The Remedy and the Turn-of-the-Century Patent Medicine Trade

Just as some advertisements outgunned others, so did the more gaudy descriptions of the beginnings of patent medicines. Alice's story is relatively modest in both length and flashiness. Her remedy came from an old Indian, who gave it to a neighbor's father, the neighbor then saving Josie Person (whom formal medicine had consigned to death). That's it, and we know that her story had at least some basis in fact. Josie's recurring illness is mentioned in Alice's correspondence, and, as was shown in the previous chapter, the ingredients of her remedy were traditional herbal medicines among nearby populations of Native Americans, who used the botanicals for largely the same purposes claimed by Alice. Whether the path of the botanicals from Native Americans to Josie Person was exactly as Alice related, or whether her anecdote is a metaphor for the literal truth — recast somewhat to fit patent medicine advertising norms— is not important. What does matter is that the tale's essence is sincere and based on fact. Alice believed in her remedy, and she had good reason to do so.

We can compare that story to the published history of the invention of another "Indian" nostrum, Judson's Mountain Herb Pills. This narrative, taken from an advertising pamphlet for that product, was summarized by James Harvey Young in his book *The Toadstool Millionaires*:

> The hero of this paperback [indeed an advertising booklet, but flavored like a Western dime novel] was Dr. Cunard. Son of a wealthy father, the physician had traveled throughout the world seeking cures for the ailments of men. He became fluent in more than thirty languages. He classified more than 10,000 plants in the Rocky Mountains alone. Living for years with various Indian tribes, Cunard met "unheard of perils and hardships, hoping only to benefit his race."
>
> One day while among the Navahoes within the borders of Mexico, the doctor came upon a fearful spectacle. "An Indian girl, with her hair floating in the wind was bound to a stake, and around her was piled the fuel, soon to be lighted for her torture." Cunard was frozen by her beauty. "The chisel of Praxiteles never formed a lovelier shape, her face and form were of faultless beauty; but the crowning beauty was her eye; before its lightning glance, her tormentors (soon to be) stood abashed.... The chief of the captors begged her to be his squaw."
>
> "Dog of a Navahoe," she replied, "I defy thee. I am the daughter of an Aztec Chief. The Eagle mates not with the thieving Hawk."
>
> The sound of this proud voice awoke Cunard from his rigid trance just as the chief applied the torch. Casting aside botanical specimens, the doctor bounded down the mountainside, scattered the startled Navahoes, hurled aside the burning faggots, cut the binding thongs, and carried the princess to the lodge of the medicine man. Then he turned and confronted the astounded Indians.
>
> "It was well that he did so." For the amazed quiet produced by his

bold action had ebbed, and the chief was already fitting an arrow to his bow.

"I demand her for my squaw," Dr. Cunard cried. "The Great Spirit has said it, and I say to you, that if you dare refuse, tomorrow you shall see sudden darkness come at noon-day, and the sun shall change to blood — nay, for a sign that I speak truly, the great sun shall be darkened tomorrow, whether you consent or not. Then keep the girl but twenty-four hours unharmed, and if it does not happen as I say, commit us both to the flames; but if it does so come about, know ye me as the 'Benisontan,' the Great Judge of the pale faces, over whom the 'Manitou' spreads his wing, and whom you cannot harm."

Cunard, of course, had perused an almanac, and when the next day his prediction was borne out and his gestures seemed to restore the sun, ceremonies were held in his honor. Then Cunard and Tula set out for her home in a secluded mountain valley. Welcomed for his heroism, the doctor dwelt with the Aztecs for nearly a year. He observed that a powder dispensed by the medicine man prevented any serious sickness among members of the tribe. Begging the formula of the Sachem Tezucho as a boon for having saved his daughter, Cunard was taken in the dead of night through labyrinthine mountain passages to the aged sorceress who alone possessed the secret. Because of his courage, she yielded to his entreaties.

"[It is] a secret," the doctor cries, "that once in my possession, shall bring healing and strength upon its wings to all the world."

Deeper into the mountain must they yet go, to a gloomy cavern containing an altar bearing a golden image of the Sun. Here Cunard takes an oath never to reveal the location of the hidden valley, and here he is shown the six herbs composing the remedy and told their proper proportions. Then, bidding farewell to the last unconquered Aztecs, he departs for the East.

Cunard returns home to find his mother on her deathbed, but the miraculous herbs effect an immediate cure. The news spreads and the demand expands. The doctor cannot compound the remedy fast enough. In order that all who suffer may be healed, Cunard conveys the secret to B.L. Judson & Co., who now compound it as Judson's Mountain Herb Pills.[6]

This is a drastically abridged rendition of the story! A schematic reduction of Young's summary reveals the same basic plot as for the invention of Mrs. Joe Person's Remedy: the eventual proprietor of a medicine is deeded a wonderful herbal recipe by an old Indian, saves a close relative's life with this concoction, and then chooses to share this miracle with the world. However, the surfaces of the stories are so very different! Which is more believable? On the other hand, which is more entertaining?

Citing Native America as a source for a patent medicine made solid advertising sense. Indians and housewives presented a pair of alternatives to the authority claimed by the expensive, intimidating army of white male doctors. In rural American culture, wives were expected to be keepers of household formulas for healing, just as they were for food, as traditional parts of their domestic responsibilities,[7] while Indians had been around "forever," and possessed mysterious eternal wisdom. Alice brought these two sources of nonestablishment authority together, as a respectable wife and mother making a remedy that had an Indian pedigree and an attractive Indian trademark.

The very first American patent medicine, Tuscarora Rice (1811), was followed by a steady stream of nostrums with Indian names, such as Wright's Indian Vegetable Pills (1837–), Dr. Morse's Indian Root Pills (1850–), Modoc Vegetable Bitters (1875–), and others.[8] Then, late in the nineteenth century, Native Americans became even better fodder for advertising due to the exciting news coming from out West about battles with the "savages," a steady diet of Western dime novels, and the visual appeal of exaggerated Plains Indian formal garb as seen first in Wild West shows and soon thereafter in enormous medicine shows. In the patent medicine business, this stunning array of emotive associations easily overshadowed the simple fact that real Indians actually did know plenty about herbal remedies. As a result, shallow advertising glitz tainted the occasional genuine Native American connection like Alice's. This became part of a general trend: the patent medicine world's dramatic marriage with advertising became a divorce from reality, simultaneously expanding the business exponentially and guaranteeing an eventual back-lash.

The Chilling Effect of the Food and Drug Act of 1906

Some proprietary medicines were actually harmful, such as William Swain's Panacea, which claimed to cure scrofula, syphilis, rheumatism, all disorders "arising from a contaminated or impure state of the blood," plus "mercurial disease," but which itself included plenty of mercury.[9] Quite a few more were marketed with breathtaking dishonesty, such as an Indian worm eradicator administered as pills which contained narrow rolls of paper that patients would pass in their stools and think were dead worms. At about the turn of the twentieth century, the American public tired of the outlandish claims made for so many patent medicines, tarred honestly marketed medicines such as Mrs. Joe Person's Remedy with the same brush as the more famous nostrums that deserved to be condemned, and welcomed legislation to require truth in advertising.

The climate of disapproval emerged gradually, and smart patent medicine promoters had time to try to adjust to it and to the many new regulations that would culminate in 1906 in the Food and Drug Act. This law required accurate labeling of ingredients, banned poisons in patent medicines, and, in applications of the law that developed quickly, banned patent medicines that weren't proven effective. A second pamphlet issued to advertise Mrs. Joe Person's Remedy (like the one discussed in the last chapter) illustrates these changes. Neither pamphlet bears a publication date. However, the first one contains testimonials dated 1878 through February of 1884, and was probably issued that year. The second contains testimonials dated December of 1884 through July of 1901. There are quite a few letters from 1899, 1900, and 1901; Alice would certainly have printed later letters if she had them. Thus, this advertising pamphlet came out no later than early 1902. It therefore dates from well before the Food and Drug Act itself but well within what we might call the gravitational field of that legislation — that is, the time when a significant percentage of the American public had reached the opinions that would eventually be reflected in that law.

This second pamphlet is shaped basically like the first one: There is a title page with attractive graphics and Alice's own claims, many pages full of testimonials, then a closing essay. The testimonials read much like those in the first pamphlet, but they gradually reveal a major development. While scrofula was the featured illness in the first brochure, it is mentioned just a half-dozen times here. Scrofula was becoming better understood as one manifestation of tuberculosis, even by the general public reading small local papers like the *Henderson Gold Leaf*. An advertisement in that paper for Doctor Pierce's Golden Medical Discovery began: "A Foot-hold for Consumption is what you are offering if your blood is impure. Consumption is simply Lung Scrofula. A scrofulous condition, with a slight cough or blood, is all that is needed to develop it."[10] The germ theory also raised its head in the *Gold Leaf*, in an ad for "Rydale's Tonic: A New Scientific Discovery for the Blood and Nerves. It purifies the blood by eliminating the waste matter and other impurities and by destroying the germs or microbes that infest the blood."[11]

Indeed, Alice dropped the word "scrofula" from the title page of this advertising brochure, and thus from her own claims for what the remedy could do, and also ceased listing most of the diseases she cited on the cover of the earlier form of the pamphlet. Her customers could write anything they wanted, but she had to play it safer now. Equally dramatic, she dropped the Indian association for the remedy. There is no picture of an Indian on the cover (she had never used that trademark in newspaper ads), no story about the discovery of the remedy on the back, no Native American link at all. She must have decided, given the lunatic antics of the Kickapoo Indian Sagwa traveling show, and given countless other irresponsible uses of live Indians in medicine shows and false claims of Indian sources for patent medicines, that continuing to share this advertising path would do more harm than good, despite the considerable truth in her own earlier Indian advertising. Instead, she finally was able to reproduce a page-long published endorsement by a physician. Dr. R.M. Miller, in an article entitled "Why Professional Endorsement of Proprietary Remedies Is Granted or Withheld," published on March 22, 1899, in the *American Journal of Health*, wrote that "there are but few among the millions of proprietary remedies (so-called) which are able to satisfy the exacting requirements of journals like this, or whose record of practical achievements as curatives of the diseases they are supposed to combat will bear the merciless search light of our investigation.... We have no hesitation in recommending Mrs. Joe Person's Remedy, offered by Mrs. Joe Person, of Kittrell, North Carolina, as a specific for rheumatism, scrofula, psoriasis, erythema, sores, and all diseases arising from impure or impoverished blood." The journal is obscure, and the endorsement seems a little over the top, but it was satisfying enough to Alice that a copy of it appeared on the back cover of this second advertising pamphlet. She thus replaced her earlier reliance on the "alternative" authority of Native American tradition with the standard and triumphant authority of the medical establishment. In addition, Alice's narrative of her old confrontation with the doctors in Raleigh, reproduced in the early pages of her earlier advertising booklet, is gone here in this later form of the brochure, in effect replaced by this published physician's endorsement.[12]

The newer title page lists far fewer ailments or general salutary qualities than that of the first pamphlet, just "blood purifier," "nervine" (sedative), "alterative," "indigestion," and being "of untold benefit" to nursing mothers and their children. That is it, even though the testimonials themselves address much the same array of ailments as before (excepting a drastic scaling back of mentions of scrofula). Thus, Alice's claims are more modest than those of her customers rather than matching them closely, as in the first brochure. She seems to be hunkering down in the anti-patent medicine atmosphere, making a smaller target for disapproval or for legal action. She is claiming little more for Mrs. Joe Person's Remedy than is asserted in the following ad, quoted on the first page of the *Gold Leaf* of December 28, 1911: "There's a Difference. Ask Your Doctor. Drink Delicious, Healthful Pepsi-Cola. The original pure food drink guaranteed under the United States Government serial 3S13. PepsiCola clarifies the brain, steadies the nerves, brightens the eye. PepsiCola is an unrivaled system-toner. It is an absolutely pure combination of pepsin (for the digestion), acid phosphate and the juices of fresh fruits.... PepsiCola bottling Co., Henderson, North Carolina."

Another publication associated with Mrs. Joe Person's Remedy is a one-

FOR SALE BY

Mrs. Joe Person's Remedy

Has established itself as the finest Blood Purifier on the market ❧ ❧ ❧

AS A NERVINE THERE IS NONE BETTER.

THE BEST ALTERATIVE KNOWN.

The Formula is published on each bottle and Physicians have given it high endorsement.

If You are suffering from Indigestion and will take MRS. JOE PERSON'S REMEDY three times a day, after each meal you will experience more benefit and comfort from its use than any medicine you ever tried. If you are a nursing mother, MRS. PERSON'S REMEDY will be of untold benefit to both mother and child.

FOR SPECIAL REMARKS AND INFORMATION SEE CIRCULAR.

OBSERVER PRINT, CHARLOTTE, N. C.

The cover of a 32-page 1901 booklet advertising the remedy (Alice Morgan Person Collection, East Carolina University).

page flyer printed front and back for her son Rufus shortly after he regained control of the company in 1916. The claims in bold print are modest, largely replicating those in the brochure of late 1901 or early 1902, though the dates on the testimonials in this late flyer suggest that it is from 1917: "Purely Vegetable; a Good Blood Medicine ... Tonic, Nervine, Alterative."[13] The most surprising thing about the flyer is its small size in comparison to the earlier pamphlets, which suggests that the company was on fragile financial footing. Alice had been deceased for several years, and it had been her personality that kept the business afloat. She had succeeded in her primary aim, to support her family well; but that success was a regional one, circumscribed by her personal rounds selling the medicine within her home state of North Carolina and in nearby parts of contiguous states. It is testimony to her unwavering determination that she did as well as she did. So many factors stood in her way. One was gender. Men were the accepted authority figures. This may have been one reason why Alice acquiesced in reproducing a somewhat inaccurate story of the origin of her medicine on the back of her own original advertising pamphlet: In the newspaper story reprinted there, her father was said to have been given the "receipt" for the medicine by an Indian rather than the female neighbor Alice cites in "The Chivalry of Man."

Mrs. Joe Person's Remedy Versus Lydia E. Pinkham's Vegetable Compound

The only dramatically successful business among the few patent medicine companies run by, and having as their spokesperson, a woman was the Pinkham company of Lynn, Massachusetts. Comparing Lydia Pinkham's operation with Alice's helps to better understand what might have been the most important complex of factors limiting the success of Alice's business, that is, the factors having to do less with product quality and with personal character, and more to do with general business affairs.

There were quite a few parallels between the two patent medicine companies. Lydia Pinkham (1819–83), like Alice, entered the business world because her husband was no longer a qualified provider. Isaac Pinkham went bankrupt in the mid–1870s as a result of an unfortunate combination of national hard times and his own adventurous but not very careful, or hardnosed, actions. He seems to have been emotionally undone by the experience.[14] In addition, the two women's advertising materials were somewhat similar. Here is the entire text of an advertising card distributed (shortly before the turn of the twentieth century) by a Pinkham retailer, preserving the original spelling, capitalization, layout, and general typographical effect:

LYDIA E. PINKHAM'S
VEGETABLE COMPOUND

IS A POSITIVE CURE

for all those painful Complaints and Weaknesses so common to our best female population.

――――――――――<>――――――――――

It will cure entirely the worst form of Female Complaints, all Ovarian troubles, Inflammation and Ulceration, Falling and Displacements and the consequent Spinal Weakness, and is particularly adapted to the Change of Life.

It will dissolve and expel tumors from the uterus in an early stage of development. The tendency to cancerous humors there is checked speedily by its use.

It removes faintness, flatulency, destroys all craving for stimulants, and relieves weakness of the Stomach. It cures Bloating, Headaches, Nervous Prostration, General Debility, Sleeplessness, Depression, and Indigestion.

That feeling of bearing down, causing pain, weight and backache, is always permanently cured by its use.

It will at all times and under all circumstances act in harmony with the laws that govern the female system.

For the cure of Kidney Complaints of either sex this Compound is unsurpassed.

LYDIA E. PINKHAM'S VEGETABLE COMPOUND is prepared at 233 and 235 Western Avenue, Lynn, Mass. Price $1. Six bottles for $5. Sent by mail in the form of pills, also in the form of lozenges, on receipt of price, $1 per box of either. Mrs. Pinkham freely answers all letters of inquiry. Send for pamphlet. Address as above.

No family should be without *LYDIA E. PINKHAM'S LIVER PILLS.* They cure constipation, billiousness, and torpidity of the liver. 25¢ per box. FOR SALE BY **HENRY D. CUSHMAN.** *Three Rivers, Mich.*

Note that Lydia's compound focused on one complex of problems (women's health issues), just as did Alice's remedy (in her case, scrofula). Also similarly, a few other problems are appended in the ad to attract a larger customer base, in the case of the vegetable compound, flatulence and kidney problems, both equal opportunity afflictions. The impression of certainty in the advertising rhetoric is parallel, as is a brief moment of restraint in assertions dealing with cancer: "It will dissolve and expel tumors from the uterus *in an early stage of development.*" The prices are customary; even the use of typefaces, which are varied in size and font, are reminiscent of Alice's ads.

There were five herbs in the vegetable compound as Lydia originally made it: unicorn root (Aletris farinosa), life root (Senecio aureus), black cohosh (Cimicifuga racemosa), pleurisy root (Asclepias tuberosa), and fenugreek seed (Foenum graceum).[15] In comparison, Alice used seven. Just one was in common, Aletris farinosa, the plant Lydia called unicorn root but which Alice called star grass. Lydia did catch up in the sheer number of herbal ingredients later. The label of a bottle likely to be from 1925 or later reads as follows:

> Lydia E. Pinkham's Vegetable Compound (with Vitamin B1) (contains 15 per cent alcohol). This is added solely as a solvent and preservative. Active ingredients: Crystalline Vitamin B1, black cohosh, true and false unicorn, life and pleurisy roots, dandelion, chamomile. Recommended as a vegetable tonic in conditions for which this preparation is adapted....[16]

The listing of ingredients probably responds to the Food and Drug Act. So does the retreat from the original claims for efficacy, the same retreat Alice had to make in describing her remedy at that time. Indeed, the Pinkham Company's advertising brochures exhibit precisely the same meticulously guarded nature as Alice's later ones: when there are emphatic and specific — that is, legally risky — claims for the medicine, these are confined within customer testimonials, while the company's own prose is more vague.

Where did this famous potion come from? Pinkham, as part of her duties as a housewife, had long made home remedies before this became a source of income for her. The basic formula for the particular home remedy that evolved into her vegetable compound was said to have been given to her husband, Isaac, in lieu of cash by a debtor, a local machinist.[17] This is somewhat comparable — at least in number of layers— to Alice getting her formula from an Indian via a neighbor, though Lydia's transaction resulted from Isaac Pinkham's reckless business practices rather than a specific illness of a specific individual (as with Alice's daughter Josie's childhood scrofula), and had been said by the debtor from whom it came to be appropriate specifically for women's health problems. Finally, Lydia, like Alice, seems to have believed in her product. Lydia radiated sincerity, and she was able to project her reassuring image over the entire country. The company's most effective advertising image was her portrait.

Lydia was at least as well educated as Alice; she taught school before she got married. She made her cure only for her family and friends until Isaac went bankrupt. When she tried to sell her compound more widely, she faced many of the same initial frustrations that Alice did. Just as Alice had trouble for years with business partners, the Pinkham family had to cope at first with unscrupulous agents. Also, Lydia's functions in the family business were partly the same as Alice's— being in charge of making the medicine, writing advertising copy (and answering letters; eventually, a team of secretaries did this), and being the public face of the company (though she didn't have to travel to sell the medicine the way Alice did). However, Lydia E. Pinkham's Vegetable Compound, sold since the 1870s up to the present (in various forms), had innumerable mercantile advantages over Mrs. Joe Person's Remedy. Lydia's father was a better role model because he was a successful businessman (although her husband, like Alice's father, was inept in that sphere). Her particular specialization, women's problems, turned what was then the disadvantage of being a woman in the business world into profitable niche targeting. She had a large family comprising children of appropriate ages to help her right away, particularly three energetic sons who shared her stunning business acumen. She and her family accumulated enough capital to advertise much more widely than Alice ever could. Also significantly, in these early years, all of the big patent medicine companies, including Lydia's, were in the North, because of collective experience and expertise in business and industry, plus the economies of scale in sales allowed by large, dense populations.

In summary, the Pinkham family business succeeded quite dramatically due to the availability of a crew of dedicated and able family members, strong capitalization allowed by quick early profits, and impeccable advertising skills employed in a fertile business environment. Alice Person, on the other hand, was an honest woman with lots of energy and a good product, but with none of the professional advantages possessed by Lydia Pinkham and by countless other patent medicine businessmen in the North.

Chapter 7

Alice and Music in Fashion

Many of the melodies Alice issued in 1889 in her *Collection of Popular Airs* were unique arrangements of blackface minstrel songs. These tunes were far from new. Indeed, most of them had first appeared in print when blackface minstrelsy as a massively popular genre was young, in the 1840s and early 1850s, before Alice Morgan was married. Her publication is quite a surprise, and very important for the history of popular music, particularly in the South. Many early minstrel songs were no longer in print by 1889, but some of these same tunes (and many similar ones) can be heard in rural folk songs that we know from the early sales of 78 rpm records in the 1920s, records labeled "hillbilly" music (i.e., early country music). Also, just a few years later, such tunes were gathered up by scholars and enthusiasts collecting folk music in rural areas, many of them connected with the Library of Congress or employed by the Works Progress Administration (in the 1930s and later).

The *Collection of Popular Airs* falls right between the early published blackface minstrel music and the first of the stream of sound recordings that would show that common people had never forgotten these lively tunes, that is, this anthology of tunes became a sort of illuminated waystation on an otherwise hidden journey through many decades, a journey from novelty to tradition and from urban-centered to essentially rural. More generally, we are reminded that the journey of culture is one contained in human hands; Alice and other long-lived members of her generation didn't just survive the long transformation of blackface minstrel music in both practice and function, they effected many of those changes themselves through their own actions and their evolving tastes.

Although this was not Alice's only venture into the world of sheet music publishing, this collection was her most significant. We can look at it from two directions. On the one hand, these are tunes with specific interesting histories worth exploring, in part due to the paucity of other evidence of this repertoire from this period. This was music that had once been in fashion. Why had it been fashionable, and why did young Alice Morgan learn these tunes? On the other hand, Alice Morgan Person's commentary, combined with some specific aspects of her forms of the tunes, offers a window into the later social history of this music. The question will be answered in this chapter, and Alice's commentary will be discussed in the next.

Blackface Minstrelsy

Blackface minstrelsy, in which white performers — made up as caricatures of African Americans — sang, danced, and performed comic sketches, was the most popular form of stage entertainment in the United States between 1843 and circa 1870.[1] However, the genre was not truly new when the Virginia Minstrels exploded into fame in 1843. Individual performers in blackface had circulated in England and the United States for decades, often as circus acts. White men performed as caricatures of blacks, and it seemed that music was far and away the most intriguing and adaptable aspect of black culture when they constructed their performances. The instruments they used helped tell the tale. The banjo was a marvelous conflation of a wide variety of West African plucked stringed instruments; an embodiment of slaves' collective memory (although as seen through outsiders' lenses; and as transformed within their technology). Two percussion instruments customarily used by blackface minstrels told a unified story, that African music in Africa, and as re-created in the New World, emphasized rhythm and the associated gigantic family of instruments that one hits to make music (actually a pair of families, as the tambourine, with its flexible head, is classified as a membranophone, while the fixed-in-shape bones belong to the other clan of percussion instruments called idiophones). This story is also a contrasting pair of narratives, since the tambourine, though there were many types in Middle Eastern and North African culture, was typical of European music by this time and thus was an adopted instrument by blacks or those imitating blacks, while the bones cleaved closer to the letter of African history. The fiddle in the shape of the violin was definitely an instrument new to blacks in the American setting, though there are plenty of bowed stringed instruments in Africa. Many male slaves were trained to fiddle at dances so that their owners who played the instrument could be socializing and dancing at parties, not working while their guests enjoyed themselves. Fiddling (of European tunes, from England but often of Scottish origin) was probably the main "black" music that whites heard!

Where does Alice's piano fit in such an array of instruments? It embodies an important part of the later history of minstrelsy as popular music, the trip from crudity to a peculiar corner of temporary refinement through fashion, the trip from stage to home. After all, people in Alice's generation and several subsequent ones couldn't "take home" a theatrical or musical performance as a CD or DVD. The most they could do was play arrangements of those tunes on instruments they personally commanded, which meant transferring melodies to the instruments of cultivated society, especially the piano.

During the heyday of minstrelsy in the decades following 1843 — that is, during Alice's youth — the typical minstrel ensemble was a quartet made up of white men playing the original blackface instruments together — the fiddle, banjo, bone castanets, and tambourine. The music they played, whether adapted from oral tradition or newly written, was often deliberately simple in terms of contour and harmonies but might feature lively rhythms meant to evoke those of African-American music. Episodic song texts, often in what was meant to be taken as dialect, generally presented blacks as "darkies" who might be cheerful and simpleminded or who might poke fun at the white "massa" in the role of a court jester of sorts. It is hard to imagine today how a body of music that was openly racist could be the most popular genre going, but there is no denying this was the case. Many white listeners needed to believe they were superior to slaves, or they just wanted to look down on *someone*.

Watching and hearing pretend slaves act silly on stage helped white Americans pursue a sad psychological strategy that was not just national, but international. For awhile, this was the most popular stage entertainment throughout the English-speaking world. Mixed with the bizarre social meanings of the stage show was, of course, music; the second-hand or imitation black music of minstrelsy was more fun as sheer sound than anything else going. We will never know exactly what mixture of motives brought these tunes into the Morgan household in Petersburg, Virginia, and into countless other American homes. Also, as time passed and such songs stayed popular in rural areas in the hearts and minds of people like Alice Morgan Person and her customers, we can't be sure precisely what about them kept them popular.

The decline of "classic" minstrelsy, with its male quartets singing jolly or plaintive dialect songs, was as gradual as the genre's ascension into popularity had been abrupt. Over the course of the 1860s and 1870s, small minstrel troupes performing music that was relatively distinct from other genres of popular music were replaced in urban, fashionable entertainment by "huge companies staging lavish extravaganzas and virtually ignoring blacks,"[2] that is, they were essentially variety shows. Some kind of minstrelsy remained central in stage entertainment for a few more decades by absorbing nearly all competing forms of popular music and spectacle, and in the process it gradually lost its own distinctive identity. But minstrelsy following earlier practice did not disappear entirely. The large troupes that appeared late in the century frequently offered an old-fashioned minstrel act as one of the many ingredients of their shows. Several of these large troupes were advertised in the *Henderson Gold Leaf* as visiting Henderson, North Carolina (just ten miles from the Person home in Kittrell).

These included Garton's New Orleans Minstrels (advertised October 17, 1890; the previous year's concert by this group was described as having been "chaste and at the same time intensely humorous— rollicking without being rude": this year's troupe featured "a real live Japanese"). The October 24 review of this concert mentioned "Frank Sommers in his original specialties, playing banjo and singing and dancing at the same time." Other groups performing in Henderson at about this time included Mizener's Old Time Minstrels, "16 artists and 12 musicians,"[3] and the Hi Henry Minstrel Company, a group of "30 stars."[4] Featuring a "real live Japanese" could not have had any link with the history of minstrelsy as musical sound, but it illustrated the unfortunate fact that the audiences of minstrelsy still needed to have someone distinctly different from themselves to stare at. At the same time, keeping Frank Sommers and his old-time one man band act traveling with a large minstrel troupe demonstrates that those audiences wanted the old-time minstrel sound and feel to persist somewhere in their evenings of entertainment. It is this old vein within the new minstrelsy that Alice would tap in her performances and music sales.

In addition to maintaining a modest niche in the big, contemporary minstrel shows, the old-time minstrel songs and stage patter survived as down-home public entertainment in the context of the medicine show; twentieth-century field recordings of banjoists and fiddlers who had performed in such shows document this clearly.[5] Mid–nineteenth-century tunes and musical style also survived in domestic performances by women like Alice who played the piano. This is not well documented because early twentieth-century folklorists didn't seek out keyboard performers when they could find players of more exotic (to these collectors, more authentic) instruments, just as they usually recorded only what they considered to be the older tunes in players' repertoires and ignored the rest.

The music of minstrelsy was marketed away from the stage (and physically preserved) as sheet music, generally in piano/vocal arrangements. These represented live performances to the same limited extent as do most piano/vocal arrangements of current popular music, that is, reproducing words, melodies, and a general idea of harmonies; mentally reconstructing the sound required applying imagination to what was on paper. Twentieth-century field recordings demonstrate that minstrel tunes had changed in oral tradition during the nineteenth century; but late nineteenth-century reprintings of songs did not illustrate these changes. They instead replicated or simplified original forms when printed in anthologies for budgetary reasons. The older songs in anthologies swelled rather than helped sell those music books, so editors felt comfortable when paying little or no attention to them. Alice Person's collection is as close as we will have to a nineteenth-century field recording. That is why it constitutes such an important body of evidence bridging the gap between blackface minstrelsy of the middle of the nineteenth century and twentieth-century southern folk music.

To understand young Alice Morgan's initial association with this music, we must think back to when she was growing up in a middle-class family in Petersburg, Virginia. When she claimed that she grew up exposed to nothing but "the elegancies and refinements of life," she must have been talking partly about her exposure to fashionable music.[6] Young ladies of her station were trained to be gracious, ornamental and useful wives. This training occurred in so-called female seminaries, finishing schools where the women studied French, crocheting, and other what were then deemed feminine skills. These included music, which for women meant singing and playing the piano or perhaps the guitar (solo instruments such as the violin and flute were reserved for males at that time). This training was meant to prepare nice girls to be good wives who were not just efficient household managers but graceful personalities. If they could master the delicacies of arts and crafts, they would have the charm and refinement to be good hostesses later in life.

When seventeen-year-old Alice married Joseph Arrington Person and moved to his prosperous farm, where they started their family, the seminary-learned skills could easily have waned, pushed aside in the excitement of new tasks and new pleasures. Maybe they were, for a while. But we must keep in mind that, at the end of the Civil War, Alice was left with a disabled husband, a large and constantly growing family to support, and no obviously marketable skills. What parts of her female seminary training could be turned into food for her family's table? Crocheting and French were little needed in the postwar South. Music emerged as a choice due to its flexibility — it wasn't inextricably tied to high (or at least ambitious) social status. Instead, the passage of time conveniently moved the tunes Alice knew from fashion to broad popularity among the common people.

Although patent medicine would end up as her mercantile focus, the musical skills of her long-past debutante days would help too. Alice's piano playing was an important part of cultivating prospective customers. In fact, her demonstrating pianos at state fairs and other expositions throughout the

South came early in her career. She described one performance in some detail in "The Chivalry of Man": "I struck up a waltz and the crowd gathered around. I went off into some gay dance tune, and the crowd rapidly increased. Then I struck up 'Billy in the Low Grounds,' and the crowd began to applaud. Then 'I Bet My Money on the Bob-Tail Nag,' and the crowd became enthusiastic, and would not have me stop."[7] The climax of this performance came with playing "Dixie." In time Alice was allowed to sell her medicine to those attracted to the piano dealers' stands by her playing.

Her various financial endeavors reached a sort of equilibrium after she moved her family and business in the mid 1880s to Kittrell, North Carolina, a small town augmented in season by visitors to nearby medicinal springs. As briefly mentioned in previous chapters, when Alice was at home bottling her medicine she played piano at one of the hotels that catered to visitors from the North.[8] Then when she traveled to sell her medicine, if a piano or organ were present in a prospective customer's home, she would sit down and entertain. Thus, her publishing of the tunes was an attempt to capitalize on something she already did regularly.

Each of Mrs. Person's Popular Airs

It should come as no surprise that Alice, a patent medicine saleswoman, shaped her *Popular Airs* like a meticulously paced live medicine show. She started and ended with obscure pieces, placing the old-fashioned hits in the middle. In such a show, there would have been pauses between tunes for sales pitches. Comments about each piece will replace the mercantile patter in the following paragraphs. These remarks will not be nearly as entertaining as Alice's must have been, but the reader won't have to buy bottles of medicine to keep the story going.

The first piece in the *Popular Airs*, "Italian Waltz," is very rare. Alice's version is possibly the only one ever committed to paper. An older North Carolina fiddler named Lauchlin Shaw has played it and claims to have learned it from a piece of sheet music owned by his mother. This sheet music is long gone and Shaw doesn't remember who it was by, but it must have been Alice's *Popular Airs*. Starting the collection with the refined elegance of the "Italian Waltz" must have been intended to set a proper tone, to assert that Alice was a dignified woman and this was a respectable collection. The following piece is also rare. It is called "Weird Waltz," but it doesn't sound "weird" in any way. To produce that effect, one must imagine it played onstage in the 1840s, with blackface performers parodying a waltz on fiddle, banjo, tambo and bones. It has to have been the history of the tune that was weird, since the musical pitches are not.

The following piece, yet another rare one, is just called "Polka." Why a polka in a medicine show? Indeed, why a polka in the early blackface minstrelsy of Alice's youth? When minstrelsy burst into national popularity in 1843, the abruptness of this leap into fashion and economic success was a surprise and minstrel troupes needed an enlarged musical repertoire to materialize just as suddenly. When the short minstrel acts before 1843 expanded into evenings of entertainment, the performers needed variety. One option was to piggyback on the popularity of other genres. Minstrel composers, in a hurry to assemble repertoire, had to be both efficient and musically omnivorous. They cast many songs in polka rhythms because the polka had just swept America; it would remain our most popular rhythm for dances and songs for decades. Consider some of those Stephen Foster songs that were initially advertised as minstrel songs, and hear in their lyrics the polka rhythm of one accented note followed by two half as long. From "Oh Susanna," there is "I come from Alabama, with my banjo on my knee." In a Foster tune reprinted in the *Popular Airs* we have, "Camptown Races, sing this song, Doo-dah, Doo-dah."

With the next piece in *Popular Arts*, we close out the "rare" section. We are still warming up in Alice's medicine show, still saving the hit tunes until a larger crowd has gathered. What should we make of the title "Carolina Racket?" Perhaps making a "racket" would associate the tune with the exuberance of minstrelsy, and the word "Carolina" made the audience feel like this was their own tune.

Next Alice edges into the good stuff, now that enough hypothetical country folk have gathered 'round her and her piano in this medicine show on paper. "Liza Jane" is the title of several minstrel songs, and it is a title still alive in the mountains. Next comes the first really famous tune in the collection, a plaintive Ethiopian (i.e., African-American) melody by Stephen Foster, "Nelly Bly." The words begin: "Nelly Bly, Nelly Bly, bring de broom along. We'll sweep de kitchen clean, my dear, and hab a little song. Poke de wood, my lady lub, and make de fire burn. And while I take de banjo down, just gib de mush a turn."[9]

Next comes "Shoo Fly,"[10] a blackface tune that was still in school songbooks when the authors of this book were boys. It was first published in 1869, after the Civil War and after Alice had become wife, mother, and breadwinner. Most girls who learned their music in female seminaries as part of becoming cultured enough to be marriageable at the right socio-economic level, stopped accumulating repertoire when they got married, and most stopped playing the piano. But in this, as in many ways, Alice was an original. While most of her tunes are prewar and pre-marriage, enough are from later that we know that piano playing wasn't just a skill she resurrected in time of need; it was an enthusiasm that she maintained faithfully through the decades.

With the next tune, a version of "Boatman Dance," we return to antebellum minstrelsy, in fact ante-popularity minstrelsy, all the way back to George P. Knauff's *Virginia Reels*. Knauff called the tune "Ohio River" in that 1839 publication.[11] A few years later, Dan Emmett, the blackface minstrel of "Dixie" fame, reissued it under his own name as "De Boatman Dance."[12] This soon became a standard festive tune for political campaigns. It remains in oral tradition and has been used in the scores of many Western movies.

Alice's "I Bet My Money" is her version of Stephen Foster's "Camptown Races."[13] It is a blackface tune, an Ethiopian melody of the specific subgenre of "walk-around" (that is, a quick tune suitable for transitions in the minstrel show). It was clearly a tune remembered. It was common in those days to refer to a well-known song by either the words of the verse or the chorus, but this is not the case here. This titling illustrates a general point and a specific point. The general point is that many songs were performed as instrumental pieces often enough that the tune could be remembered with just one complete set of words. And the specific point is that Alice *played* rather than *played and sang* these tunes, or she would have called this one "Camptown Races" or the first words of the chorus, "Gwine to Run All Night." Instead, for her it was "I Bet My Money." The next piece is called "I'm Gwine Down Town." I suppose the dialect word "gwine" associates this tune with minstrelsy, and maybe it is in the *Popular Airs* in this position in the collection because "Camptown Races," which preceded it in the collection, has the word "gwine" starting off the chorus.

Now we are at about two-thirds of the way through the collection — time for a monster hit. It is time for "Dixie." "Dixie" has been a hit since the time Dan Emmett borrowed it from a black family in his Ohio hometown[14] up to the modern day, a hit because it is both cheerful in tune and nostalgic in text. It was incredibly popular not just in its original published form, but in countless arrangements, both for specific instruments (or ensembles) and with new texts. And then we have the other giant hit in this collection, "De Year of Jubilo" (like "Dixie," common as a contrafactum, that is, a new song that is made by fitting new words onto an existing tune), a re-titled form of Henry Clay Work's "Kingdom Coming."[15] This mockery of a hypocritical and cowardly slave owner was nearly as big as "Dixie" back in 1889. "Kingdom Coming" is still in oral tradition today and is found sometimes in print, but no longer on the same grand scale as "Dixie." Consider again the psychological labyrinth of Reconstruction. The rich, who owned slaves, had sent the poor to war. The country folk who loved Alice's character, and her medicine and her music, could never have been fully in tune with the affluent slave owners of what at the time was not so very long in the past. The words of this song include: "Have you seen the massa with the mustache on his face" (that is, in disguise), the man "gwine to leave this place?"

The next tune, "Billy in the Low Grounds," was a rare Scottish fiddle tune earlier called "Johnny in the Nether Mains."[16] (There is another fiddle tune called "Billy in the Low Grounds" that is quite common, but this one is less so.) With this tune, widely known but certainly not a lasting hit, we are starting to tail off in Alice's medicine show. The second-to-the-last tune is called "Oh! Carry Me Back." We are to be carried back to "Old Virginia," but this isn't the later and still famous tune by James Bland that starts with the words "Carry Me Back to Old Virginny."[17] Both were minstrel tunes, and both were nostalgic. This earlier tune was popularized by E.P. Christy of Christy's Minstrels, and perhaps was written by him.[18]

Finally, our replication of a medicine show ends with a walk-around (named exactly that) just as blackface minstrel performances did for decades in the nineteenth century. This particular walk-around isn't a well-known piece — in fact, it is as rare as a couple of the tunes from the beginning of the *Popular Airs*. As in the case of "Billy in the Low Grounds," you might hear echoes of Scotland in this tune. There is a hint of a circular ending here, which is a typical Scottish dance tune device. (In a circular ending, the final cadence isn't on the tonic — the only note that sounds truly final — so that "cadencing" satisfactorily means going back to the beginning of the tune.) But the hypothetical country folk crowding around our hypothetical minstrel performance (by the very real Alice) would not have cared if a tune at this point in the show was obscure. They would have either pushed to the front to buy some of Alice's tonic or they would have crept away, cheapskates who didn't want to cough up the informal (but real) price of the half-hour of stirring and nostalgic music.

When Alice finally decided to publish these pieces, ones she had played for many years, she traveled to Richmond, Virginia, not far from her childhood home of Petersburg, and appealed to her friend George Minor for help. Minor, of the firm of Hume and Minor that would publish her collection, referred her to a man named John Baseler, who transcribed her tunes from her playing in two days, free of charge. Alice may have originally learned some or all of these pieces from sheet music, since she was doubtless at least somewhat musically literate. The fact she didn't transcribe the tunes herself suggests that she was passively musically literate, that is, able to read notes but not write music on her own. Whether Alice learned her repertoire from published sources, by ear, or through a mixture of these methods, differences between her versions of tunes and their original forms make clear that these melodies lived in her memory, in her personal oral tradition, by the time she had them published.

How large a proportion of Alice's repertoire did her publishing represent? In addition to the *Popular Airs*, she put out one shorter collection including "Blue Alsatian Mountains," "Down-Town Girls" (a version of "Buffalo Gals"), and a repeat of "Boatman Dance" at about the same time. That appears to complete her published record! However, tucked away in one of her journals is a piece of stationary embossed with the words "The Manor" (probably a hotel at which she was staying during her travels to sell her remedy). On it, she wrote the names of quite a few tunes, apparently as much of her repertoire as came to mind just then. She then drew lines across many titles, then fit in some numbering, indicating with that last step the tunes she intended (at least at that moment) to anthologize in the *Popular Airs*. Here is her list, starting at the top of the right side of the folded stationary (as it seems she did). The numbers preceding some of the titles are those assigned by Alice. In the interest of legibility, the titles she marked through on her list are underlined here:

> 1 Italian Waltz, 2 I'll bet my money, 3 Dixie, 4 Year of Jubilo, Dixie, Yankee Doodle, 5 Weird Waltz and 6 Polka, 7 Eliza Jane, 8 I'm gwine down town, 9 Walk-around, Rory O'Moore, Campbells are coming, I'm gwine back to Dixie, Lauterbach Waltz, Saratoga Waltz, Darkie's Dream, Shortening Bread, 10 Billy in the lowgrounds, 11 Dance the Boatman Dance, One more River, I'm a jolly good fellow, 12 Oh carry me back, 13 Boatman dance, Hush Miss Lucy, Mississippi Sawyer, Johnny get your hair cut,14 Carolina Racket, Johnny get your hair cut, Zip Coon or Natchez on the Hill, Hop light ladies, Jim crack corn and I don't care, Marching through Georgia, When the leaves begin to turn, Rosa Lee, 15 Shoo Fly, 16 Nelly Bly [and continuing on the left side of the fold], Kentucky Home, Old wooden rocker, Coe's Scottische, Smith's March, Atlantic City Boardwalk, Hold the fort, Evening Star Waltz, Kittrell Waltz, Peek a boo [waltz, I assume], Ehrin on the Boyne, 17 Alsatian Mts, Rainbow Scottische, Susannah, Old Black Joe, Down town gals.

The next steps in her thought process, not evidenced in this doodled list, would likely be to separate "Blue Alsatian Mountains" from the pack for its own mini-anthology (and adding its companion pieces), and then to put the tunes in order for the pair of anthologies (some of the marked tunes would be left out in the final process of selection). There is sufficient overlap between this list and the various citations of tunes that Alice performed to suggest that this list represents nearly all of her repertoire. In addition, an article in the *Henderson Gold Leaf* of November 20, 1880, mentioned that she played "Old Bob Ridley" and "Old Folks at Home." Perhaps these two tunes had dropped out of her repertoire by the time she was planning her publications, perhaps not. Assuming she didn't remember quite everything as she penned that list, her active repertoire might include about sixty pieces, which is roughly the average number of tunes in contemporary old-time fiddlers' repertoires. That seems to be about how many tunes a typical American folk instrumentalist holds in his or her mental and tactile memory.

It would have been nice for posterity if Alice had published more! However, careful analysis of the list she wrote down at The Manor suggests that her published repertoire is a fair sample of the whole. Just as in her collections, there are additional old and new tunes, more tunes with their original titles, tunes with slightly changed titles, and more elegant waltzes resting next to lively walk-arounds. Above all, this list helps show that she had grown up during an amazing time in the history of American music. Her own musical activities and musical taste help us understand that time just a little better. The fact her repertoire joined obscure pieces with hits illustrates how popular music, then as now, encompasses thousands of tunes of varying quality that experience a multitude of fates. Pieces destined to succeed — some even to last through the decades — are rare jewels originally surrounded by plenty of flotsam and jetsam.

The most striking thing about Alice's repertoire is the most obvious — that it was dominated by blackface minstrel tunes. Despite how reprehensible the genre was when it first coalesced, minstrelsy marked several laudable turning points in the history of American music. It was the first genre of truly American popular music, and, as such, it reversed the prevailing cultural flow. Americans had imported tunes and taste from England up to this point; they became exporters from then on. Minstrelsy is the first distinctly American source of "old standards," and the earliest really substantial batch of such songs that Americans remember across the generations. As we remember minstrel tunes today, we don't think of the original racist associations. In fact, we either have preserved ones in which those associations were never prominent (such as "Camptown Races," Alice's "I Bet My Money") or revised them to minimize that factor. Foster's "Oh Susanna," which Alice also played, lost its one explicitly racist verse long ago.[19]

How quickly did the essence of Southerners' affection for walk-arounds tilt away from emphasizing the initial ghastly racist associations to appreciating the sheer sonic fun of the music? Alice loved these tunes, stuck them next to refined waltzes in her performances, and included them in her personal classification of "music for the home circle." If she had been notably racist, we would have known it, given how thoroughly and unreservedly she expressed herself in a rich array of surviving documents. The sounds of music mean what we want them to mean, while words are more explicit and thus also more difficult to reinterpret. But Alice was a pianist, not a singer, so words mattered less to her than pitches. In the end, her enthusiasm for blackface minstrel tunes constitutes remarkable evidence concerning how incredibly quickly meanings of music can be adjusted by an individual, and in turn by a society.

Chapter 8

Popular Airs, Blue Alsatian Mountains, *and Nostalgia*

Alice Person stated in "The Chivalry of Man" that her music was "so different from that of the present day that it touched a responsive chord in the hearts of many a one present" at her performances at expositions; she advertised it as "essentially music for the home circle."[1] These claims deal with Alice's audience. Who still liked this mid–nineteenth-century music late in the century? Why did they like it? Who would be interested in buying copies? These are all questions of taste, concerning especially the endurance of affection.

Which responsive chord did Alice's music activate? Many bodies of song bear one complex of associations when new, then find much of those meanings displaced in later decades by nostalgia. Think of the protest songs of the 1960s, born as rallying standards for a turbulent time. Those that survive into the twenty-first century now seem comforting echoes of an era that we choose to remember as principled and pure at heart, with uncomfortable complexities concerning patriotism and intergenerational conflicts leached of their venom by the passage of the years. Memories of "flower children" now hover in a lovely glow, symbolizing generosity and desire for peace, while the often ugly disdain in which those idealists held their parents' values has dropped out of collective memory. Of course, the nasty social factors that were an indispensable ingredient in the gestation and initial popularity of blackface minstrelsy remained in place in the age of Jim Crow, and those factors must have been part of why some people continued to enjoy early minstrel songs. However, Alice referred specifically and exclusively to the antiquity of her tunes as appealing.

Early minstrel tunes like those Alice played, though long past their days on the leading edge of fashion, remained reasonably well known in 1889. *The Board of Music Trade Complete Catalogue of Sheet Music and Musical Work* of

1870 — a remarkable list of sale items — offered many older pieces to potential customers, including quite a few early minstrel tunes. For instance, no fewer than five editions of "Boatman Dance" are listed in a section of the catalog entitled "Dances, Hornpipes, and One-Page Pieces," a section that was the home for many older pieces.[2] A widely distributed songbook from around the turn of the century, *Minstrel Songs Old and New*, listed among about one hundred pieces several genuinely old songs played in instrumental versions by Alice: "Boatman Dance," "Camptown Races" (also indexed as "Gwine to Run All Night"), "Carry Me Back to Old Virginny" (also indexed as "Floating Scow of Old Virginny"), "Kingdom Coming," "Nelly Bly," "Old Bob Ridley," and "Way Down Upon de Swanee Ribber"— that is, Foster's "Old Folks at Home."[3] The fact this repertoire maintained a niche in later nineteenth-century popular music does not mean it was unusually long-lived in print: many songs from even earlier in the century continued to be marketed. Before Tin Pan Alley transformed popular music processes at the end of the century, turnover of repertoire was no more common than accumulation, and music merchants seem to have had room on their shelves for quite a varied inventory.

Was it odd for these particular older — but not forgotten — pieces to please many people who heard Alice play? The general theme of nostalgia thoroughly permeated nineteenth-century American song and literature and certainly was considered an appealing emotion in the post–Civil War South.[4] Since many early minstrel songs had nostalgia built into their lyrics or melodies, these were natural vehicles for later nineteenth-century nostalgia, an emotion that didn't just hold its own in the late nineteenth and early twentieth centuries but took on new vigor with the passage of time. This then became not just nostalgia for a better past, but nostalgia for memories of the comforting feeling of nostalgia. Songs such as "Old Folks at Home" were originally written to evoke a picture of a rosy past. Other, livelier songs, such as "Nelly Bly" and "Camptown Races," presented jolly, simple-minded blacks, ideal characters to people a severely and willfully edited retrospective of plantation life. However, some of Alice's prospective customers perceived these clearly old-fashioned songs as disreputable rather than comfortably and reassuringly quaint. Her assertion that her music was essentially music for the home circle had been true in her youth, when the pieces were newly composed. Even this may be a little hard to swallow, since capering blackface banjoists and crinoline-clad debutantes would seem not to square after time removed the patina of fashion.

Alice's *Popular Airs* was along the lines of, for instance, one mid–nineteenth-century publication clearly destined for the use of respectable young ladies; *The Cottages Duett, a popular collection of Melodies, arranged* [anonymously] *for two performers on the piano forte* includes, along with such tunes as "Chorus from Norma," "Jenny Lind Polka," "Salut a la F[r]ance," and "Erin Is My Home," several minstrel tunes: "Dandy Jim of Caroline," "Old Dan Tucker," and "Lucy Neal."[5] However, by 1889, many of the same fashion-conscious homes that had welcomed *The Cottages Duett* had come to shun minstrel tunes. Alice encountered this attitude several times. In one instance, a prospective customer stated that she liked the music but would not have it in her house. In another case, she visited a home to which she had been referred by a local piano teacher and got this reaction from an aspiring pianist's mother: "She was aghast with amazement, that 'my daughter's' teacher should have sent that kind of music here for 'my daughter' to play! She plays classic music and standard music, and I cannot think that her teacher should have meant for her to play this kind of music! 'The Boatman Dance!' 'Walk-Around!' No, no, there must be some mistake. 'My daughter' wouldn't play that kind of music. Oh no!"[6]

This mixed reception ought not to surprise. As a measure of prosperity began to return to the South, so did the option of purchasing the latest in clothes, home furnishings, and entertainment. Slowly but surely the South became once again a profitable market for northern music publishers. A modest vogue for southern regional literature, much of it written by women, materialized in the 1880s,[7] but this seems not to have stimulated interest in the other arts as practiced specifically in the South. Old standards like "Dixie" and various songs by Foster met any need for referring to the South in song. These pieces were sporadically republished in anthologies, but their style was not emulated in new compositions. Alice's *Popular Airs*, destined for a persisting but marginal corner of popular taste, did not interest the affluent part of the public who could keep up with fashion and purchase substantial amounts of sheet music. So who bought Alice's music? The poor could not, and the rich would not. Nevertheless, it must have appealed strongly to someone with money to spare, or she would not have issued several editions! Perhaps her best audience consisted of those on the cusp between poverty and affluence, people rurally oriented but with a little money to spare — a real slice of the population, however modest in size.

Was it significant that Alice referred to her collection as a gathering of "popular" airs? What did the word "popular" mean to her? What we now regard as the pop music of the nineteenth century, that is, the sorts of pieces that were issued as sheet music for general consumption, was advertised as being "fashionable," "the latest," or "salon," as often as it was called "popular." At the same time, the word "popular" in the sense of "of the people" was often encountered in descriptions of music in oral tradition, music that today would generally be called folk music. For instance, the article titled

"Popular Ancient English Music" in the 1889 edition of *Grove's Dictionary of Music and Musicians*[8] is an extended reference to Chappell's *Popular Music of the Olden Time*,[9] a collection rich in pieces from oral tradition. Elsewhere in this same dictionary volume, in an article on the music of Scotland, that country's "national music" is described as having been handed down partly through "mere tradition," as "popular music" and "folk music."[10] Perhaps some of the widespread use of these terms as near synonyms was the result of confusion, but the accepted meanings do seem to have overlapped considerably. While Alice may have used the word "popular" to mean generally liked, or belonging to the people, she may well have also meant that many people knew the tunes that she played, that they were in oral tradition.

Why might it be that we have not encountered other collections similar to this one? The precise circumstances inspiring this collection were quite unusual. Alice's *Popular Airs* consists of tunes performed and eventually published in connection with the sale of patent medicines, the main forum in which mid-century blackface minstrel airs continued to be performed as public entertainment, and the only place where this repertoire remained central. Respectable women like Alice, who would have learned to play the piano as debutantes, were rare in the environment; most of the few women music performers in the world of proprietary medicine bore sobriquets like "Princess Iola" and wore peacock feathers and such.

Alice's Arrangement of "The Blue Alsatian Mountains"

In addition to the *Popular Airs*, Alice published a smaller collection, one containing one big piece — her arrangement of the hit waltz song "Blue Alsatian Mountains" — and two one-page tunes, "Down-Town Girls" and "Boatman Dance." Each of the three pieces illustrates some aspect of the broad theme of nostalgia in music, even though "Blue Alsatian Mountains" was far and away the youngest tune she ever published. Two English musicians collaborated to create it. Clara Alington Barnard, working under her usual pen name of Claribel, wrote the lyrics, and Michael Mayrich, under the pen name Stephen Adams, wrote the music early in his distinguished career as a prolific composer of light music. The song was an immediate hit when it came out in 1879. A dozen or more arrangements followed in the next four years in the U.S., several in the customary business pattern in which a publisher in a given city hopped on the bandwagon.[11] Other publishers then recast it for a variety of performance media. It was heard everywhere for those few years, then enthusiasm died down, at least on the part of publishers. Alice's arrangement, though a relatively quick follow-up in the context of *her* choices of pieces to reissue, was tardy within the broad rhythms of the northern-dominated music business; it came out well after the song had lost its mercantile luster.

What about "Blue Alsatian Mountains" allowed it to fit into a repertoire that Alice claimed was "so different from that of the present day that it touched a responsive chord in the hearts of many a one present?"[12] Although it was a young composition, it evoked nostalgia with every word and every note. Each of the three verses begins with the phrase "by the blue Alsatian mountains." Verse one describes a "maiden young and fair" in tender detail, but that description ends with the sad notice that her "song will pass away." Verse two introduces a "stranger" listening to her song, but "such dreams may pass away." The protagonists do not meet in the third verse. Instead, "the years have passed away, but the blue Alsatian mountains seem to watch and wait alway." The lyrics move gently, with wistful inevitability, through this territory of long ago and far away. There is enough repetition and parallelism between verses that the text would have been easy to remember. Also, the music is just as simple and smoothly catchy, with conjunct melodies swaying predictably in waltz time.

Though the genre of the waltz song was just entering the process of becoming the dominant model for popular music for the next few decades, waltz tunes had permeated European and American popular song since the 1820s. This song was a slightly new take on a venerable model — an instant folksy standard. Alice's piano arrangement was, as was typical for her, somewhat simpler than the batch of arrangements of the song that came out from 1879 through 1883. The accompaniment is a bit easier, the key quite accessible (C major), and the harmonies have just a little less chromaticism, thus making for fewer moments in the written music that might confuse the average pianist. Even though this song was not old when she arranged it, her version gives the impression of a venerable song remembered and translated through the vagaries of memory to broad accessibility, to the down-home friendliness of folk music, just like the rest of Alice's repertoire.

Why did Alice append arrangements of two spritely minstrel songs to that of this sweeping, weepy waltz? There are several reasonable explanations, each probably partly accurate. The most straightforward factor concerns the publication as a physical assembly of pieces of paper. Given the length of her "Blue Alsatian Mountains" (four pages) the easiest way to put the piece of sheet music together leaves two blank pages. Imagine two wide rectangular sheets of paper, folded left to right, one sheet within the other. That creates a tidy nested double folio of eight pages: a title page, two openings of two pages each for "The Blue Alsatian Mountains," then an opening of two pages for something else (the back page of the collection was left blank). Putting two short pieces in that last opening could be construed as a simple competitive bonus, raising the value of this arrangement of "The Blue Alsatian Mountains" by having those extras seemingly inserted for free. But why these two pieces? If we compare this little collection with the much more substantial *Popular Airs*, we see that both start with a proper, elegant waltz (two waltzes, in the *Popular Airs*). The composer and initial performer, Alice herself, is establishing respectability before cutting loose, which is then done in a long string of minstrel tunes in the *Popular Airs* but in just two tunes with impeccable minstrel credentials following the "Blue Alsatian Mountains." In short, she was trying for roughly the same aesthetic progression (and moral progression, in a way) in her two published collections.

The last piece, "Boatman Dance," is the only tune found in both of her collections. It must have been a favorite of both Alice and her audiences from innumerable performances at dances, at county fairs, and in political rallies. Alice's arrangement of this piece in this collection is different in a few interesting ways from her *Popular Airs* presentation of this well-known minstrel tune. It is a little easier to play. The flashy introduction from her first version doesn't appear here. Also, by shifting to the key of F major from C major (both are easy keys on the piano), she was able to get the melody off of the high ledger lines and fully onto the staff, so that a beginning pianist (or a veteran whose music reading skills remained rudimentary) would have a less stressful time figuring out where to place their fingers.

However, the most interesting difference is neutral in terms of technical difficulty. In this arrangement, the accompaniment pattern (what the left hand plays) resembles what Alice did for most of her pieces that are in duple time (in two) in both collections. Each beat includes the three members of a chord, with the lower two members played on the beat, then the remaining upper member played off the beat. It was more common then, and remains more usual now, to play a single low note on the beat, then the two other members of the chord off the beat. Alice's reversal of the normal guitaristic "boom-chick," with the "boom" having two notes rather than the "chick," actually has a deep meaning beyond the sound itself, though that deep meaning was a subtle one then and would not ring a bell with modern listeners. The explicitly nostalgic Scottish tune "Auld Lang Syne," a tune endlessly reprinted in America during the nineteenth century, almost always featured that exact accompaniment pattern, and it spilled over into arrangements of lots of Scottish tunes. Nostalgia in English popular music had been associated with Scotland for centuries, and much of that association carried over when English popular music entered the colonies and the United States.

The more striking accompaniment pattern in Alice's second "Boatman

Dance" brings that accompaniment into line with most of her other left hand parts, and gently evokes nostalgia by doing so. Other under-the-radar musical elements do the same thing. She not only employs less chromaticism (i.e., sharps and flats), she uses fewer different chords per song than in her published models, even when it seems like those models have few chords to start with. She could not reduce harmony below the absolute minimum. That is, she could not avoid the two most basic chords, the tonic and the dominant, but she does cut back on employment of the third most common chord, the subdominant. This evokes memories of older five-string banjo playing, which doesn't easily or customarily include a variety of full chords. You naturally hear plenty of the tonic in banjo tunes, and the short string offers a drone on the dominant, but the subdominant tends to be deemphasized. Indeed, the simple variation techniques Alice offers in some of her arrangements place just enough rhythmic emphasis off the beat to unobtrusively remind the listener of the syncopation characteristic of old-time minstrel banjo performance.

We can clarify what all these factors add up to by considering the middle piece in this tiny collection, the one Alice called "Down-Town Girls." It is a nice, easy arrangement of the tune best known today as "Buffalo Gals." All of the stylistic factors mentioned in the previous paragraph are there: just two chords, the "Scottish" accompaniment figure, the slight banjo-like variation. Also, it is old. Just like "Boatman Dance" and another tune from the *Popular Airs*, "Billy in the Low Grounds," this tune first came out in the U.S. in 1839 in George P. Knauff's *Virginia Reels*. Although Cool White (pen and stage name of John Hodges) generally gets credit for the first "Buffalo Gals" in his "Lubly Fan" of 1844, the first published form of the tune is Knauff's "Midnight Serenade" in the *Virginia Reels*. The association with Knauff matters for two reasons. One is that he was the music instructor at a female seminary in Farmville, Virginia (located just about 30 miles from Petersburg) when Alice probably was studying piano through a seminary in Petersburg. She said that her collections were old Virginia and North Carolina melodies and we see that we can accept that claim quite literally. Even more important, Knauff was not composing in this collection, but rather arranging tunes from oral tradition.[13] While the tunes were all published in 1839, each originated at a different time prior to that. Thus, just as "Blue Alsatian Mountains" was Alice's youngest tune, its companion pieces, "Down-Town Girls" and "Boatman Dance, were among her oldest. Since the young "Blue Alsatian Mountains" was designed to seem old in every way, this little collection matches Alice's *Popular Airs* not just in the careful balancing of the impeccably proper with the rambunctiously informal, but in the constant evocation of nostalgia.

An Opportunity Missed

An article from the *Knoxville Sentinal* described Alice's playing style: "Her style of performance is extremely novel, her touch being remarkably vigorous and exact, heavy yet sympathetic; her repertoire is composed almost exclusively of old ante-wartime melodies and songs."[14] This brings us to a tantalizing missed opportunity: we might actually have heard Alice play if history had followed a slightly different path:

> FOR VICTOR COMPANY: Mrs. Joe Person Plays for Big Talking Machine Corporation. Mrs. Joe Person, known personally all over the State, and by reputation over a greater part of the entire country, has added another laurel to her already notable collection by making several records for the Victor Talking Machine Company at the factory in Camden, N.J. Mrs. Person was in Pennsylvania on a visit to a son, and while there completed arrangements with the factory to make a number of records of the old time Southern songs, such as "Dixie," "Sewanee [sic] River," and others of her repertoire.
>
> Mrs. Person is one of the most accomplished pianists in the country and although she has passed the three score and ten, she is as bright and active as a woman many years her junior.
>
> When the coming issues of the Victor catalogue are issued, Mrs. Person's picture will rank with the most famous artists that are employed by this company to make records. It is a difficult proposition for any company to get a clear and satisfactory record of a piano [referring here to the vicissitudes of acoustic recording], and it was some time before Mrs. Person knew whether or not her records had been taken clearly or not. When the disks were finished, it was found that they were among the best and clearest piano records that had been made.[15]

The tunes recorded were a nice cross section of her repertoire as detailed in chapter seven of this book. If the sessions went so well, why weren't these recordings released? Perhaps it was a matter of timing. Had the recording session taken place just one decade later, it would have fit into a new context, a more favorable climate for traditional music: these tunes might have been heard as members of a brand new commercially successful genre of recordings of old music, "hillbilly" recordings.

Many families in the South were in financial trouble after the Civil War and were forced to make what must have felt like shocking adjustments. But however commonplace the Person family's plight, Alice's solution seems to have been unusual. She transformed her finishing school graces of polite conversation and ornamental piano playing into hard-driving sales talk coupled with tireless functional keyboard performance. She played old-fashioned music because that was what she knew, and because her minstrel tunes pleased the country folk who were her customers. She played these tunes on the piano because that was what she could play. It was not the most practical choice: many places where she stopped to sell her remedy would not have had a keyboard on hand. Alice may indeed have been the only, or at least one of very few, solo patent medicine acts that featured piano playing, which would help explain why her collections seem to be unique. But one would suspect that many other women of her vintage were playing this and similar music on keyboard instruments too, some from print, and some not — but not as a business. Alice's *Popular Airs*, an unusual collection published under unusual circumstances, may represent a widespread tradition of domestic performances in oral tradition of early blackface minstrel music. Alice's determination and creativity when faced with the need to piece together an income inspired both a surprisingly successful patent medicine business and a pair of remarkable publications of music. Her collections are a no-longer-missing link, filling gaps in our knowledge of the interaction of oral and written traditions in nineteenth-century America and illustrating some of the nuances of late nineteenth-century Southern nostalgia.

Appendix: Timeline of Alice Morgan Person and Her Company

1804 (September 4): Father, Samuel Wilson Morgan, born in Nottoway County, Virginia.[1]

1814 (January 23): Husband-to-be, Joseph Arrington Person, born in Franklin County, North Carolina.[2]

1818 (February 9): Mother, Esther Jane Robinson, born in Greensville County, Virginia.[3]

1832 (March 13): Father marries first wife, Elizabeth Dorothy Rivers, in Shelby, TN.[4]

1833 (August 9): Father's first wife dies in Nottaway County, Virginia.

1834 (July 24): Parents married in Greensville County, Virginia.[5]

183?: Older brother, Joseph, born.[6]

1840 (June 4): Older brother dies.

1840 (July 28): Alice Morgan born in Greensville County, Virginia.

1847 (April 1): Husband-to-be inherits 466 acres and a country home from his father Presley Carter Person.[7]

1848 (July 21): Father purchases a home on the corner of Walnut and Marshall streets in Petersburg.[8]

1852 (January 2): Father becomes indebted to the Exchange Bank for ten thousand dollars and mortgages his Walnut Street home and life insurance policy to cover the debt.

1852 (January 5): Mother formally relinquishes her dower (i.e., the Walnut Street home).[9]

1852 (April 3): Father's home sold by the mortgagee; family relocates to Old Street in Petersburg.

1854 (November 1): Father enters the ice business and forms a three-year partnership with two men from Rockport, ME.

1856 (July 18): Father mortgages the family's household and kitchen furniture to pay additional debts.

1856: Meets husband-to-be at the North Carolina wedding of a maternal relative to Presley Carter Person, Jr., brother of her husband-to-be.[10]

1857 (December 17): Marries in Grace Church in Petersburg and relocates to Franklin County, North Carolina.

1859 (August 31): First child, Alice Gibson, born.[11]

1861 (April 9): Second child, Esther Morgan, born.[12]

1861 (April 12): Civil War begins; parents and siblings relocate to Warrenton, North Carolina.[13]

1862 (August 24): Third child, Wiley Mangum, born.[14]

1863: Husband volunteers for Civil War service, but is honorably discharged due to an injury sustained earlier in life.

1863: Confirmed a member of the Episcopal Church.

1863 (October 1): Father dies.

1864 (4): Stroke leaves husband permanently paralyzed.[15]

1864 (November 10): Fourth child, Josephine Arrington, born.[16]

1865 (April 9): Civil War ends.

1866 (November 16): Fifth child, Robert Lee, born.[17]

1871 (February 24): Sixth child, Rufus Morgan, born.[18]

1872: Daughter Josephine very ill and near death; neighbor offers the remedy, and Josephine is cured.

1872 (August 1): Sells a tract of land to William Montgomery.[19]

1872 (October): First uses the remedy on something other than Scrofula (husband's facial sore) and finds it to be effective.

1872–1878: Trials the remedy by sharing it with friends and neighbors.

1873 (October 3): Seventh child, Henry Harris, born.[20]

1874 (December): Josephine very ill and near death for the second time, but survives once again.

1875: Mother moves to Hickory where sister, Lucy, lives.[21]

1875 (February 19): Mother very ill.

1875 (November 3): Eighth child, Levin King, born.[22]

1876 (March 4): Mother dies in Hickory, North Carolina.

1878 (January 22): Files application to register the remedy trademark with the U.S. Patent and Trademark Office; registration becomes effective August 20, 1878.

1878 (April 22): Ninth child, William Montgomery, born.[23]

1879 (January): Brother Rufus relocates to California.[24]

1879 (August 11): Rufus' wife, Mary, and their two children, Bayard and Samuel, reside with the Persons while Rufus is in California.[25]

1879 (October): Poor harvest results in poor remedy sales.

1879: Alice enlists the aid of her children in preparing the remedy.

1880 (April 5): Brother Rufus dies after eating poisonous mushrooms.[26]

1882 (January 11): Daughter Gibson marries William Harris.[27]
1882 (February): Travels to Raleigh to market the remedy to the medical community, but is unsuccessful.
1882 (fall): Travels to Charlotte to market the remedy, and does so with some success.
1883 (January 29): Sells another tract of land to William Montgomery.[28]
1883 (February 23): Mortgages farm to Wyatt McGhee.
1883 (May): Enters into a preliminary agreement with Salisbury, North Carolina, businessman George Davidson for the sale of the remedy trademark and rights for twenty thousand dollars and a royalty on each bottle; Davidson defaults the following August.
1883 (October 4): Mortgages farm to Wyatt McGhee for the second time.
1884 (January 24): Registers herself as a free trader.
1884 (January 25): Enters into a five-year partnership with Charlotte businessman, Charles R. Jones.
1884 (March 5): Daughter Esther marries William Blacknall.[29]
1884 (April 8): Husband dies.
1884 (November): Mortgage due date comes and goes; McGhee grants an extension.
1884 (December 9): Dissolves partnership with Charles Jones after discovering he had been embezzling.
1885 (April): Enters into a partnership with Tarboro, North Carolina, businessman E.B. Hodges.
1885 (November 24): Farm sold at public auction to Franklin County businessman E.B. Clegg.
1885 (December 10): Clegg, unable to make the down payment, sells the farm to Wyatt McGhee.
1886 (April): Dissolves partnership with E.B. Hodges and settles in Kittrell, North Carolina.
1887: Son Rufus joins Alice in the remedy business.[30]
1887 (March 17): Son Levin dies.
1888 (April 13): Daughter Esther dies.[31]
1889: Copyrights and publishes *Popular Airs* collection; publishes *Blue Alsatian Mountains* collection.
1889 (July-September): Wages copyright battle with Boston music publisher Oliver Ditson.
1889 (September-October): Continues her trademark battle with George Davidson.
1895 (November 28): Son Robert marries Mollie Kent in Macon, Georgia.[32]
1897 (March): Son Wiley marries his first cousin, Prudence Person, in Louisburg, North Carolina.[33]

1897: Completes the first part of *The Chivalry of Man*.[34]
1898 (December 3): Kittrell laboratory burns to the ground.
1903: Completes the second part of *The Chivalry of Man*.[35]
1904: Sells eight thousand packages of the remedy.
1904 (March): Relocates to Charlotte, along with Rufus and his family.
1904 (June 22): Son Henry dies.[36]
1906 (January 6): Son Robert dies.[37]
1907: Sells fifteen thousand packages of the remedy.
1907 (January 16): Son William marries Mary Haywood.[38]
1908 (June–October): Travels with sister Lucy to the western U.S. to visit the grave of their brother, Rufus.
1910 (March 25): Sells remedy formula and trademark to son Rufus.
1910 (March 30): Remedy company incorporated under the name Mrs. Joe Person's Remedy Company.
1910 (May 25): Rufus subleases the remedy formula and trademark to Guy Barnes.
1911 (June–August): Takes a second trip to the western U.S. with Lucy.
1912 (October): Records folk tune arrangements for the Victor Talking Machine Company in Camden, N.J.
1913 (June 10): Sets out on third trip to the western U.S with Lucy.
1913 (June 12): Dies of a stroke in Santa Fe, N.M.
1913 (June 17): Buried in Charlottte's Elmwood Cemetery.
1916 (February): Guy Barnes dies.[39]
1916 (April 6): Remedy company reincorporated under the name Person Remedy Company.
1916 (April 24): Rufus begins to work for the reincorporated remedy company.[40]
1917 (August): Rufus announces he is sole owner and proprietor of Person Remedy Company.
1939–1941: Rufus makes numerous unsuccessful attempts to sell the remedy company.
1943: Person Remedy Company closes during World War II.
1947 (January 17): State of North Carolina suspends the Person Remedy Company's certificate of incorporation for failure to pay taxes.

Chapter Notes

Introduction

1. Chris Goertzen, "Mrs. Joe Person's *Popular Airs*." The second publication is Pearce, "The Persistence of Mrs. Joe Person."
2. "Spring Blossoms," *Eastern Reflector*, March 21, 1898.
3. See page 7 of the present work.
4. See page 58 of the present work.

BOOK II: A Life Out of the Ordinary

Chapter 1

1. Alice Person family Bible, private collection of Harmon Person.
2. Journal of Alice Morgan Person, (1902–1906), hereafter referred to as "Journal," 189, Person Collection (#1116).
3. Alice Morgan Person, letter to Lucy Morgan Beard, 19 February 1875, private collection of Mary Barden.
4. Claiborne, *Seventy-Five Years in Old Virginia* (New York: Neale, 1904), 66.
5. Deed, Morgan to Hurt, 2 January 1852, Petersburg, VA, deed book 19, pp. 139–40.
6. Deed, Morgan to Ragland, 3 April 1852, Petersburg, VA, deed book 19, p. 284.
7. Deed of trust, Morgan to Lyon, 18 July 1856, Petersburg, VA, deed book 23, p. 54.
8. Contract, Morgan with Carlton and Gould, 26 July 1855, Petersburg, VA, deed book 22, pp. 210–211.
9. Deed of trust, Morgan to Lyon, 18 July 1856.
10. Claiborne, *Seventy-Five Years in Old Virginia*, 59.
11. Person to Morgan, 22 October 1879, private collection of Mary Barden.
12. Stephen E. Massengill and Robert M. Topkins, eds., "Letters Written from San Diego County, 1879–1880: By Rufus Morgan, North Carolina Apiarist and Photographer," *Journal of San Diego History* 40, no. 4 (1994): 144.
13. See page 11 of the present work.
14. Claiborne, *Seventy-Five Years in Old Virginia*, 97.
15. Journal (1902–1906), p. 187, Person Collection (#1116).
16. Suzanne Lebsock, *The Free Women of Petersburg: Status and Culture in a Southern Town, 1784–1860* (New York: Norton, 1984), 172–75.
17. U.S. Bureau of the Census, *Inhabitants in City of Petersburg in the County of Dinwiddie, State of Virginia* (Washington, DC), 1850.
18. Lebsock, *Free Women of Petersburg*, 175.
19. Ibid.
20. Claiborne, *Seventy-Five Years in Old Virginia*, 70–90.
21. "Mrs. Joe Person Talks," *Charlotte Daily Observer*, July 21, 1907.
22. Grace Church Parish Register (now Christ and Grace Episcopal Church), Bristol Parish, Petersburg, VA, 139.
23. Journal (1901–1904), p. 29, Person Collection (#1116).
24. Alice Morgan Person, letter to Thomas Arrington Person, 29 April 1864, Person Family Papers.
25. Mary E. Montgomery, letter to Abiah Whitehead Culpepper Person, 9 May 1864, Person Family Papers.
26. Alice Morgan Person, letter to Mary Temperance Person, 8 August 1865, Person Family Papers.
27. Person to Beard, 19 February 1875, private collection of Mary Barden.

28. Journal (1902–1906), p. 189, Person Collection (#1116).
29. Alice's niece, Mary Bayard Morgan, later married Charles Wootten and established herself as a renowned photographer and artist under the name Bayard Wootten. At the age of twenty-seven she developed the first Pepsi-Cola trademark for the New Bern, North Carolina, pharmacist who invented the drink (*Dictionary of North Carolina Biography*, s.v., "Wootten, Mary Bayard Morgan").
30. Person Morgan, 22 October 1879, private collection of Mary Barden.
31. This undated letter, found in the pages of Alice's 1911 journal, appears to be a draft and may never have been sent. It does, however, provide an excellent example of the extent of Alice's moral convictions.
32. Person to Morgan, [1911?], Person Collection (#1116).
33. Alice Person, will dated April 30, 1912, proved June 27, 1913, Record of Wills, 1907–1915, vol. Q, p. 376, Mecklenburg County, NC.
34. Journal (1902–1906), p. 73, Person Collection (#1116).
35. Person to Morgan, 29 December 1874, private collection of Mary Barden.
36. Ibid., 15 November 1878, private collection of Mary Barden.
37. Ibid., 22 October 1879, private collection of Mary Barden.
38. Massengill and Topkins, eds., "Letters Written from San Diego County," 144.
39. To supplement his bee-keeping income, Rufus created and sold mottos ornamented with dried wild ferns, which he gathered in the country surrounding his farm (Massengill and Topkins, eds., "Letters Written from San Diego County," 168–171).
40. Person to Morgan, 22 May 1880, private collection of Mary Barden.
41. "Found Brother's Far-West Grave," *Charlotte Evening News*, August 11, 1908.
42. Journal (1906–1908), pp. 96–100, Person Collection (#1116).
43. Journal (1909–1912), pp. 81–83, Person Collection (#1116).
44. "Mrs. Joe Person Laid to Rest Today," *Charlotte News*, June 17, 1913.
45. Diary of Lucy Morgan Beard, pp. 1–4, Person Papers (#3987).
46. Ibid., p. 5, Person Papers (#3987).

Chapter 2

1. "Mrs. Joe Person Dies in New Mexico of Apoplexy," *Charlotte News*, June 13, 1913.
2. Joseph E. Elmore, *The Person Place: Sketches of Its Owners* (Louisburg, NC: Person Place Preservation Society, 1981), 15.
3. Grace Church Parish Register (now Christ and Grace Episcopal Church), Bristol Parish, Petersburg, VA, 139. This register contains information regarding the professions of registrants and also whether they were widowed or single. Joseph's entry indicates he was single.
4. Ibid.
5. Picnic invitation, Person Papers (#3987).
6. "McGhee-Person House," *Louisburg (NC) Franklin Times*, October 11, 1984.
7. See page 12 of the present work.
8. See page 11 of the present work.
9. Alice Person, letter to Thomas Arrington Person, 29 April 1864, Person Family Papers.
10. Massengill and Topkins, eds., "Letters Written from San Diego County," 144.
11. Person to Morgan, 15 November 1878, private collection of Mary Barden.
12. Person to Morgan, 22 March 1880, private collection of Mary Barden.
13. See page 12 of the present work.
14. See page 14 of the present work.
15. See page 15 of the present work.
16. Contract, Alice Person with Joseph Person, 23 January 1884, Franklin County, NC, deed book 63, p. 54.
17. North Carolina General Assembly, Public Laws, 1871–72 session, pp. 334–36.
18. Contract, Alice Person with Charles R. Jones, 9 December 1884, Mecklenburg County, NC, deed book 44, p. 77.
19. See pages 22–28 of the present work. Salisbury, NC, businessman George Davidson was the first. In May of 1883 Davidson made plans to purchase the Remedy from Alice, but he later withdrew his offer.
20. Deed, Joseph and Alice Person to Wyatt L. McGhee, 24 February 1883, Franklin County, NC, deed book 62, pp. 145–46.
21. See page 30 of the present work.
22. University of North Carolina commencement invitation, June 1884, Person Family Papers.
23. *Dictionary of North Carolina Biography*, s.v., "Clarke, Mary Bayard Devereux."
24. Clarke to Person, 15 May 1884, Person Family Papers.
25. Contract, Alice Person with Charles R. Jones, 9 December 1884, Mecklenburg County, NC, deed book 44, p. 77–78; and see page 000 of the present work.
26. See pages 47–54 of the present work.
27. Deed, Joseph and Alice Person to Wyatt L. McGhee, 4 October 1883, Franklin County, NC, deed book 63, pp. 205–6.
28. J.H. Conyers to Wyatt L. McGhee, statement, 13 August 1895, private collection of Wyatt L. McGhee III.

29. E. Ragsdale to Wyatt L. McGhee, statement, 24 August 1895, private collection of Wyatt L. McGhee III.
30. L.T. McGhee to Wyatt L. McGhee, statement, 5 August 1895, private collection of Wyatt L. McGhee III; and Deed, E.B. Clegg to Wyatt L. McGhee, 10 December 1885, Franklin County, NC, deed book 71, pp. 144–145. In "Chivalry of Man," Alice states her home was sold "in the fall of '84," but public records indicate it was the next year. This was probably an instance in which Alice's memory failed her; approximately thirteen years passed from the time she sold her home until she completed "Chivalry of Man" (see page 53 of the present work).
31. "McGhee-Person House," *Louisburg (NC) Franklin Times*, October 11, 1984.
32. Person to Montgomery, 25 January 1887, Person Family Papers.
33. Rufus Person to Peabody Drug Co., 31 March 1939, Person Collection (#1116).
34. Journal (1902–1906), p. 189, Person Collection (#1116).
35. Ibid.
36. Journal (1901–1904), p. 83, Person Collection (#1116).
37. Journal (1902–1906), p. 92, Person Collection (#1116).
38. Person to Montgomery, 3 January 1889, Person Family Papers.
39. Person to Montgomery, 28 January 1889.
40. Person to Montgomery, 27 September 1889.
41. Alice's youngest daughter, Josie, also did not marry, but all indications point to the fact that, unlike Henry, she was not mentally and emotionally capable of doing so.
42. Alice Person, letter to Henry Person, 13 August 1897, Person Family Papers.
43. A. Person, letter to H. Person, 13 September 1897, Person Family Papers.
44. Alice Person, letter to William Person, undated letter copied into journal (1901–1904), p. 29, Person Collection (#1116).
45. William Person, letter to Alice Person, 30 November 1908, Person Collection (#1116).
46. Diary of Jessie Person (wife of Rufus Morgan Person), 21 March 1904, private collection of Michael Boyce.
47. Mary Morgan, letter to Rufus Morgan, 6 October 1879, private collection of Mary Barden.
48. M. Morgan to R. Morgan, 10 November 1879, private collection of Mary Barden.
49. Alice Person, letter to Wiley Person, 17 April 1890, Person Family Papers.
50. "McGhee-Person House," *Louisburg (NC) Franklin Times*, October 11, 1984.
51. Alice Person to Wiley Person, undated draft letter, Person Collection (#1116).

52. Alice Person, will dated April 30, 1912, proved June 27, 1913, Record of Wills, 1907–1915, vol. Q, p. 376, Mecklenburg County, NC.
53. Journals (1901–1914), Person Collection (#1116). Alice's journals indicate regular payment of board to Rufus or his wife, Jessie, when she was in Kittrell (1901–1904) and Charlotte (1904–1911).
54. Alice Person, letter to Rufus Person, 8 March 1911, Person Collection (#1116).
55. Cousin of Wiley Person, letter to Wiley Person, 2 May 1884, Person Family Papers.
56. Person to Harris, 7 November 1912, letter copied into journal (1909–1912), p. 170, Person Collection (#1116).
57. Josie Person, letters to Mary Temperance Person Montgomery, 24 February 1892 and 13 August 1894, Person Family Papers.
58. Cousin of Wiley Person, letter to Wiley Person, 2 May 1884, Person Family Papers; Alice Person, letter to William Montogomery, 27 September 1889, Person Family Papers; Josie Person, letters to Mary Temperance Person Montgomery, 24 February 1892 and 13 August 1894, Person Family Papers; Alice Person to Josie Person, 18 February 1901, private collection of Michael Boyce; and Wiley Person, letter to Alice Person, 6 January 1913, Person Collection (#1116).
59. Journal (1907–1910), p. 91, Person Collection (#1116).
60. Alice Person, will dated April 30, 1912, proved June 27, 1913, Record of Wills, 1907–1915, vol. Q, p. 376, Mecklenburg County, NC.
61. Mary Morgan, letter to Rufus Morgan, 21 September 1879, private collection of Mary Barden.
62. See page 12 of the present work.
63. Person to Morgan, 29 December 1874, private collection of Mary Barden.
64. Mrs. Joe Person Remedy Co., *Mrs. Joe Person's Remedy: Is a Specific for All Blood Diseases* (Charlotte: [1884?]), 31.

Chapter 3

1. "A Woman's Enterprise," *Durham (NC) Globe*, n.d., included in Album (1884–1902), p. 12, Person Papers (#3987).
2. Mrs. Joe Person Remedy Co., *Mrs. Joe Person's Remedy: A Specific for All Blood Diseases* (Charlotte: [1884?]), 39.
3. Mrs. Joe Person Remedy Co., *Mrs. Joe Person's Remedy: Is a Specific*, 31–32.
4. Ibid., forematter.
5. "A Woman's Enterprise," *Durham (NC) Globe*, n.d., included in Album (1884–1902), p. 12, Person Papers (#3987).
6. Alice Person, 1878, trademark for a me-

dicinal preparation, U.S. Trademark 6,495, filed January 22, 1878, and registered August 20, 1878.

7. "Two Parts Man Is Mrs. Person," *Raleigh Daily News and Observer*, June 25, 1905.

8. Mrs. Joe Person's Old Time Medicine bottle, ca. 1940, private collection of Libby and Wyatt McGhee III.

9. Person to Morgan, 15 November 1878, private collection of Mary Barden.

10. Mrs. Joe Person Remedy Co., *Mrs. Joe Person's Remedy: A Specific*, 40.

11. Ibid.

12. Ibid.

13. Ibid., 41.

14. Ibid., 40.

15. Mrs. Joe Person's Remedy Co., untitled circular, [1914?], private collection of Steve Massengill.

16. See page 49 of the present work.

17. Mary Morgan to Rufus Morgan, 10 November 1879, private collection of Mary Barden.

18. Person to Morgan, 22 October 1879, private collection of Mary Barden.

19. Samuel Thomas Peace, *"Zeb's Black Baby": Vance County, North Carolina, a Short History* (Durham: Seeman, 1955), 357–59.

20. Ibid., 358.

21. See page 55 of the present work.

22. Deed, Robinson Cator to Rufus Person, 17 June 1896, Vance County, NC, deed book 11, p. 85.

23. "Fire at Kittrell," *Henderson (NC) Goldleaf*, Dec. 8, 1898.

24. Southeast Bottle Club, Jan/Feb 2004 Newsletter, Mrs. Joe Person's Remedy trade card, http://www.antiquebottles.com/southeast/raleigh/2004/Jan/MrsJoe2.jpg.

25. See page 57 of the present work.

26. Deed, Samuel Morgan to S.J. Hurt, 2 January 1852, Petersburg, VA, deed book 19, pp. 139–40.

27. See page 55 of the present work.

28. See page 55 of the present work.

29. Concordia Historical Institute, Lutheran Church Missouri Synod, "Today in History," http://chi.lcms.org/history/tih1207.htm.

30. See page 58 of the present work.

31. Alice Person to Wiley Person, 29 September 1889, Person Family Papers.

32. Mrs. Joe Person, *Popular Airs*, cover.

33. Folded stationary sheet, Person Collection (#1116). This piece of stationary—found in one of Alice's journals—is headed by the words "The Manor" and is perhaps from one of the establishments at which Alice boarded while on one of her remedy selling trips. It contains a list—in Alice's hand—of the titles of fifty songs, among them those contained in her published music collections. Two of the songs, "Dixie" and "Johnny Get Your Hair Cut" are repeated. While these repetitions could be distinct pieces with the same titles, or an error on Alice's part, they are most likely the result of Alice's attempt to creatively group appropriate pieces.

34. Later editions and printings indicate Alice's location as Charlotte rather than Kittrell.

35. Alice Person, letter to William Montgomery, 27 September 1889, Person Family Papers.

36. The fifteen pieces were assigned copyright registration numbers 9952 to 9966.

37. See page 19 of the present work.

38. Alice Person, letter to Wiley Person, 29 September 1889, Person Family Papers.

39. Ditson Co. to Person, 9 July 1889, Person Family Papers.

40. Ibid., 13 September 1889, Person Family Papers.

41. Alice Person, letter to Wiley Person, 29 September 1889, Person Family Papers.

42. A. Person to W. Person, 4 October 1889, Person Family Papers.

43. Alice Person, letter to William Montgomery, 27 September 1889, Person Family Papers.

44. See page 22 of the present work.

45. Alice Person, letter to Wiley Person, 4 October 1889, Person Family Papers.

46. A. Person to W. Person, 29 September 1889, Person Family Papers.

47. A. Person to W. Person, 4 October 1889, Person Family Papers.

48. See page 28 of the present work.

49. "Fire at Kittrell," *Henderson (NC) Goldleaf*, December 8, 1898.

50. "Mrs. Joe Person's Misfortune," *Durham Recorder*, December 22, 1898.

51. Deed, A.S. Woodlief to Rufus Person, 14 December 1898, Vance County, NC, deed book 11, p. 364; Deed, Charles Williams to Alice Person, 23 October 1899, Vance County, NC, deed book 11, p. 451; Deed, J.M. Woodlief to Alice Person, 16 November 1903, deed book 15, p. 486; and Deed, Rufus Person to Alice Person, 19 November 1903, deed book 15, p. 484.

52. Diary of Jessie Person (wife of Rufus Morgan Person), 21 March 1904, private collection of Michael Boyce.

53. Ibid.

54. Journal (1901–1904), p. 80, Person Collection (#1116).

55. Seaboard Air Line Railway brochure, Person Collection (#1116).

56. Deed, Rufus Person to E.L. Keesler, 1 January 1904, Mecklenburg County, NC, deed book 181, p. 313.

57. Deed, Rufus Person to Alice Person, 23 November 1904, Mecklenburg County, NC, deed book 192, pp. 612–13.
58. "Two Parts Man Is Mrs. Person," *Raleigh Daily News and Observer*, June 25, 1905.
59. Ibid.
60. Journals (1901–1914), Person Collection (#1116).
61. "Two Parts Man is Mrs. Person," *Raleigh Daily News and Observer*, June 25, 1905.
62. Agreement, Guy Barnes and Mrs. Joe Person's Remedy Company, 25 May 1910, Vance County, NC, deed book 55, pp. 193–99.
63. Person to Morgan, 15 November 1878, private collection of Mary Barden.
64. Southeast Bottle Club, Jan/Feb 2004 Newsletter, Mrs. Joe Person's Remedy trade card, http://www.antiquebottles.com/southeast/raleigh/2004/Jan/MrsJoe2.jpg.
65. Mrs. Joe Person Remedy Co., *Mrs. Joe Person's Remedy: Has Established Itself as the Finest Blood Purifier on the Market* (Charlotte: [1901?]), 14.
66. Ibid., 27
67. Kelly to Person, n.d., Person Collection (#1116).
68. Griffithe to Person, 9 July 1900, Person Collection (#1116).
69. John to Person, 24 March 1903, Person Collection (#1116).
70. Powell to Person, 30 May 1900, Person Collection (#1116).
71. Mrs. Joe Person Remedy Co., *Mrs. Joe Person's Remedy: A Specific*, 19–20.
72. Ibid., 20.
73. Ibid.
74. Ibid.
75. Ibid., 21.
76. "Democratic Rule for Good Government," advertisement, *Greenville (NC) Daily Reflector*, May 17, 1898.
77. "It Takes Pure Blood for Good Health," clipped newspaper advertisement, Person Collection (#1116).
78. "Miss M'Craw Wins," *Raleigh News and Observer*, n.d., included in Album (1884–1902), p. 7, Person Papers (#3987).
79. Journals (1901–1914), Person Collection (#1116).
80. Contract, Alice Person and Rufus Person, 25 March 1910, Mecklenburg County, NC, deed book 263, p. 362.
81. "Three Charters Yesterday," unidentified newspaper article, included in Person Collection (#1116).
82. Diary of Jessie Person (wife of Rufus Morgan Person), private collection of Michael Boyce.
83. Agreement, Guy Barnes and Mrs. Joe Person's Remedy Company, 25 May 1910, Vance County, NC, deed book 55, pp. 193–99.
84. Journal (1909–1912), Person Collection (#1116).
85. Person Remedy Co. billing statements, Person Collection (#1116).
86. Alice Person, letter to Rufus Person, 8 March 1911, Person Collection (#1116).
87. Journal (1911–1914), pp. 68–69, Person Collection (#1116).
88. "Mrs. Joe Person Dies in New Mexico of Apoplexy," *Charlotte News*, June 13, 1913.
89. Sam Brylawski, ed., "Encyclopedic Discography of Victor Recordings" (forthcoming), e-mail message to author, June 6, 2005.
90. "Mrs. Person, Medicine Maker, Recalled Here," *Halifax (VA) Record-Advertiser*, March 30, 1972.
91. Sam Brylawski, ed., "Encyclopedic Discography of Victor Recordings" (forthcoming), e-mail message to author, June 6, 2005.
92. North Carolina, Department of the Secretary of State, Corporations Division, Certificate of Incorporation of Person Remedy Company, filed April 6, 1916.
93. "Mrs. Joe Person's Remedy," one-page advertisement circular, North Carolina Collection, Wilson Library, University of North Carolina at Chapel Hill.
94. Minutes of the Person Remedy Company, 10 April 1917, Person Collection (#1116).
95. Alice Person, 1909, trademark for remedies for certain diseases, U.S. Trademark 72,472, filed Feb. 6, 1908, and registered Jan. 26, 1909.
96. Rufus Person, letter to H.C. Starling, 3 December 1941, Person Collection (#1116).
97. Rufus Person, letter to J.G. Fulmer, 26 April 1941, Person Collection (#1116).
98. Bessie C. Boyer, letter to Rufus Person, 26 April 1941; L.N. Patrick, letter to Rufus Person, 21 April 1941; H.C. Starling, letter to Rufus Person, 28 November 1941; and E. Linden, letter to Rufus Person, 23 December 1940, Person Collection (#1116).
99. Person to Chatham, 1 November 1940, Person Collection (#1116).
100. Rufus Person, letter to H.C. Starling, 3 December 1941, Person Collection (#1116).
101. H.C. Starling, letter to Rufus Person, 6 December 1941, Person Collection (#1116).
102. North Carolina, Department of Revenue, Franchise Tax Division, Annual Franchise Tax Report for Person Remedy Co., 1943, Person Collection (#1116).
103. North Carolina, Department of State, announcement of suspensions of certificates of incorporation, 1947.
104. Michael Boyce, conversation with the author, June 2007.

Chapter 4

1. "Two Parts Man Is Mrs. Person," *Raleigh Daily News and Observer*, June 25, 1905.
2. Ibid.
3. Untitled newspaper article, *(Charlotte?) Observer*, n.d., included in Album (1884–1902), p. 7, Person Papers (#3987).
4. Untitled newspaper article, *(Louisburg, NC?) Franklin Times*, August 25, 1909, included in Person Collection (#1116).
5. "A Story Worth Reading," unidentified newspaper article, included in Album (1884–1902), p. 2, Person Papers (#3987).
6. "Mrs. Person Sick," unidentified newspaper article, included in Album (1884–1902), p. 2, Person Papers (#3987).
7. "Found Brother's Far-West Grave," *Charlotte Evening News*, August 11, 1908.
8. "Among the Exhibits," *(Dallas?) News*, n.d., included in Album (1884–1902), p. 14, Person Papers (#3987).
9. "Likened Unto the Queen of Sheba," *(Dallas?) News*, n.d., included in Album (1884–1902), p. 15, Person Papers (#3987).
10. "A Unique Musical Genius," *Knoxville Sentinel*, n.d., included in Album (1884–1902), p. 14, Person Papers (#3987).
11. Journals (1901–1914), Person Collection (#1116).
12. Alice Person, letter to Rufus Person, 8 March 1911, Person Collection (#1116).
13. Journal (1909–1912), p. 170, Person Collection (#1116).
14. Journal (1901–1902), p. 171, Person Collection (#1116).
15. Alice Person, letter to Josie Person, 18 February 1901, private collection of Michael Boyce.
16. Alice Person, letter to William Person, undated letter copied into journal (1901–1904), p. 29, Person Collection (#1116).
17. Journal (1911–1914), p. 73, Person Collection (#1116).
18. Ibid., 74.
19. "Mrs. Joe Person Dies in New Mexico of Apoplexy," *Charlotte News*, June 13, 1913.
20. Journal (1911–1914), pp. 73–75, Person Collection (#1116).
21. "Mrs. Joe Person Dies Suddenly," *Charlotte Daily Observer*, June 13, 1913.
22. "Mrs. Joe Person Dies in New Mexico of Apoplexy," *Charlotte News*, June 13, 1913.
23. "Mrs. Joe Person Laid to Rest Today," *Charlotte News*, June 17, 1913.
24. "Mrs. Joe Person Dies Suddenly While on Her Way to California," *Charlotte Evening Chronicle*, June 13, 1913.
25. "Mrs. Joe Person Laid to Rest Today," *Charlotte News*, June 17, 1913.
26. Ibid.
27. Ibid.
28. See page 67 of the present work.

Chapter 5

1. Mrs. Joe Person Remedy Co., *Mrs. Joe Person's Remedy: A Specific*, [1884?], cover.
2. Judith Sumner, *American Household Botany: A History of Useful Plants 1620–1900* (Portland, OR: Timber Press, 2004), 231.
3. Alma R. Hutcheons, *Indian Herbalogy of North America* (Boston: Shambhala, 1991).
4. Virgil J. Vogel, *American Indian Medicine* (Norman: University of Oklahoma Press, 1970).
5. Daniel E. Moermann, *Native American Ethnobotany* (Portland, OR: Timber Press, 1998).
6. J. T. Garrett, *The Cherokee Herbal: Native Plant Medicine from the Four Directions* (Rochester, VT: Bear and Company, 2003).
7. Locklear Boughman and Loretta O. Oxendine, *Herbal Remedies of the Lumbee Indians* (Jefferson, NC: McFarland Publishers, 2004).
8. By 1837, Andrew Jackson's administration had removed well over 40,000 Indians from their land east of the Mississippi in order to give the land to white settlers. Most members of the five largest southeastern nations had been relocated west, though many Choctaw remained in Mississippi and nearby, and a fair number of Cherokee managed to stay in North Carolina, as did parts of smaller groups such as those now known as the Lumbee and the Haliwa-Saponi.
9. Varro E. Tyler, *Herbs of Choice: The Therapeutic Use of Phytomedicinals* (New York: Pharmaceutical Products Press, 1994), 3.
10. Ibid., 130, 175–76.
11. *Ichthyol: Its History, Properties, and Therapeutics* (New York: Merck & Co., 1913), 100–111.

Chapter 6

1. See pages 16-17 of the present work.
2. James Le Fanu, *The Rise and Fall of Modern Medicine* (New York: Carroll and Graf Publishers, 1999), 3.
3. Steven M. Stowe, *Doctoring the South: Southern Physicians and Everyday Medicine in the Mid-Nineteenth Century* (Chapel Hill: University of North Carolina Press, 2004), 8.
4. John Odell, *Indian Bottles and Brands* (Bend, OR: Maverick Publications, 1977), 42.
5. *Henderson (NC) Gold Leaf*, February 21, 1884, p. 4.

6. James Harvey Young, *The Toadstool Millionaires: A Social History of Patent Medicines in America before Federal Regulation* (Princeton, NJ: Princeton University Press, 1961), 177–79.

7. Anthony Cavender, *Folk Medicine in Southern Appalachia* (Chapel Hill: University of North Carolina Press, 2003), 147; Sumner, *American Household Botany*, 230.

8. See Odell, *Indian Bottles and Brands*, for hundreds of such listings.

9. Young, *The Toadstool Millionaires*, 59.

10. *Henderson Gold Leaf*, January 4, 1894, p. 2.

11. Ibid., January 7, 1904, p. 1.

12. Mrs. Joe Person Remedy Co., *Mrs. Joe Person's Remedy: Has Established*, [1901?], back cover.

13. "Mrs. Joe Person's Remedy," one-page advertisement circular, North Carolina Collection, Wilson Library, Univ. of NC at Chapel Hill.

14. Sarah Stage, *Female Complaints: Lydia Pinkham and the Business of Women's Medicine* (New York: Norton, 1979), 30.

15. Ibid., 32.

16. Ibid., 150.

17. Young, *The Toadstool Millionaires*, 58.

Chapter 7

1. See Charles Hamm, *Yesterdays: Popular Song in America* (New York: Norton, 1979), 109–40; Hans Nathan, *Dan Emmett and the Rise of Early Negro Minstrelsy* (Norman: University of Oklahoma Press, 1962); Robert C. Toll, *Blacking Up: The Minstrel Show in Nineteenth Century America* (New York: Oxford University Press, 1974); and others.

2. Toll, *Blacking Up*, 135.

3. *Henderson Gold Leaf*, January 16, 1890.

4. *Henderson Gold Leaf*, October 30, 1880.

5. Ralph and Richard Rinzler, notes, *Old-Time Music at Clarence Ashley's* (Folkways Records FA2355, 1961), 1–2.

6. See page 11 of the present work.

7. See page 56 of the present work.

8. Peace, "*Zeb's Black Baby*," 358.

9. Stephen Foster, "Nelly Bly" (New York: Firth, Pond, and Company, 1850), and many other editions.

10. T. Brigham Bishop, "Shew! Fly, Don't Bother Me" (Boston: White, Smith and Perry, 1869).

11. George P. Knauff, *Virginia Reels*, 4 vols. (Baltimore: Willig, 1939).

12. Daniel Decatur Emmett, "De Boatman Dance" (Boston: C.H. Keith, 1843).

13. Stephen Collins Foster, "Camptown Races" (Baltimore: Benteen; New Orleans: W.T. Mayo, 1850).

14. Howard L. Sacks and Judith Rose Sacks, *Way Up North in Dixie: A Black Family's Claim to the Confederate Anthem* (Washington, D.C.: Smithsonian Institute, 1993).

15. Henry Clay Work, "Kingdom Coming" (Chicago: Root and Cady, 1862).

16. Printed in Neil Gow and Sons, *Part Second of the Complete Repository of Original Scots Slow Strathspeys and Dances*, 3rd ed. (Edinburgh: Robert Purdie, [1828]), 2.

17. James Bland, "Carry Me Back to Old Virginny" (Boston: Ditson, 1878).

18. Edwin Christy, "Carry Me Back to Old Virginny" (New York: Jacques and Brother, 1847).

19. Stephen Collins Foster, "Oh! Susanna" (New York: C. Holt, Jr., 1848). The unexpurgated text and music are reprinted in *Popular Songs of Nineteenth-Century America: Complete Original Sheet Music for 64 Songs*, edited by Richard Jackson (New York: Dover Publications, Inc., 1976), 152–55.

Chapter 8

1. *Henderson Gold Leaf*, April 17, 1890.

2. Board of Music Trade, *Complete Catalogue of Sheet Music and Musical Work* (New York: Board of Music Trade of the United States of America, 1870; reprint, with a new introduction by Dena Epstein, New York: Da Capo, 1973), 506–13.

3. *Minstrel Songs Old and New* (Boston: Ditson, [ca. 1890]), 146, 94, 132, 180, 98, 122, and 3 respectively.

4. Hamm, *Yesterdays*, 54.

5. *The Cottages Duett* [sic], *a Popular Collection of Melodies, Arranged* [anonymously] *for Two Performers on the Piano Forte* (Baltimore, Willig, ca. 1845–50).

6. See page 60 of the present work.

7. Merrill Maguire Skaggs, *The Folk of Southern Fiction* (Athens: University of Georgia Press, 1972).

8. William Barclay Squire, "Popular Ancient English Music," in *Grove's Dictionary of Music and Musicians*, by Sir George Grove, vol. 3 (London: MacMillan, 1889).

9. William Chappell, *Popular Music of the Olden Time* (London: Cramer, Beale and Chappell, 1855–59).

10. J. Muir Wood and T.L. Stillie, "Scotland," in *Grove's Dictionary of Music and Musicians*, by Sir George Grove, vol. 3 (London: MacMillan, 1889).

11. A sample American edition was published in Boston by Russell in 1879.

12. See page 000 of the present work.
13. See Chris Goertzen and Alan Jabbour, "George P. Knauff's *Virginia Reels*" and "Fiddling in the Antebellum South," *American Music* 5 (Summer 1987): 121–44.
14. A Unique Musical Genius, *Knoxville Sentinel*, n.d. Included in: Album (1884–1902), p.14, Person Papers (#3987).
15. Mrs. Person, Medicine Maker, Recalled Here, *The Halifax (VA) Record-Advertiser*, March 30, 1972.

Appendix

1. Journal (1902–1906), p. 187, Person Collection (#1116).
2. Alice Person family Bible, private collection of Harmon Person.
3. Journal (1902–1906), p. 187, Person Collection (#1116).
4. Alice Person family Bible, private collection of Harmon Person.
5. Ibid.
6. Ibid.
7. Deed, Presley Carter Person to children, 1 April 1847, Franklin County, NC, deed book 30, pp. 87–93.
8. Deed, Ludovick Colquhoun to Morgan, 21 July 1848, Petersburg, VA, deed book 19, pp. 280–83.
9. Deed, Morgan and wife to Samuel J. Hurt, 5 January 1852, Petersburg, VA, deed book 19, pp. 164–5.
10. "Mrs. Joe Person Dies in New Mexico of Apoplexy," *Charlotte News*, June 13, 1913.
11. Alice Person family Bible, private collection of Harmon Person.
12. Ibid.
13. Massengill and Topkins, eds., "Letters Written from San Diego County," 143.
14. Alice Person family Bible, private collection of Harmon Person.
15. Alice Morgan Person, letter to Thomas Arrington Person, 29 April 1864, Person Family Papers.
16. Alice Person family Bible, private collection of Harmon Person.
17. Ibid.
18. Ibid.
19. Deed, Joseph Person to William Montgomery, 1 August 1872, Franklin County, NC, deed book 62, pp. 20–21.
20. Alice Person family Bible, private collection of Harmon Person.
21. Lucy Morgan, letter to unknown person with given name of Mary, 20 December 1874, private collection of Mary Barden.
22. Alice Person family Bible, private collection of Harmon Person.
23. Ibid.
24. Massengill and Topkins, eds., "Letters Written from San Diego County," 144.
25. Mary Morgan, letter to Rufus Morgan, various letters from 15 August 1879 to 10 November 1879, private collection of Mary Barden.
26. Massengill and Topkins, eds., "Letters Written from San Diego County," 144.
27. Alice Person family Bible, private collection of Harmon Person.
28. Deed, Joseph Person to William Montgomery, 29 January 1873, Franklin County, NC, deed book 62, pp. 21–22.
29. Journal (1902–1906), p. 186, Person Collection (#1116).
30. Rufus Person, letter to Peabody Drug Co., 31 March 1939, Person Collection (#1116).
31. Journal (1902–1906), p. 189, Person Collection (#1116).
32. Alice Person family Bible, private collection of Harmon Person.
33. "Mr. W.M. Person and Miss Prudence Person United in Wedlock," unidentified newspaper clipping with handwritten date of March 10, 1897, in Prudence Person scrapbook, North Carolina Collection, Wilson Library, University of North Carolina at Chapel Hill. After they married, Prudence and Wiley lived in what has become known as the Person Place located on the campus of Louisburg College in Louisburg, North Carolina (Elmore, *Person Place*, 19).
34. See pages 11, 15, and 53 of the present work.
35. "Mrs. Joe Person Dies in New Mexico of Apoplexy," *Charlotte News*, June 13, 1913.
36. Diary of Jessie Person (wife of Rufus Morgan Person), 20 June 1904, private collection of Michael Boyce.
37. Journal (1902–1906), p. 92, Person Collection (#1116).
38. Journal (1907–1910), p. 50, Person Collection (#1116).
39. Diary of Jessie Person (wife of Rufus Morgan Person), February 1916, private collection of Michael Boyce.
40. Ibid., 27 April 1916, private collection of Michael Boyce.

Bibliography

Bishop, T. Brigham. "Shew! Fly, Don't Bother Me." Boston: White, Smith and Perry, 1869.
Bland, James. "Carry Me Back to Old Virginny." Boston: Ditson, 1878.
Board of Music Trade. 1870. *Complete Catalogue of Sheet Music and Musical Work.* With a new introduction by Dena Epstein. New York: Board of Music Trade of the United States of America. Reprint, New York: Da Capo, 1973.
Boughman, Arvis Locklear, and Loretta O. Oxendine. *Herbal Remedies of the Lumbee Indians.* Jefferson, NC: McFarland Publishers, 2004.
Cavender, Anthony. *Folk Medicine in Southern Appalachia.* Chapel Hill: University of North Carolina Press, 2003.
Chappell, William. *Popular Music of the Olden Time.* London: Cramer, Beale and Chappell, 1855–1859.
Christy, Edwin. "Carry Me Back to Old Virginny." New York: Jacques and Brother, 1847.
Claiborne, John Herbert. *Seventy-Five Years in Old Virginia.* New York: Neale, 1904.
Cottages Duett [sic]. *The Cottages Duett, a Popular Collection of Melodies, Arranged for Two Performers on the Piano Forte.* Baltimore: Willig, ca. 1845–1850.
Elmore, Joseph E. *The Person Place: Sketches of Its Owners.* Louisburg, NC: Person Place Preservation Society, 1981.
Emmett, Daniel Decatur. "De Boatman Dance." Boston: C.H. Keith, 1843.
Foster, Stephen Collins. "Camptown Races." Baltimore: Benteen; New Orleans: W.T. Mayo, 1850.
_____. "Nelly Bly." New York: Firth, Pond, and Company, 1850.
_____. "Oh! Susanna." New York: C. Holt, Jr., 1848.
Garrett, J.T. *The Cherokee Herbal: Native Plant Medicine from the Four Directions.* Rochester, VT: Bear and Company, 2003.
Goertzen, Chris. "Mrs. Joe Person's *Popular Airs*: Early Blackface Minstrel Tunes in Oral Tradition." *Ethnomusicology* 35, no. 1 (Winter 1991): 31–53.
_____. *Southern Fiddlers and Fiddle Contests.* Jackson: University Press of Mississippi, 2008.
_____, and Alan Jabbour. "George P. Knauff's *Virginia Reels* and Fiddling in the Antebellum South." *American Music* 5 (Summer 1987): 121–44.
Gow, Neil, and Sons. *Part Second of the Complete Repository of Original Scots Slow Strathspeys and Dances.* 3d ed. Edinburgh: Robert Purdie [1828].
Grzybowski, Stefan, and Edward Allen. "History and Importance of Scrofula." *Lancet* 346 (December 2, 1995): 1472–1474.

Hamm, Charles. *Yesterdays: Popular Song in America*. New York: Norton, 1979.
Hatfield, Gabrielle. *Encyclopedia of Folk Medicine: Old World and New World Traditions*. Santa Barbara, CA: ABC-CLIO, 2004.
Henderson Gold Leaf. Henderson, NC.
Holbrook, Stewart H. *The Golden Age of Quackery*. New York: MacMillan, 1959.
Hutcheons, Alma R. *Indian Herbalogy of North America*. Boston: Shambhala, 1991.
Ichthyol: Its History, Properties, and Therapeutics. New York: Merck & Co., 1913.
Knauff, George P. *Virginia Reels*. 4 Vols. Baltimore: Willig, 1839.
Lebsock, Suzanne. *The Free Women of Petersburg: Status and Culture in a Southern Town, 1784–1860*. New York: Norton, 1984.
Le Fanu, James. *The Rise and Fall of Modern Medicine*. New York: Carroll and Graf, 1999.
Lover, Samuel. "Rory O'Moore." Philadelphia: Thomas G. Chase, 1839.
Massengill, Stephen E., and Robert M. Topkins, eds. "Letters Written from San Diego County, 1879–1880: By Rufus Morgan, North Carolina Apiarist and Photographer." *Journal of San Diego History* 40, no. 4 (1994): 142–177.
Minstrel Songs Old and New. Boston: Ditson, ca. 1890.
Moerman, Daniel E. *Native American Ethnobotany*. Portland, OR: Timber Press, 1998.
Mrs. Joe Person Remedy Co. *Mrs. Joe Person's Remedy: A Specific for All Blood Diseases*. Charlotte: Mrs. Joe Person Remedy Co. [1884?]. Advertising Ephemera Collection. Rare Book, Manuscript, and Special Collections Library, Duke University, Durham, NC.
Mrs. Joe Person Remedy Co. *Mrs. Joe Person's Remedy: Has Established Itself as the Finest Blood Purifier on the Market*. Charlotte: Mrs. Joe Person Remedy Co. [1901?]. Alice Morgan Person Collection (#1116, unprocessed). Special Collections Department, J.Y. Joyner Library, East Carolina University, Greenville, NC, USA.
Mrs. Joe Person Remedy Co. *Mrs. Joe Person's Remedy: Is a Specific for All Blood Diseases*. Charlotte: Mrs. Joe Person Remedy Co. [1884?]. Alice Morgan Person Collection (#1116, unprocessed). Special Collections Department, J.Y. Joyner Library, East Carolina University, Greenville, NC, USA.
Nathan, Hans. *Dan Emmett and the Rise of Early Negro Minstrelsy*. Norman: University of Oklahoma Press, 1962.
North Carolina. General Assembly. Public Laws of the State of North Carolina. 1871–72 session.
Odell, John. *Indian Bottles and Brands*. Bend, OR: Maverick Publications, 1977.
Peace, Samuel Thomas. *"Zeb's Black Baby": Vance County, North Carolina, a Short History*. Durham, NC: Seeman Printery, 1955.
Pearce, T.H. "The Persistence of Mrs. Joe Person." *The State* 54, no. 5 (October 1986): 22–24.
Person, Alice Morgan, Collection (#1116, unprocessed). Special Collections Department, J.Y. Joyner Library, East Carolina University, Greenville, NC, USA.
Person, Alice Morgan, Papers (#3987). Southern Historical Collection. Manuscripts Department, Wilson Library, University of North Carolina at Chapel Hill.
Person Family Papers. Rare Book, Manuscript, and Special Collections Library, Duke University, Durham, NC.
Person, Mrs. Joe. *A Collection of Popular Airs: As Arranged and Played Only by Mrs. Joe Person at the Southern Expositions*. Richmond: Hume, Minor, & Co., 1889.
Rinzler, Ralph, and Richard Rinzler. Notes to *Old-Time Music at Clarence Ashley's*. Folkways Records FA2355, 1961.
Sacks, Howard L., and Judith Rose Sacks. *Way Up North in Dixie: A Black Family's Claim to the Confederate Anthem*. Washington, D.C.: Smithsonian Institution, 1993.

Skaggs, Merrill Maguire. *The Folk of Southern Fiction*. Athens: University of Georgia Press, 1972.
Squire, William Barclay. "Popular Ancient English Music." In *Grove's Dictionary of Music and Musicians*, by Sir George Grove. Vol. 3. London: MacMillan, 1889.
Stage, Sarah. *Female Complaints: Lydia Pinkham and the Business of Women's Medicine*. New York: Norton, 1979.
Stowe, Steven M. *Doctoring the South: Southern Physicians and Everyday Medicine in the Mid-Nineteenth Century*. Chapel Hill: University of North Carolina Press, 2004.
Sumner, Judith. *American Household Botany: A History of Useful Plants, 1620–1900*. Portland, OR: Timber Press, 2004.
Toll, Robert C. *Blacking Up: The Minstrel Show in Nineteenth Century America*. New York: Oxford University Press, 1974.
Tyler, Varro E. *Herbs of Choice: The Therapeutic Use of Phytomedicinals*. New York: Pharmaceutical Products Press, 1994.
U.S. Bureau of the Census. *Inhabitants in City of Petersburg in the County of Dinwiddie, State of Virginia*. Washington, DC, 1850.
Vogel, Virgil J. *American Indian Medicine*. Norman: University of Oklahoma Press, 1970.
Wood, J. Muir, and T.L. Stillie. "Scotland." In *Grove's Dictionary of Music and Musicians*, by Sir George Grove. Vol 3. London: MacMillan, 1889.
Work, Henry Clay. "Kingdom Coming." Chicago: Root and Cady, 1862.
Young, James Harvey. *The Toadstool Millionaires: A Social History of Patent Medicines in America before Federal Regulation*. Princeton, NJ: Princeton University Press, 1961.

Index

Numbers in **_bold italics_** indicate pages with photographs.

Adams, Stephen 182; see also Mayrich, Michael
advertising 104–105, 116–123, **_124_**, 138, 151, 160–161, **_162_**, 163–166
alcohol 140, 142–143, 165
Aletris farinose 142, 164–165; see also star grass; unicorn root
Alvita Black Cohosh Root Tea 149
American Journal of Health 161
ammonium bituminosulfonate 147; see also ichthammol; ichthyol
Anderson Seminary 73
antibiotics 145, 155
Aralia nudicalis 142–143, 146; see also sarsaparilla; wild sarsaparilla
Asclepias tuberosa 164; see also pleurisy root
Ayers Company 156

Baker, Dr. Julian 41–45
banjo 168–170, 172–173, 185
The Bank of Virginia 71
Barden, Mary Moulton ix
Barnard, Clara Alington 182; see also Claribel
Barnes, Guy V. 125–126, 136, 192
Baseler, John 3, 58, 175
Beard, Lucy Morgan 71, 75, 78–79, 80, 82, 84, 100, 133, 135–136, 190, 192
Beckham, T.T. x
"Billy in the Low Grounds" 56, 172, 175–176, 185; see also "Johnny in the Nether Mains"
bitters 105–106, 108, 117–118, 121, 140, 159
black cohosh 149, 164–165; see also Cimicifuga racemosa; squaw root
blackface: minstrelsy 167–173, 179; music 167–168, 172–175, 177–179, 182, 187; racist aspects 169–170, 177
Bland, James 175
bleeding 154–156
blood: diseases 118, 138; impurity 15–16, 43, 105, 153, 156, 159–161; purifiers 32, 105, 117–118, 123, 138–139, 141–142, 146, 160–161

Blue Alsatian Mountains (collection) 111, **_112_**, 126, 179, 183–185, 191
"Blue Alsatian Mountains" (piece) 176, 182–185
"Boatman Dance" 60, 126, 174, 176, 180–182, 184–185; see also "Dance, the Boatman Dance"; "Ohio River"
Boyce, Michael x, 2, 137, 143
"Buffalo Gals" 176, 185; see also "Down-Town Girls"; "Lubly Fan"; "Midnight Serenade"

"Camptown Races" 173–174, 177, 180; see also "Gwine to Run All Night"; "I Bet My Money"; "I Bet My Money on the Bob-Tail Nag"
cancer 103–105, 118, 138–139, 141–142, 146
"Carolina Racket" 173, 176
"Carry Me Back to Old Virginny" 175, 180; see also "Floating Scow of Old Virginny"
Caswell County, North Carolina 66
catarrh 138–139, 156
Chamaelirium luteum 141, 144; see also false unicorn; helonias
Cherokee 141–144, 198
Chimaphila 141; see also pipsissewa
"Chivalry of Man" x, 2, 7, 108, 114, 152–153, 163, 172, 179, 192
Christy, E.P. 175
Cimifuga racemosa 149, 164; see also black cohosh; squaw root
Claribel 182; see also Barnard, Clara Alington
Clarke, Mary Bayard 33, 89
colic 118, 138–139
A Collection of Popular Airs 109, **_110_**, 111, 114, 126, 167, 172–176, 179–182, 184–185, 187, 191

"Dance, the Boatman Dance" 111, 176; see also "Boatman Dance"; "Ohio River"

Davidson, George 22–28, 114–115, 133, 191, 194
Davidson Female College 73
Davis Hotel 154; see also Glass House
"De Year of Jubilo" 174, 176; see also "Kingdom Coming"
"Dixie" 57, 112–113, 126, 172, 174, 176, 181, 186, 196
Dr. Clark Johnson's Indian Blood Syrup 156
Dr. Morse's Indian Root Pills 159
Doctor Pierce's Golden Medical Discovery 160
"Down-Town Girls" 126, 176, 182, 185; see also "Buffalo Gals"; "Lubly Fan"; "Midnight Serenade"

"Eliza Jane" 176; see also "Liza Jane"
Elmore, Joseph x
Emmett, Dan 172
erysipelas 118, 138–139, 156
Ethiopian melody 173–174
Exchange Bank 71–72, 189

false unicorn 141, 148, 165; see also Chamaelirium luteum; helonias
Farmers Bank 71
"Floating Scow of Old Virginny" 180; see also "Carry Me Back to Old Virginny"
Food and Drug Act of 1906 137, 159–160, 165
Foster, Stephen Collins 113, 173–174, 177, 180–181
Franklinton, North Carolina 12, 16, 20, 25, 27, 31, 85, 90, 137, 152
free trader 88, 191

Garton's New Orleans Minstrels 170
Glass House 108, 154; see also Davis Hotel
Grace Church 73, 85, 190
Green County, North Carolina 66
Greenwood 85, 88–90, 108
"Gwine to Run All Night" 174, 180; see also "Camptown Races"; "I Bet My Money"; "I Bet My Money on the Bob-Tail Nag"

Haliwa-Saponi 144–145, 198
heart disease 30, 118, 138–139, 156
helonias 105, 141, 144, 148; see also Chamaelirium luteum; false unicorn
Hi Henry Minstrel Company 170
Hickory, North Carolina 75, 84, 100, 133–134, 190
Hodges, E.B. 46–49, 89, 133, 191
Hodges, John 185; see also White, Cool
Hume, Minor & Co. 109, 113, 175
Humours 153–154
Hurt, Samuel 71
Hyde County, North Carolina 66

"I Bet My Money" 174, 176–177; see also "Camptown Races"; "Gwine to Run All Night"; "I Bet My Money on the Bob-Tail Nag"
"I Bet My Money on the Bob-Tail Nag" 56, 172; see also "Camptown Races"; "Gwine to Run All Night"; "I Bet My Money"
ichthammol 147; see also ammonium bituminosulfonate; ichthyol
ichthyol 147; see also ammonium bituminosulfonate; ichthammol
"I'm Gwine Down Town" 174, 176
indigestion 118, 138–139, 142, 155–156, 161, 164
"Italian Waltz" 59, 126, 172, 176

"Johnny Get Your Hair Cut" 176, 196
"Johnny in the Nether Mains" 175; see also "Billy in the Low Grounds"
Jones, Charles R. 88–89, 133, 191
Judson's Mountain Herb Pills 157–158

Kickapoo Indian Medicine Company 137
Kickapoo Indian Sagwa 160
"Kingdom Coming" 174, 180; see also "De Year of Jubilo"
Kittrell, North Carolina x–xi, 53, 90–91, 108–109, 115–116, 118, 123, 125, 152, 154, 156, 161, 170, 172, 191–192, 195
Knauff, George P. 174, 185

laboratory: Charlotte 116, *117*, 125; fire 115–116, 192; Kittrell x, 49–50, 109
Lane's Liver Pills 147
Leavenworth's Female Seminary 73
"Liza Jane" 126, 173; see also "Eliza Jane"
"Lubly Fan" 185; see also "Buffalo Gals"; "Down-Town Girls"; "Midnight Serenade"
Lumbee 143–144, 198

Marlboro County, South Carolina 66
Massengill, Steve ix
Mayrich, Michael 182; see also Adams, Stephen
McGhee, Libby x, 2, 90, *107*, 137
McGhee, Wyatt L. 88–89, *90*, 91, 191
McGhee, Wyatt, III x, 2, 90, *107*, 137
McLeod, Elaine 148
McLeod, George 147–148
medicine shows 137, 159, 161, 170, 172–173, 175
Mexican sarsaparilla 105, 141–142; see also sarsaparilla; Smilax medica
"Midnight Serenade" 185; see also "Buffalo Gals"; "Down-Town Girls"; "Lubly Fan"
Minor, George A. 58, 109, 111, 175
Mizener's Old Time Minstrels 170
Modoc Vegetable Bitters 159
Montgomery, Mary Temperance (nee Person) 74–75, 86, 91, 100
Montgomery, William P. (Billy) 86, 92–93, 96–97, 100, 114, 190–191

Morgan, Alfred 71, 75–79
Morgan, Anna 77
Morgan, Esther Jane (nee Robinson) 71–75, 189
Morgan, Joseph 71, 189
Morgan, Laura 77
Morgan, Mary Bayard 75, 194
Morgan, Mary Clarke 95, 101; see also Moulton, Mary Morgan
Morgan, Rufus ix, x, 71, 72, 74–76, 78, 80, *81*, 85–87, 89, 97–98, 101–102, 105, 108, 190, 192, 194
Morgan, Samuel (son of Rufus Morgan) 72, 75, 190
Morgan, Samuel Wilson 71–74, 189
Moulton, Mary Morgan ix; see also Morgan, Mary Clarke

"Nelly Bly" 112, 173, 176, 180
New Market Races 72

"Oh! Carry Me Back" 175–176
"Oh, Susanna" 173, 176–177, 199
"Ohio River" 174; see also "Boatman Dance"; "Dance, the Boatman Dance"
"Old Bob Ridley" 131, 176, 180
Oliver Ditson Company 111, 113, 191

Pearce, Joseph, Jr. x
Pearce, Thilbert x, *107*
Person, Abiah Whitehead Culpepper 74–75
Person, Alice Gibson 79, 85, 91, 93, 98–99, 101, 116, 133–134, 190–191
Person, Esther Morgan 85, 91, 190–191
Person, Harmon ix–x
Person, Henry Harris 85, 91–94, 98, 190, 192
Person, Jessie (nee Allen) 93, 116, 126, 195
Person, Joseph Arrington 11, 74, 85–89, 98, 171, 189, 194; stroke and paralysis 12, 86–87, 190
Person, Josephine Arrington 78, 84–85, 93, 99–102, 119, 133, 134, 140, 148, 152, 157, 165, 190, 195; illness 12–13, 101–102, 157, 190
Person, Levin King 85, 91, 98, 190–191
Person, Robert Lee 26, 85, 89–90, 92–94, 190–192
Person, Rufus Morgan x, 53, 85, 91, 93–94, 97–100, 106, 109, 116, *117*, 123, 125–128, 132–134, 163, 190–192
Person, Thomas Arrington 74, 86
Person, Wiley Mangum 85, 93, 95–97, 113–115, 134, 190–191, 200
Person, William Montgomery 74, 85–86, 91, 93, 94–95, 98, 116, 134, 190, 192
Person County, North Carolina 66
Petersburg, Virginia ix, 2, 11, 71–73, 85, 169, 171, 175, 185, 189–190
Petersburg Female College 73
Pinkham, Lydia 163–166

Pinkham's Liver Pills 164
Pinkham's Vegetable Compound 149, 163–166
pipsissewa 105, 141, 144, 146; see also Chimaphila
pleurisy root 164–165; see also Asclepias tuberosa
"Polka" 173, 176
prickly ash bark 105, 141–142, 144, 146, 148; see also Zanthoxylum

queen's root 105, 141–142, 144; see also Stillingia sylvatica

Red Indian Brand: blood pills 106; cathartic pills 106; diuretic pills 106; kidney pills 106, 108; liver pills 106, 108
Rees, Franceine Perry x
remedy ingredients 105, 141–143
rheumatism 118, 138–139, 141–142, 156, 159, 161
Richardson, Arnold 144
Richardson, Maxella 144, 147
Richmond County, North Carolina 66
Ritter, Alice ix–x
Rub-It-On — Ezit 106

Sarsaparilla 142–144, 146, 148, 150, 156; see also Aralia nudicalis; Smilax herbacea; Smilax medica
scrofula 12–13, 15–16, 18, 87, 101, 103–105, 118, 121–122, 138–145, 147–148, 152–153, 156, 159–161, 164–165, 190
Shaw, Lauchlin 172
"Shoo Fly" 173, 176
Smilax aristolochiaefolia 142; see also Smilax medica
Smilax herbacea 142; see also sarsaparilla
Smilax medica 142; see also Mexican sarsaparilla; sarsaparilla
Spartanburg, South Carolina 60, 124
springs, Kittrell, North Carolina 108, 152, 154, 172
squaw root 149; see also black cohosh; Cimifuga racemosa
star grass 105, 141–142, 144, 146, 165; see also Aletris farinosa; unicorn root
Staton, Mary 40–45
Stephenson, Louise Scott ix–x, xi, 1–2
Stillingia sylvatica 142, 144; see also queen's root
Stubbs, Harry xi, 1

Tarboro, North Carolina ix, 2, 40–49, *50*, 51–53, 89–90, 108, 191
tetter 118, 141–142
trademark 23, 29, 36–37, 47–49, 52, 104, 114, 125–126, 159–160, 190–192
Trail of Tears 144, 198
trillium 105, 141–142

tuberculosis 12, 139–140, 142, 145–146, 148, 160
Tuscarora Rice 159
Tutt's Pills 156

unicorn root 142, 164–165; *see also* Aletris farinosa; star grass

Vance County "Cubans" 144–145
Victor Talking Machine Company 126, 186, 192
Virginia Minstrels 168

walk-around (genre) 174–175, 177
"Walk-Around" (piece) 60, 126, 175–176, 181

wash 40, 46, 86, 105–106, 117–119, 121, 125
"Weird Waltz" 172, 176
whiskey 35–36, 86, 95, 118, 140, 152
White, Cool 185; *see also* Hodges, John
wild sarsaparilla 142, 146; *see also* Aralia nudicalis
William Swain's Panacea 159
Work, Henry Clay 174
Wright's Indian Vegetable Pills 159

"Yankee Doodle" 126, 176
Yates, E.A. 30–34, 38

Zanthoxylum 142, 148; *see also* prickly ash bark

www.ingramcontent.com/pod-product-compliance
Lightning Source LLC
Chambersburg PA
CBHW032055300426
44116CB00007B/748